Rough Writing

NATION OF NEWCOMERS

Immigrant History as American History

Matthew Jacobson and Werner Sollors
GENERAL EDITORS

Beyond the Shadow of Camptown: Korean Military Brides in America
Ji-Yeon Yuh

Feeling Italian: The Art of Ethnicity in America
Thomas J. Ferraro

Constructing Black Selves: Caribbean American Narratives and the Second Generation
Lisa D. McGill

Transnational Adoption: A Cultural Economy of Race, Gender, and Kinship
Sara K. Dorow

Immigration and American Popular Culture: An Introduction
Jeffrey Melnick and Rachel Rubin

From Arrival to Incorporation: Migrants to the U.S. in a Global Era
Edited by Elliott R. Barkan, Hasia Diner, and Alan M. Kraut

Migrant Imaginaries: Latino Cultural Politics in the U.S.-Mexico Borderlands
Alicia Schmidt Camacho

The Force of Domesticity: Filipina Migrants and Globalization
Rhacel Salazar Parreñas

Immigrant Rights in the Shadows of Citizenship
Edited by Rachel Ida Buff

Rough Writing: Ethnic Authorship in Theodore Roosevelt's America
Aviva F. Taubenfeld

AVIVA F. TAUBENFELD

Rough Writing

Ethnic Authorship in Theodore Roosevelt's America

NEW YORK UNIVERSITY PRESS
New York and London

NEW YORK UNIVERSITY PRESS
New York and London
www.nyupress.org

© 2008 by New York University
All rights reserved

Library of Congress Cataloging-in-Publication Data
Taubenfeld, Aviva F.
Rough writing : ethnic authorship in Theodore Roosevelt's America / Aviva F. Taubenfeld.
  p. cm.—(Nation of newcomers)
Includes bibliographical references and index.
ISBN-13: 978-0-8147-8290-3 (cl : alk. paper)
ISBN-10: 0-8147-8290-6 (cl : alk. paper)
ISBN-13: 978-0-8147-8291-0 (pb : alk. paper)
ISBN-10: 0-8147-8291-4 (pb : alk. paper)
 1. Roosevelt, Theodore, 1858–1919—Influence. 2. Roosevelt, Theodore, 1858–1919—Political and social views. 3. Roosevelt, Theodore, 1858–1919—Literary art. 4. Rhetoric—Political aspects—United States—History. 5. Ethnicity in literature. 6. National characteristics, American, in literature. 7. American literature—History and criticism. 8. American literature—Minority authors—History and criticism. 9. Immigrants—United States—ntellectual life. 10. United States—Intellectual life—1865–1918. I. Title.
E757.T33   2008
973.91'1092—dc22   2008023920

New York University Press books are printed on acid-free paper, and their binding materials are chosen for strength and durability. We strive to use environmentally responsible suppliers and materials to the greatest extent possible in publishing our books.

Manufactured in the United States of America
c 10 9 8 7 6 5 4 3 2 1
p 10 9 8 7 6 5 4 3 2 1

For My Parents

CONTENTS

Acknowledgments   ix

Introduction   1

1. Mendel's Melting Pot: Israel Zangwill and the Science of the Crucible   13

2. Two Flags to Love: Jacob Riis and the Transnational American at the Turn of the Twentieth Century   41

3. Making American Homes and America Home: Theodore Roosevelt and Elizabeth Stern in the Pages of the *Ladies' Home Journal*   77

4. "Threatin' Him as a Akel": Finley Peter Dunne's Ethnic Critique of "True Americanism"   121

Epilogue   159

Notes   163

Bibliography   215

Index   227

About the Author   241

ACKNOWLEDGMENTS

Through the rough writing of this book, I have been fortunate to have had the support of many remarkable institutions and individuals. I would like to thank the Woodrow Wilson Fellowship Foundation and Columbia University for backing the research and writing of the earliest drafts, and Purchase College, State University of New York, for granting me funding and leave to complete it. I am greatly indebted to the outstanding archivists and librarians at Columbia, Harvard University, Haverford College, the New York Public Library, the Museum of the City of New York, the University of Pennsylvania, and the Central Zionist Archives, who patiently helped me to track down materials. I am especially grateful in this regard to Wallace Dailey, curator of the Theodore Roosevelt Collection at Harvard College Library, and to Simone Schliachter and Michal Zaft of the Central Zionist Archives in Jerusalem, Israel.

I would also like to thank the editors and staff at NYU Press, especially Eric Zinner, Despina Papazoglou Gimbel, Ciara McLaughlin, Emily Park, and Susan Ecklund. *Rough Writing* would not have taken its present form without them or without the suggestions of the anonymous readers for the press.

During my time at Columbia, I was blessed with many outstanding teachers and advisers. Priscilla Wald first introduced me to the richness of these texts and provided me with a language in which to talk about them. Herbert Gans and Elizabeth Blackmar generously read portions and provided much-needed perspective. Robert O'Meally and Andrew Delbanco were instrumental not only in providing suggestions and support but also in creating rare opportunities for me to develop as both a scholar and a teacher and for never letting me lose sight of either. Werner Sollors adopted me as his student and gave unstintingly of his vast intellect, diverse resources, limited time, and warm spirit. His genuine love of knowledge and commitment to nurturing young scholars have been my boon, and I consider myself extremely fortunate to have had such a mentor. This book could not have been completed, however, without the tough questions, careful reading, steady encouragement, wisdom, and good sense of Robert A. Ferguson; for all of these and for his exceptional dedication, I am ever grateful.

I have been most fortunate to find a home at Purchase College among such stimulating and supportive colleagues and students. I am especially grateful to Bill Baskin, Laura Chmielewski, Rachel Hallote, Elizabeth Langland, Elise Lemire, Jonathan Levin, Kathleen McCormick, Gaura Narayan, Charles Ponce de Leon, Brenda DiMartini Squires, Lee Schelsinger, Tom Schwartz, Bob Stein, Nina Straus, Jennie Uleman, and Louise Yelin, who have supported this project in myriad ways, and to the wonderful Rosalie Reutershan and Stephanie Acton, who make everything happen. I also wish to thank Michelle Spigonardo, Tim Coakley, Crystal Boerschig, Cora Oberst, Jeana Bonacci, and all of my students who have shared their ideas so enthusiastically and who have pushed me to refine my own. Particular thanks goes to my friends Rebecca Kobrin and Elisabeth Levi, who voluntarily read multiple drafts of each chapter.

Finally, I must thank my family. The stories of the Taubenfeld and Zabusky families, woven into the fabric of my childhood, and of the Schloss and Wimmer families, more recently appended, have inspired my work. I am particularly grateful to David Sudaley, Jonathan and Devorah Schloss, and Vincent Burke for their indulgence and good humor, and to Jack and Betty Schloss for their constant support. Amy Sudaley Burke has been the greatest friend and cheerleader anyone could ask for, and I am truly blessed to have her as my sister. At every step of the way, my husband, Daniel Schloss, listened, read, prodded, and praised. His friendship, integrity, impeccable judgment, and love sustain me daily, and I am most fortunate to have him as my in-house counsel. I also must thank our light and joy, Leora Gila, who provided the much-needed doses of reality, laughter, and playtime that enabled me to complete this work and enjoy it, and Jonah Samuel, who arrived just in time and slept through its final stages. My best and most enthusiastic readers have been my parents, Isaac Taubenfeld and Sylvia Zabusky Taubenfeld. They continually inspire me with their tenacious pursuit of their dreams and unflaggingly support me in my own. To them this work is dedicated with the utmost love and appreciation.

Introduction

"What meaning . . . can continue to attach to such a term as the 'American' character?" questioned Henry James upon his return to the United States in 1904. It is a "challenge to speculation"; the native-born observer "doesn't know, he can't say, before the facts, and he doesn't even want to know or say; the facts themselves loom . . . in too large a mass."[1] The question of who and what is an American, as old as the nation itself, took on urgent intensity as the turn from the nineteenth to the twentieth century brought to the United States a massive influx of ethnically diverse foreigners largely from eastern and southern Europe. Their arrival between 1880, when the wave began, and 1924, when the legislation of a national quota system ended it, provoked extreme anxiety among native-born Americans struggling to maintain power and a sense of nation and self.

Not even one generation after the close of the Civil War, this forty-four-year period began at a time when the very existence and nature of the Union seemed tenuous. Americans still questioned whether North and South would be able to reunite and under what conditions. The status and fate of the new population of freedmen remained under violent debate. Rapid industrialization and its attendant internal migrations and urbanization produced unprecedented opportunities and problems. The move away from a home-based economy shifted the sites of gender construction with as yet unknown consequences. And the simultaneous incursions of the United States into empire challenged the nation's republican identity. Race, economy, class, gender, citizenship—all major constituents of individual and national identity—now stood in flux.

Inseparable from these shifts, massive numbers of immigrants began to arrive. Between 1880 and 1924, more than twenty million newcomers landed on U.S. shores.² Not only unprecedented in number, they were unprecedented in kind. No longer predominantly from northern and western Europe, these new immigrants came from southern and eastern Europe and Asia, with languages, customs, religions, ideologies, and economic experiences deemed radically different from those of the earlier arrivals. Confronting what Henry James called "a sense of chill" at this torrent of newcomers, native-born Americans wondered what the next generations would look like, how they would earn their living, what would become of their language, political systems, ways of life.³ "We are submerged beneath a conquest so complete that the very name of us means something not ourselves," said Harvard professor Barrett Wendell, despairing at the threat to national and individual self-recognition this "conquest" wrought.⁴

Everything seemed up for grabs; anything seemed possible. It became more critical than ever to establish a definition of "us," an ethic and narrative of belonging by which Americanness could be established, transmitted, maintained, and judged. A period of intense imaginings followed, as Americans of all stripes called upon a host of ideological, scientific, and literary discourses in an attempt to articulate and enforce their visions of the nation's past, present, and future.

Central to these attempts was Theodore Roosevelt. A rising political star who, though a child of the elite, made his reputation by claiming to speak for the people against special interests and for what he would later call a "square deal," Roosevelt was soon to become one of the best-known and most influential men of the period.⁵ "Americanism is a question of spirit, conviction, and purpose, not of creed or birthplace," he declared in his defining essay "True Americanism" (1894).⁶ Like later theorists of nationalism, Roosevelt realized that a nation is an intangible entity located in the minds of its inhabitants.⁷ He insisted that Americanism is an animating principle, a system of beliefs, a shared story with "grandeur . . . lying before the eyes of every man who can read the book of America's past and the book of America's present."⁸

Better than any president before him, Roosevelt understood from early on the narrative component of American identity and nationalism. He believed that America's story needed to be told and told right in order to unite and rally its inhabitants and to ensure that "their first loyalty [be] to nation and to decency in citizenship."⁹ To this end, he wrote his own histories. He framed *The Winning of the West* as part of a larger narrative of the "spread of the English-speaking peoples over the world's waste spaces" and as a story of the power of the American wilderness to fuse mixed blood into a uniquely American race, forging its character and destiny.[10] He told the story of *New York* as a progressive nationalist morality tale, "a lesson in Americanism—a lesson that he among us who wishes to win honor in our life, and to play his part honestly and manfully, must be indeed an American in spirit and purpose, in heart and thought and deed."[11] He told *Hero Tales from American History* and depicted the life of a statesman in *Gouverneur Morris* as models of "those qualities of daring and lofty disinterestedness which we like to associate with the name American."[12] And he presented his own life story as proof that "no exercise of collective power will ever avail if the average individual does not keep his or her sense of personal duty, initiative, and responsibility."[13] With these books and more, Roosevelt deliberately sought to craft a narrative of Americanness—American exceptionalism, race, manhood, character, responsibility, and mission.

At the same time, he called upon other writers with similar visions of America to construct a distinctive national literature. "These new surroundings and the new strains in our blood interact with one another in such a fashion that our national type must certainly be new; and it will either develop no art and no literature or else the art and literature must be distinctly our own," he declared.[14] While contemporaneous European nationalists sought to locate national distinctiveness in the seemingly timeless folk, its "race spirit," and epic tales, Roosevelt, as we shall find, invented a new, composite American race and insisted that its spirit be revealed through the creation of a new, characteristic literature. He charged its authors "partly [to] express the soul of the nation, partly . . . [to] lead and guide the soul of the nation"; they were simultaneously to articulate America and to create America through the articulation.[15]

Roosevelt's national literary project is well known.[16] He praised contemporaneous authors, male and female, whom he thought contributed significantly: Owen Wister, Mark Twain, Joel Chandler Harris, Edward Arlington Robinson, Sarah Orne Jewett, and Mary Wilkins Freeman, to name just a few. Their work "smack[s] of our own soil, mental and moral, no less than physical."[17] Less understood, however, is Roosevelt's realization that with the swell and shift in immigration, these authors could not fully represent or speak to the populace. A more encompassing national literature was needed to "express . . . and guide the soul of the nation." To this end, Roosevelt promoted the work of a select group of ethnic authors writing about the immigrant. As he used his "Rough Riders" to establish a narrative of American masculinity and race, so Roosevelt used these "rough writers" to articulate a narrative of Americanism. *Rough Writing: Ethnic Authorship in Theodore Roosevelt's America* examines the surprising place and implications of the immigrant and of ethnic writing in Roosevelt's America and American literature.

"Learn to Think, Talk and Be United States": Making Immigrants into Americans

In including the immigrant in American literature, Roosevelt had no intention of creating a multicultural canon or multiculturalism more generally. He had a very particular view of who an immigrant must be and what he or she must accomplish to enter into American life and letters. "The mighty tide of immigration to our shores has brought in its train much of good and much of evil," he declared in "True Americanism," "and whether the good or the evil shall predominate depends mainly on whether these newcomers do or do not throw themselves heartily into our national life, cease to be Europeans, and become Americans like the rest of us."[18] Roosevelt demanded the cessation of one identity and the creation of a new one. He demanded a complete shift in national loyalty and political ideology as well:

> There are certain ideas which [the immigrant] must give up. For instance, he must learn that American life is incompatible with the existence of any form of anarchy, . . . and he must learn that we exact full religious toleration and the complete separation of Church and State. Moreover, he must not bring in his Old World religious, race, and national antipathies but must merge them into love for our common country, and must take pride in the things we can all take pride in. He must revere only our flag; not only must it come first, but no other flag should even come second. He must learn to celebrate Washington's Birthday rather than that of the Queen or Kaiser, and the Fourth of July instead of St. Patrick's Day.[19]

Insisting that "we have a right, and it is our duty to demand . . . so," Roosevelt charged immigrants to divest themselves of prior national attachments and to join America on its terms.[20]

Roosevelt believed such transformation was both necessary and possible. For if, as he said, "Americanism is a question of spirit, conviction, and purpose, not of creed or birthplace," then anyone can share its convictions, join wholeheartedly in its purpose, and convert to its "civil religion"[21]—anyone, that is, with the innate capacity and adequate civilization to practice Americanism.[22] For while the once scrawny, asthmatic Roosevelt believed in the power of will to transform the individual and the power of environment to alter the character and body of both an organism and its offspring, he nonetheless held that not all individuals or races could yet be remade and fused into America. "It is urgently necessary to check and regulate our immigration . . . to keep out races which do not assimilate readily with our own, and unworthy individuals of all races—not only criminals, idiots, and paupers, but anarchists."[23] Race was central to Roosevelt's thinking. As we will discover, defining "our own race" as a composite of northern and western European races made over in the "American crucible," Roosevelt quite radically, among his peers, held that all Europeans immigrants, even those from eastern and southern Europe, could be absorbed into that race without altering its composition or character a jot. But other races—being either too different (the Japanese) or as yet too uncivilized (the Chinese and Africans)—could not be absorbed, nor could the mentally, morally, or politically defective. Roosevelt's America was simultaneously a racial and a civic construct; not all could join, and those who could needed to learn to "think, talk, and be United States."[24]

If newcomers accomplished this, then, Roosevelt insisted, native-born Americans had an obligation to stand with them "shoulder to shoulder, not asking as to the ancestry or creed of our comrades, but only demanding that they be in very truth Americans, and that we work together, heart, hand, and head, for the honor and greatness of our country."[25] This was a progressive vision of civic responsibility that enabled the right newcomers to join the nation through their devotion and actions. Their willingness to put the good of the nation above all else, and to work for it, entitled them to equal status among its citizens.

Of course, many in this era would not agree with Roosevelt's conception of the nation or with his notion of the possibility and means of joining it.

As the nativist Alfred P. Schultz observed derisively in 1908, "We know that nature is more powerful than theory, and that the individual is the product of many generations, and yet we believe that the reading of the Declaration of Independence will change the essence of the child." Refuting Roosevelt's claims, he argued instead, "This is the truth: schools, political institutions, and environment are utterly incapable to produce anything. No man can ever become anything else than he is already potentially and essentially."[26] Defining America as Anglo-Saxon and even its European newcomers as racially other, inferior, and nonwhite,[27] Schultz insisted that these arrivals were entirely lacking the physical stuff of Americanness. Famed eugenicist Madison Grant would further popularize such claims, arguing in 1916 that it was "pathetic and fatuous" to believe "in the efficacy of American institutions and environment to reverse or obliterate immemorial hereditary tendencies."[28] Along with a growing chorus of nativists, Grant and Schultz concluded that since it is impossible to turn immigrants into Americans, the nation must slam shut its doors and adopt a eugenic policy to deal with the non-Anglo-Saxon already within its borders.

Similarly defining national identity and heritage racially, the philosopher Horace Kallen, who would go on to cofound the New School for Social Research, declared in 1915, "Men may change their clothes, their politics, their wives, their religions, their philosophies, to a greater or lesser extent: they cannot change their grandfathers."[29] For Kallen, as for Schultz and Grant, the distinctive character of the immigrant is a biological essence that could not be cast off. But rather than fearing these unalterable distinctions, Kallen embraced them. Articulating an ideology of what he would later term "cultural pluralism," Kallen argued that "as in an orchestra, every type of instrument has its specific timbre and tonality, founded in its substance and form; as every type has its appropriate theme and melody in the whole symphony, so in society each ethnic group is the natural instrument, its spirit and culture are its theme and melody, and the harmony and dissonances and discords of them all make the symphony of civilization."[30] Each immigrant group and its descendants would retain its own spirit, sound, and ways, contributing these unaltered to the harmonious pluralist collective that would be the United States.

Like Kallen, leading intellectual and famed pacifist Randolph Bourne insisted in 1916: "What we emphatically do not want is that these distinctive qualities should be washed out into a tasteless, colorless fluid of uniformity. Already we have far too much of this insipidity." But rather than limiting each immigrant to the legacy of his grandfather, Bourne called for the inhabitants of the United States to create for themselves a "new spiritual citizenship . . . of the world," "a trans-nationality, a weaving back and forth, with the other lands, of many threads of all sizes and colors."[31] Living in the United States among peoples of all different origins and experiences, both the individual and the nation at large have the opportunity to select their affinities and affiliations, forging a cosmopolitan identity that would indeed revise the horrific errors of European nationalism and usher in a millennial era of peace. Bourne, Kallen, Schultz, and Grant exemplified alternative ways of thinking about immigrants and their potential impact on the nation, for good and ill.

But despite growing arguments for recognition in some circles of what Jane Addams called "immigrant gifts," changing the nation for the better, and in others of the "immigrant menace" threatening to overwhelm it, Roosevelt held fast to the claim that America had altered little since its founding. Despite the developing science of genetics, which asserted that the nature of races and individuals was fixed, Roosevelt continued to assert the earlier ideas of Jean-Baptist Lamarck, that bodies and peoples could be altered by environment; thus immigrants could be made into Americans in the United States. And despite his own increasing anxiety during World War I over the political loyalties of European émigrés, Roosevelt continued to insist stridently in 1915 that "a hyphenated American is not an American at all. . . . But if he is heartily and singly loyal to this Republic, then no matter where he was born, he is just as good an American as any one else."[32] As *Rough Writing* reveals, science, race, gender, class, economics, politics, progressivism, and the desire to believe in an America that was simultaneously open yet impermeable underlay Roosevelt's claims and shaped his interactions with both immigrants and their stories. And while the claims of Schultz and Grant would be embraced by the increasingly influential eugenics movement of the 1920s and 1930s, and the ideas of Kallen and Bourne would be revived later in the century by multiculturalists, until the end of his life in 1919, the views Theodore Roosevelt represented held sway, shaping the nation's official claims, policies, and narrative.[33]

Roosevelt addresses a crowd, Evanston, IL 1903 (Theodore Roosevelt Collection, Harvard College Library).

"The Book of America's Past and the Book of America's Present"

It is no coincidence that "True Americanism," Roosevelt's first major essay laying out the obligations of and to new immigrants, was simultaneously a call to literary arms. Roosevelt recognized that for America to become the primary source of identity and belonging for *all* its citizens, it needed to be narrated, broadcast, and promoted in popular form. This was to be a national and nationalist literature, not a sectional, international, or transnational one, Roosevelt insisted, eschewing "the patriotism of the village," along with "lack of all patriotism," "hyphenated" patriotism, and their literary expressions.[34] Inserting himself into the debate over literary regionalism, Roosevelt maintained that "we should keep steadily in mind the futility of talking of a Northern literature or a Southern literature, an Eastern or a Western school of art or science. Joel Chandler Harris is emphatically a national writer; so is Mark Twain. . . . They write as Americans for all people who can read English."[35] While some saw literature focused on the particularities of place as a means of preserving regional distinctiveness and independence against the increasingly centralized state, Roosevelt saw it as a means of consolidating the state, of building a unified American story and nation through its diverse parts.[36] As he wrote elsewhere, American literature must represent regional diversity in a way that is "representative of all the local features of our *composite* nationality."[37] It must be national, not sectional, he insisted less than thirty years after the Civil War. At the same time, American literature and its authors should not "mold themselves in conventional European forms," exhibiting a "spirit of colonial dependence on, and exaggerated deference to, European opinion."[38] "Thus it is with the undersized man of letters who flees his country because he, with his delicate, effeminate sensitiveness, finds the conditions of life on this side of the water crude and raw; in other words, because he finds that he cannot play a man's part among men, and so goes where he will be sheltered from the winds that harden stouter souls," Roosevelt added, with an assault on both the Americanness and the masculinity of expatriate writers in particular.[39] Americans and American literature must be nationalist, not parochial, internationalist, or cosmopolitan.

Roosevelt clearly feared not only for the loyalties of the immigrant but for the "true Americanness" of the native born. "It is not only necessary to Americanize the immigrants of foreign birth who settle among us, but it is even more necessary for those of us who are by birth and descent already Americans not to throw away our birthright," he declared.[40] And popular literature was a central means of Americanizing them all.[41]

Though "True Americanism" does not explicitly mention immigrant literature, Roosevelt's anxiety over the values and national orientation of native-born Americans and their writings created a space for alternative sites of production. "I for one would heartily throw in my fate with the men of alien stock who were true to the old American principles rather than with the men of the old American stock who were traitors to the old American principles," Roosevelt proclaimed in his speech "Race Decadence" (1911).[42] In the face of a failing native stock, Roosevelt looked to immigrants of the "right ideals" for both the biological and cultural reproduction of the nation. He called upon them to make America and Americans—to have more children, to work actively to reform social ills, and to create a new, distinctly American literature.

To articulate and disseminate a truer Americanism, Roosevelt fostered the writings of non-Anglo writers of the "right principles," actively promoting or involving himself in the literary production of writers of diverse European backgrounds explored here, including Jacob Riis, Elizabeth Stern, and Finley Peter Dunne. He also backed the "American work" of the British Jew Israel Zangwill, whose play *The Melting Pot* set the terms of the discussion for years to come.[43] The social reformer, autobiographer/novelist, humorist, and dramatist, respectively, provided diverse public forums for the articulation of "true Americanness" in popular form. Their explicit focus on assimilation, race, nationalism, domesticity, class, manhood, and reform provided ideal opportunities to present key positions to the public. Through these writers, Roosevelt could spread his ideas to new audiences in plays, books, women's magazines, and newspapers. Through them, he could model for immigrants the terms of assimilation, enflame old-stock Americans with the passion of the new recruits, and demonstrate his own progressivism, his "square deal" to folks of (almost) any background with the right American values.

And what of the writers themselves? The apparently increasing abandonment of national ideals and responsibilities by old-stock Americans and particularly old-stock American writers created a frightening ideological and cultural gap for the nation. But for ethnic writers with dreams of establishing themselves, this breach produced a unique opportunity. They could reassert for the nation the values it wanted to believe defined it, creating in the process a place for themselves and their ethnic communities in America.

What did it mean for these authors to win the patronage of a president of the United States? The sense of flattery and chosenness was unimaginable, but so, often, were the attendant demands. To win Roosevelt's support—to have him author a preface, favorable review, or blurb—these writers generally had to conform in some way to his notion of the "true American." The pressure was sometimes indirect, but so huge a national presence had Roosevelt become, so dominant his narrative of Americanness and the means of achieving it, that for all, he was their imagined audience, and his vision had to be engaged.

But the stories these writers told were not always the stories Roosevelt wanted to hear or even the ones he thought he heard. Israel Zangwill's scientific vision of the melting pot was radically different from Roosevelt's, threatening the stability of the "American race" as the president imagined it. Jacob Riis's proud dual loyalty and active transnationalism challenged Roosevelt's demand for "only one flag." Elizabeth Stern's subtle questioning of progressive domesticity undercut the gender and class assumptions on which race and nationalism relied. And Finley Peter Dunne's brazen ethnic challenge to Roosevelt's articulations of masculinity, race, nation, and progressivism—indeed to his very "true Americanism"—shook the president's carefully constructed image of himself and the nation. Still, Roosevelt backed these authors and their work.

The direct connection between Roosevelt and these writers and the complexities of their associations demonstrate again the impact of "official narratives" on the lives and stories of individuals: all but one of these authors, for instance, tell their story as a narrative of transformation, of becoming American.[44] But this was never a one-way street. Not only do these authors anxiously or boldly revise or contest this convention and its scientific, racial, nationalist, class, gender, and political underpinnings, but they do so before its primary champion, Theodore Roosevelt, pushing him and the nation he represented to confront the realities of their America. In supporting them, Roosevelt engulfed their work into a particular nationalist framework, but simultaneously and inadvertently he opened the narrative of Americanism to alternative notions of race, nationalism, gender, class, and politics. The rhetoric and dream of "true Americanism" afforded both the immigrant and the native born the flexibility to shift emphasis and make room for diversity as the occasion arose, while at the same time setting and modifying the limits of acceptability.

In examining this give-and-take, *Rough Writing* confronts as well the ways in which the official rhetoric of the period continues to confound our understanding of how America was written and lived by both "new and old stock." The popularity of the "melting-pot" trope has obscured its contested scientific underpinnings and their ramifications. The World War I calls to "100% Americanism" and later claims of national unity and consensus muffled not only the reality but the tolerance of immigrant transnationalism during this prior period. The increased acceptance of progressive middle-class norms for gender and the home has hidden early resistance, just as the accepted history of progressivism has covered over the critique of its exclusions from ethnic quarters. Understandings, experiences, and representations of American life were far more complex and contradictory in this period than previously realized. And yet, they were brought together in this literature, a meeting place of diverse ideas and people who drew on each other to foster their own often disparate goals and visions of America.

Though only particular types of narratives by or about particular types of immigrants were officially sanctioned by Roosevelt, nonetheless, his powerful assertion of the Americanness of these fraught "ethnic texts" opened a space for other immigrant and ethnic writers, providing models for subsequent generations to imitate and revise. And though the boundaries remained circumscribed, they stretched, expanding the canon of American literature in a way that, at a later time and under other circumstances, would authorize and direct the creation of a broader, multicultural national literature. In exposing the early origins of this development, *Rough Writing* complicates our notions of power relations, narrative processes, true Americanness, and the creation of a national American literature at the turn of the twentieth century with implications into the twenty-first.

CHAPTER 1

Mendel's Melting Pot

Israel Zangwill and the Science of the Crucible

> The real American has not yet arrived. He is only in the Crucible, I tell you— he will be the fusion of all races, the coming superman.
> —Israel Zangwill, *The Melting Pot,* 1908[1]

> We Americans are the children of the crucible. The crucible does not do its work unless it turns out those cast into it in one national mould; and that must be the mould established by Washington and his fellows when they made us into a nation.
> —Theodore Roosevelt, "The Children of the Crucible," 1917[2]

"Dear President Roosevelt," began the August 1908 letter from British-Jewish author Israel Zangwill to the president of the United States: "I don't know if the fifth of October will find you in Washington, but if so, I should like to offer you or any members of your family a box for the first performance of my new play 'The Melting Pot' which dramatises your own idea of America as

MR. ROOSEVELT says:

"IT'S A GREAT PLAY! A GREAT PLAY!"

JACOB H. SCHIFF says:

"Perhaps a hundred years hence the world will know an American Race. Today it doesn't exist. It is in the making, and the conditions concerning this melting can apparently not be more forcibly portrayed than in Israel Zangwill's great play, 'The Melting Pot'."

OSCAR S. STRAUS, Secretary of Commerce and Labor, says:

"It is a great play . . . The feat of a genius. Incarnates the underlying spirit of our American patriotism . . . A great human canvas."

Roosevelt's reaction to *The Melting Pot* was featured in its publicity material years to come. (Central Zionist Archive A120/163, Jerusalem, Israel).

a crucible in which the races are fusing into the future American."[3] The invitation was formal but audacious, requesting the president to attend the world premiere of a melodrama on the basis of the play's ideology. Even more remarkable was the president's response. Roosevelt, his wife, and nearly half his cabinet accepted the invitation, and the morning after the performance, papers reported that "certain strong lines caused Mr. Roosevelt to lean forward in his box and say in a perfectly audible tone: 'That's all right!'"[4] Subsequent ads for the drama quoted Roosevelt as saying, "A great play. I do not know when I have seen a play that stirred me as much."[5]

The publicity generated by the premiere and the reaction of its most notable audience member did wonders for ticket sales. So did widespread reports that the president had invited Zangwill to lunch at the White House to express his displeasure with one of the lines, which joked about Americans' propensity for divorce. Headlines proclaiming "Roosevelt Criticizes Play" only added to popular interest,[6] and the president's desire to get every line just right, "in order not to mar your extraordinarily able and powerful play," reaffirmed his support of the drama as a whole.[7] When the play was published in 1909, it included a dedication to Theodore Roosevelt "by his kind permission," in "respectful recognition of his strenuous struggle against the forces that threaten to shipwreck the great Republic which carries mankind in its fortunes." For the next three-quarters of a century, the term the "melting pot," popularized by Zangwill's play and Roosevelt's backing, would dominate national debates over immigration and assimilation. The playwright and the president had truly grasped the power of popular literature to dramatize America. But what was the America it told?

Many assumed that Zangwill's words reflected Roosevelt's own ideology. "It is not too hard to understand why President Roosevelt was so intensely interested in [*The Melting Pot*] and why he suggested certain slight changes in the text," wrote one Chicago paper. "Americanism—the lofty high ideal of true Americanism—depicted by a Jew and an Englishman, is the keynote of the Zangwill drama."[8] As we have seen, for Roosevelt "true Americanism" was "a question of spirit, conviction, and purpose, not of creed or birthplace." It promised that all members of the "assimilable races" (i.e., all Europeans) could become complete Americans if they would just "throw themselves heartily into our national life, cease to be European, and become Americans like the rest of us." Once they gave up their old identities and allegiances and "learned to think, talk, and be United States," they would be accepted unconditionally into the nation and could be relied upon to perpetuate its ideals even more readily than native-born citizens.[9]

It is true that all facets of the president's notion of "true Americanism" are articulated in popular form in Zangwill's drama—from the imperative that native-born Americans stop "throw[ing] away their birthrights" to the demand that immigrants become Americans in every way and that the nation accept them as such.[10] The drama's main characters are drawn exactly to Roosevelt's models of the good immigrant, the unfortunate hyphenated immigrant, and the despicable native-born worshiper of Europe.

The characters even speak like Roosevelt, with the hero shouting, "Ah, it was bully!"—Roosevelt's trademark phrase.[11]

Undoubtedly aware of the president's ideas, Zangwill deliberately wrote his play with Roosevelt in mind. In the years after the bloody pogrom against the Jews of Kishineff described in the play,[12] the British dramatist was increasingly worried about the security of the Jews of eastern Europe. He worked to establish and maintain safe havens for them, supporting the World Zionist Congress's attempts to create an autonomous Jewish colony while simultaneously struggling to ensure that the United States remain open to refugees. Drawing on Roosevelt's prescriptions for what immigrants must do to become "true Americans," Zangwill crafted *The Melting Pot* as a deliberate political intervention, using his play to demonstrate just what wonderful Americans Jews in particular could become. And he looked to Roosevelt to back both his political and literary endeavors.[13]

For his part, Roosevelt saw in Zangwill's play a unique opportunity to popularize his imperatives for being and becoming American. Roosevelt's very entourage at the performance, which included the first Jewish U.S. cabinet member, Oscar Straus,[14] enacted the opportunities available to those who Americanized, while the play's premiere performance on the night of the most sacred Jewish holiday, Yom Kippur, indicated what the immigrant should and indeed would give up for the privilege of becoming a "true American."[15] The president and the playwright took full advantage of these very public onstage and offstage performances of the ideals, obligations, and possibilities of Americanism.

But Zangwill claimed that his drama represented not only Roosevelt's ideas of Americanization but also his notions of the "American race." As Zangwill said in his invitation, the drama portrays "your own idea of America as a crucible in which the races are fusing into the future American." For neither the president nor the playwright, nor even J. Hector St. John de Crèvecoeur, who first applied the terms to American society, did the words "crucible" or "melting pot" suggest a locus of cultural assimilation, as they are used by many today.[16] Rather, they imagined America as a crucible in which the races of the world were losing their distinctiveness and amalgamating into a single, unified race connected by blood. The process was seen as not only social but biological. Because virtually all traits were viewed as located in the blood, the only way to truly alter an individual's or a group's physical or cultural attributes was thought to be through intervention in the processes of heredity. Becoming an American at this time, then, meant changing not only one's customs, language, and loyalties but one's very biology or, at least, the biological makeup of one's descendents. Unlike Alfred P. Schultz or Horace Kallen, Zangwill and Roosevelt agreed that physical, as well as national and ideological, transformation was both possible and necessary.

But despite the playwright's insistence that his work mirrored Roosevelt's precisely, the two men had completely different ideas about the mechanism and the product of America's crucible. As we shall find, Zangwill believed that race mixture in the melting pot would produce an entirely new race, superior to its component parts. Roosevelt, on the other hand, insisted that contact would create nothing new at all; rather, it would erase biological difference, enabling newcomers to join the preexisting "race" of the founders without altering it in the least. And both men proclaimed their visions the "melting pot."

The significance of their fundamental disagreement goes beyond how a British playwright and an American president envisioned the past and future of the American people. The conflict between Zangwill and Roosevelt over the nature of the melting pot marks a moment of transition in the dominant scientific paradigms of race and heredity in the United States. This scientific shift had far-reaching social implications, impacting both immigration policy and narratives of Americanness. How the biological future of the nation was imagined depended on the theories of heredity one adopted. At the same time, as is always the case, the choice of a scientific worldview often had less to do with the merits of the science itself than with how one wished to imagine the future it foretold. And Zangwill and Roosevelt chose to imagine that future very differently. This chapter examines their competing racial visions and the science that underwrote them only to reveal how the metaphor and drama of the "melting pot" enabled both to be brought simultaneously into an increasingly complex narrative of America.

Melting and Fusing: Zangwill's Racial Vision of the Melting-Pot Millennium

For the hero of Zangwill's play, America's future was clear:

> America is God's Crucible, the great Melting-Pot where all the races of Europe are melting and re-forming! Here you stand . . . in your fifty groups,

with your fifty languages and histories, and your fifty blood hatreds and rivalries. But you won't be long like that, brothers, for these are the fires of God you've come to—these are the fires of God. A fig for your feuds and vendettas! Germans and Frenchmen, Irishmen and Englishmen, Jews and Russians—into the Crucible with you all! God is making the American.... The real American has not yet arrived. He is only in the Crucible, I tell you—he will be the fusion of all races, the coming superman.[17]

To David Quixano, victim of the pogroms of Kishineff instigated by the czarist government against the Jews, the United States holds out the apocalyptic hope of an end to all race hatred. It promises, as Roosevelt claimed, that antipathies will be forgotten and "merge[d] into love for our common country."[18] For Quixano, it promises further to merge through love of one another. The key is interbreeding. Joined in a new nation, former enemies will unite their bloodlines and become kin. They will fuse their races and produce a composite superrace, superior to each of its component parts.[19]

But as David discovers, it is far more difficult to overcome historical enmities and allegiances in practice than in theory. Zangwill's drama centers on the love story between the Russian Jewish immigrant composer, David, and Vera Revendal, an immigrant of Russian Christian nobility. Defying his family and what his Uncle Mendel refers to as "the call of our blood through immemorial generations," David betroths Vera, hoping to forget "all that nightmare of religions and races . . . by holding out my hands with prayer and music toward the Republic of Man and the Kingdom of God!"[20] But just as they are ready to marry, Vera's father arrives from Russia, brought to the United States to prevent the marriage by the decadent American millionaire Quincy Davenport, who wishes to wed Vera himself, despite the fact that he is already married. David soon discovers that Vera's father is none other than the Butcher of Kishineff, the very man who oversaw the slaughter of his parents and siblings. Torn apart by the "river of blood" between them, David proclaims that he can no longer marry Vera. He cannot deny his past, forgive his enemy, and join their families together. In Vera's kiss, he feels "blood on his lips," in her arms "the cold dead pushing."[21] The blood of the massacred forces their bloodlines apart.

But in the end, Vera and David reunite. They must in order to salvage David's (and Zangwill's) vision of America. The play ends with the lovers joined on the rooftop of the settlement house where David's great

Against the backdrop of New York City and the Statue of Liberty, David Quixano (Walker Whiteside) and Vera Revendal (Grace Lane) reunite on the rooftop of a settlement house in the final scene of *The Melting Pot*. London production, 1914. (Central Zionist Archive A120/163, Jerusalem, Israel).

American symphony has just been performed. Gazing at the sun setting behind the Statue of Liberty, they proclaim:

> David: There she lies, the great Melting-Pot—listen! Can't you hear the roaring and the bubbling? There gapes her mouth—the harbour where a thousand mammoth feeders come from the ends of the world to pour in their human freight. Ah, what a stirring and a seething! Celt and Latin, Slav and Teuton, Greek and Syrian,—black and yellow—
> Vera: [Softly, nestling to him.] Jew and Gentile.
> David: Yes, East and West, and North and South, the palm and the pine, the pole and the equator, the crescent and the cross—how the great Alchemist melts and fuses them with his purging flame! Here shall they all unite to build the Republic of Man and the Kingdom of God. Ah, Vera, what is the glory of Rome and Jerusalem where all nations and races

come to worship and look back, compared with the glory of America, where all races and nations come to labour and look forward!

[He raises his hands in benediction over the shining city.]

Peace, peace, to all ye unborn millions, fated to fill this giant continent—the God of our children give you Peace.[22]

Looking forward toward their children, the product of their individual and racial union, David and Vera imagine the coming millennium with America as its focal point. Their vision is a religious one. God is the great Alchemist who melts down all difference and fuses all races into a blessed, new entity. The United States, in phrases repeated in the play, is both the "Republic of Man" and the "Kingdom of God," the new Rome and the new Jerusalem. This notion of America as the new promised land is as old as the first Puritan settlement on the continent.[23] But arguing that the "Pilgrim Fathers came straight out of his Old Testament," David reverses the Puritan typology.[24] He claims old Israel as the new Puritan, thereby creating a place for himself and for his uniquely Jewish millennialism in America and suggesting that in fact to be Jewish is by definition to be American.[25]

But there is something else new in David's millennialism. It is not only Jewish and national but also evolutionary. As historian Gail Bederman has suggested, with Darwin shaking the belief in a divinely ordered human history progressing toward the ultimate rule of Christ, turn-of-the-century thinkers sought to substitute evolution for God. Instead of believing that God was working to perfect the world through the battle of good against evil, they believed that evolution was working to perfect the world through the competition between superior and inferior races, leading to the advancement of civilization and the ultimate perfection of the human race.[26] Roosevelt is often, though somewhat mistakenly, seen as one of the key proponents of this idea of the advancement of humanity through conquest, domination, and tutelage by the civilized races.[27] In *The Melting Pot*, Zangwill too combines religious and evolutionary millennialism, but he revises the prevalent Darwinian model. He imagines the perfectibility of the human race—the coming of the "superman"—not through racial strife but through racial fusion in a crucible stirred by God.

This God, "the great Alchemist, melts and fuses [all] with his purging flame," David tells us, and while the image is violent, replete with roaring and bubbling, stirring and seething,[28] its prophet reminds us that these are not "the fires of hate" but "the fires of love. That is what melts."[29] His Uncle Mendel, opposed to the intermarriage of Jew and Gentile, sneers at this claim, insinuating that it is David's desire for Vera that has changed him. But David insists: "The love that melted me was not Vera's—it was the love *America* showed me—the day she gathered me to her breast."[30] His metaphor is of maternal love, and David juxtaposes America's motherly embrace of her diverse newcomers, particularly of Jews, to the hatred shown them by other nations. But Uncle Mendel is not far off. In exhibiting political tolerance to all people, America, Zangwill believes, will encourage social tolerance among its people, leading to interaction and ultimately to intermarriage.[31] Though mothers may melt hatred and prejudice, the fusing fires of the crucible are ultimately the fires of passion.

By the end of the play, David genders the melting pot as female, a woman lying suggestively in New York harbor, "her mouth" agape, open to "human freight" from the ends of the earth.[32] It is only through promiscuous sexuality that the melting pot can do its work. Zangwill, who perceives race as a biological phenomenon fixed in blood, believes that the only way to alter one's racial line is to combine it with another through a sexual union producing hybrid offspring. Sexuality, and in particular, sex that transgresses racial borders, is thus, by necessity, at the heart of David's vision for America and sanctioned by his God. For it is transgressive desire that will usher in the new millennium.[33]

Passion and Compassion: Sex and Empathy in the Making of Americans

Because of its capacity to alter biology, sexual passion is the primary engine of racial development; yet within the world of *The Melting Pot*, compassion and its social influence must precede and accompany passion in creating the future American. This idea is expressed most poignantly through the relationship between the Irish Catholic maid in the Quixano household and the elderly grandmother figure of Frau Quixano, an observant Jew who detests America for destroying her family's practice of Judaism. The maid, Kathleen's uniquely American mixture of Yiddish and Irish brogue ("*Wu geht Ihr,* bedad?") and Jewish and Catholic worldviews ("Her father was a Rabbi." "What's that? A priest?")[34] have led some readers to view her relationship with the Frau as a model of ethnic accommodation and cooperation posed as an alternative to David's insistence on sexual and racial fusion.[35] It suggests the possibility of a blending of languages and traditions based on an ethic of mutual understanding rather than an act of physical intermixing. In his 1914 afterword to the play, Zangwill claims that such blending, what he calls "spiritual miscegenation," has occurred and will continue to occur in the United States. "The action of the crucible is thus not exclusively physical—a consideration particularly important as regards the Jew. The Jew may be Americanised and the American Judaised without any gamic interaction."[36] But for Zangwill, such interaction has the capacity to alter the tenor of a nationality, not of a race. It cannot lead to the creation of the new American "superman." As we shall see, assimilation without amalgamation is problematic and incomplete for Zangwill. Within the framework of his play, spiritual intermarriage is a present, but certainly not preferred or even sustainable, option.[37]

The relationship between Kathleen and Frau Quixano exemplifies spiritual fusion. At first, Kathleen resents the old woman and her odd ways. "Pots and pans and plates and knives. Sure 'tis enough to make a saint chrazy," she exclaims in frustration with the laws of *kashrut*.[38] "Bad luck to me if iver I take sarvice again with haythen Jews," she proclaims, planning to leave the Quixano home immediately.[39] She is persuaded to stay only upon hearing the sorrowful story of the old woman's life and the full account of her loneliness in America, where "nobody understands her, and she sits all the livelong day alone—alone with her book and her religion and her memories."[40] "'Oh, Mr. David,'" the maid cries, "[hysterically bursting into tears, dropping her parcel and untying her bonnet strings]. 'Oh, Mr. David, I won't mix the crockery, I won't –.'"[41] Through an act of empathy, Kathleen is able to overcome her prejudice and frustration and become the old lady's most devoted companion and protector of her faith. She walks up flights of stairs with her on the Sabbath in order to see David after the performance of his symphony; she goes to Hester Street to purchase masks for the holiday of Purim, encourages the men of the household to give joy to the old woman by celebrating the holiday with her, and even learns to speak a few words of Yiddish in order to communicate with Frau Quixano.

Not only is Kathleen Judaized, as several critics have suggested,[42] but in a very real sense, these two most ethnically marked women in the play are Americanized through their relationship with one another. The opportunity for empathetic and cooperative contact between peoples of different origins is a unique feature of the United States, according to Zangwill. "In America alone can be found the synthesis in which the extremest antithesis can be reconciled."[43] Through compassion, cooperation, and family feeling, Kathleen and Frau Quixano are transformed into Americans of a sort and can celebrate the Fourth of July together, as they do in the final act of the play.

But Kathleen and the Frau are not the play's heroes. Kathleen is portrayed as a comic fool. Her relationship with the old woman is not one of equals but of employee and employer, subject to the power dynamics implied therein. Furthermore, it is a transient phenomenon that will die with these two first-generation immigrants.

David and Vera's relationship, the focus of the play, also includes an act of empathic blending, but in this case it creates the potential for physical blending and, as such, contains the promise of the future. David believes that he must forget his past in order to cast himself wholeheartedly into the melting pot and become a true American. When Mendel urges him to look backward to Jewish history, David cries, "hysterically": "To what? To Kishineff? . . . To that butcher's face directing the slaughter? . . . [H]ow else shall I calm myself save by forgetting all that nightmare of religions and races . . . !"[44] The past is filled with maddening pain for him, and he longs to find sanity and health through a deliberate act of forgetting. But David finds that this cannot be achieved. Whenever he plays his violin, a stabbing pain in his shoulder reminds him of the Butcher of Kishineff, who inflicted the wound. The actual sight of the baron leads him to recall not only his personal history but the long history of Jewish persecution, and to cry out with the traditional plaint: "O God, shall we always be broken on the wheel of history? How long, O Lord, how long?"[45] And when he kisses Revendal's daughter, he is confronted with images of the pogrom, of the three kisses on the mouth "in token of peace and good will" shared by the Christians on that Easter Sunday that turned into a day of massacre.[46]

Despite David's dearest hopes, America cannot make him forget; what it does instead is to cause Vera to remember as he does. "I had not realized that crimson flood. Now I see it day and night. O God!" she shudders.[47] David's memories have become hers; like Kathleen with Frau Quixano, she understands the other by sharing his past through an act of empathy.

"There lies my failure—to have brought it to your eyes, instead of blotting it from my own," David laments, but his cry is misplaced.[48] It is because Vera can share his pain and his history that they can unite. She becomes a victim of Kishineff as well, with nightmares of her own and a butcher-father who, she sobs, "thought you were ordering your soldiers to fire at the Jews, but it was my heart they pierced."[49] David's pain is eased only when Vera takes up his burden of remembering, forgetting that her family was on the side of the murderers and his on the side of the murdered. And with this shared burden comes its own remedy—the creation of children who will have no such memories.

The centrality of forgetting to national unity was famously articulated by the French intellectual Ernest Renan in his lecture "What Is a Nation?" (1882). Renan argued: "Forgetting, I would even go so far as to say historical error, is a crucial factor in the creation of a nation. . . . The essence of a nation is that all individuals have many things in common and also that they have forgotten many things. No French citizen knows whether he is a Burgundian, an Alan, a Taifale, or a Visigoth, yet every French citizen has to have forgotten the massacre of Saint Bartholomew, or the massacres that took place in the Midi in the thirteenth century."[50] Though Renan speaks of forgetting who was the perpetrator and who the victim of the violence done to create the nation, his notion of forgetting is nonetheless useful in the American melting-pot context, where, according to both Zangwill and Roosevelt, immigrants must forget the enmities of their pre-American past. This is achieved in Zangwill's play through the act of reimagining the past from the perspective of the other, thereby forgetting the distance between their historical experiences. Only then can Vera and David hope to merge their blood within the crucible, building a future together that will annihilate their separate and violently opposed origins through the creation of a new united line.

Empathy like Kathleen's may be necessary, but it is not enough to forge the nation. Ultimately, as Renan's Frenchman must "emerge out of the cauldron in which . . . the most diverse elements have together been simmering,"[51] Zangwill's American must emerge from the heat of passion in the melting pot where different races are together procreating. Race must be altered along with nationality. Passion must follow compassion.

Within the world of Zangwill's play, relationships of desire are valued above relationships of friendship or even of birth. In his classic study,

Beyond Ethnicity, Werner Sollors has shown how U.S. ethnic literatures sacralize volitional relationships based on love and desire over kinship relationships based on blood. Immigrants have consistently used the distinction between descent and consent to argue that they, who have chosen America as their home, are more loyally in love with it than those placed there by accidents of birth.[52] The contrast between David Quixano and his rival and nominal inverse, Quincy Davenport, demonstrates just this point.[53] If David represents Roosevelt's "true American," Davenport represents his "silly and undesirable citizen," about whom Roosevelt wrote: "It is not only necessary to Americanize the immigrants of foreign birth who settle among us, but it is even more necessary for those among us who are by birth and descent already Americans not to throw away our birthright, and, with incredible and contemptible folly, wander back to bow down before the alien gods whom our forefathers forsook."[54] Davenport, a "dude" living decadently off of his father's money, has done just this, spending ten months out of the year in Europe, aping old-world ways, and consistently denigrating the United States.

If marriage is the model for the immigrant's relationship to America, adultery is the paradigm for the native born who has turned his back on his country's values. "A man who loves another country as much as he does his own is quite as noxious a member of society as a man who loves other women as much as he loves his wife," Roosevelt wrote, speaking of the native-born lover of Europe.[55] In an apparently deliberate appeal to the president, Zangwill makes his expatriate a philanderer. Davenport wants Vera, flirts with her unabashedly, and is willing to divorce his wife to have her. When Quincy expresses his delight upon discovering that Vera and David are only engaged, not wed, Vera berates him, saying, "We are not native-born Americans; we hold our troth eternal!"[56]

This was the line to which Roosevelt took exception, feeling, despite his own attacks on the neglective native born and on divorce, that Zangwill's words were an unjust slight to all Americans. Roosevelt urged Zangwill to revise Vera's words to: "Not being members of the Four Hundred, we hold even our troth sacred," thereby attacking the morals of only the very wealthy, the un-American in America.[57] Zangwill reluctantly made the change, which he later edited to "not being unemployed millionaires like Mr. Davenport, we hold even our troth eternal," attacking an even tinier percentage of native-born Americans.[58]

Even with this emendation, however, Zangwill shows that it is immigrants who are more faithful to their chosen loves, and thus by extension to their chosen land, than the very descendants of the founding fathers. Residual love for mother and motherland is not at issue for David, who was orphaned in a pogrom that simultaneously cut all affective ties to Russia for the Jewish immigrant. David is free to love America exclusively.[59] Davenport cannot understand this, and when David declares that the millionaire and his type are "killing my America," he replies, "*Your* America, forsooth, you Jew-immigrant!"[60] Davenport believes that America is his by virtue of his ancestry. He values breed and bloodlines, desiring Vera not for her goodness or for the future that he can create with her but for her aristocratic birth. She is, in his words, "the right breed—the true blue blood of Europe."[61]

It is probably not accidental that Quincy Davenport's name recalls that of one of the United States' most famed eugenicists, Charles Davenport. In his emphasis on descent, claims to America by birth, and desire to "stop all alien immigration,"[62] Quincy mirrors his real-life counterpart, who claimed that nationality was a function of race and would later argue that the idea of melting and re-forming races within the American crucible was scientifically impossible.[63] Zangwill does away with Davenport and his ideas by casting him into the melting pot himself. "You shall not kill my dream!" David declares. "There shall come a fire round the Crucible that will melt you and your breed like wax in a blowpipe. . . . America *shall* make good . . . !"[64] But though David Quixano replaces Quincy Davenport as the true American, it is too much to claim with Sollors that Americans by consent replace Americans by descent entirely within Zangwill's play.

This drama is primarily about race—not race abrogated but race reformulated. And it is not only about love and marriage but, as we have seen, about sex and offspring. Though Vera and David reject the rules of endogamy dictated by their fathers and their peoples, they do so in order to create a new line of descent. True, all races are invited and urged to contribute to this new mixed American blood, and it remains ever-changing and unfixed, but the children of the melting pot are meant to celebrate their mixed ancestry and prize their hybrid blood.[65] This blood is what entitles them and their descendants to America, and it is what will forge the American superman.

To suggest that Zangwill reified blood does not entirely discount the liberalism of his vision. His notion of hybrid superiority is a direct response to those who foretold the horrors of interracialism. Alfred Schultz, for instance, warned in 1908:

> We are told that our truly amazing assimilative power will produce the finest human race that has ever been known. . . . No dog fancier ever thought that the promiscuous crossing of bloodhound, terrier, greyhound, St. Bernard, pug, Newfoundland, and spaniel produces anything but worthless mongrel curs. Moral lepers. . . . Promiscuous crossing never produces a homogeneous race, and it destroys every race, even the strongest race.[66]

Schultz vehemently argued that interbreeding leads to racial chaos, degeneration, and destruction. Others believed that the product of intermixture would represent the lowest common denominator of its components, leading to the deterioration of the higher race.[67] Some claimed that the race already established on the geographic site of interbreeding would dominate.[68] Still others insisted, despite all evidence to the contrary, that human racial intermixtures would ultimately prove as infertile as mules.[69] Virtually all agreed that the success of interbreeding depended on how closely related the component races were to one another.[70] Yet Zangwill promiscuously cast all races into his melting pot—"Celt and Latin, Slav and Teuton, . . . black and yellow"—confident that what would emerge would be not only viable but far superior to anything seen before.[71] What gave him this confidence? The answer lies in Zangwill's understanding of new hereditary science and the place of the Jew within.

The Jew as Race Pioneer

Throughout his career, Zangwill took an active part in transatlantic debates over race, heredity, and nationalism. Invited to serve as the Jewish spokesperson at the First Universal Races Congress in 1911,[72] he used this opportunity to attempt to disprove claims that races were too different to survive contact and that divergent races needed to be kept apart and immigrants of these races kept out of Britain and the United States.[73]

Attempting to counteract such claims, Zangwill turned to the example of the ubiquitous Jew, present in every nation and mixed with every race. He argued first from Jewish assimilability:

> If the Jew . . . displays simultaneously with the most tenacious preservation of his past the swiftest surrender of it that the planet has ever witnessed, if we find him entering with such passionate patriotism into almost every life on earth but his own, may not even the Jewish patriot draw the compensating conclusion that the Jew therein demonstrates the comparative superficiality of all these human differences?[74]

At the same time that he condemns Jews for not holding on to their own traditions and reproves them for their extreme patriotic allegiance to every nationality and land but their own, Zangwill argues that their extraordinary ability to assimilate proves that the races are not so far apart. For Zangwill, assimilation into a foreign nation without amalgamation into its racial mixture is largely a matter of performance, and the Jew is the consummate actor.[75] "What wonder that Jews are the chief ornaments of the stage, that his chameleon quality finds its profit in artistic mimicry as well as in biological," Zangwill adds, claiming unique access for himself as a dramatist and for Jewish actors to the performative arts.[76] Zangwill understands assimilative performance—including name changes, exaggerated local patriotism, disengagement from Jewish affairs, and even "mimetically absorbed" anti-Semitism—in Darwinian terms, as a mode of adaptation for survival. It is for him "an exemplification of the Darwinian theory of protective coloring," changing one's colors to fit into an environment without changing one's essential self.[77] Though Zangwill believes that by constantly acting like other peoples, Jews will wear down their own traditions and void them of meaning, he assumes that they nonetheless remain Jews by blood even while easily mimicking aspects of their host environment. Assimilation is a performance that does not alter the essential racial Jewishness of the actor, he insists. But the fact that the extreme outsider, the Jew, can slip into the national drama of another people and mimic the characteristic features of another race proves for Zangwill that racial types are not as distinct as many wished to claim. "Could Jews so readily assimilate to all these types, were these types fundamentally different?" he asks.[78] Even acting would be impossible were race types so vastly diverse.

Pushing his arguments further, Zangwill ultimately rests his case for the unity of the human species on the racial intermixture of the Jew. "Not only is every race akin to every other but every people is a hotch-potch of races," he asserts:

> The Jews, though mainly a white people, are not even devoid of a colored fringe, black, brown or yellow. . . . If the Jews are in no metaphorical sense brothers of all these peoples, then all these peoples are brothers to one another. If the Jew has been able to enter into all incarnations of humanity and to be at home in every environment, it is because he is a common measure of humanity. He is the pioneer by which the true race-theory has been experimentally demonstrated.[79]

The mongrel Jew, who, for Zangwill is every Jew, is the prototype of the future. That the Jew can successfully breed with every race means that each race can successfully breed with the others. "One touch of Jewry makes the whole world kin," he said.[80] And each race should breed with the others, his drama insists.

Mendel's Melting Pot

What kinds of peoples will all of this racial intermixture produce? Here Zangwill turned to the recently rediscovered work of Gregor Mendel for clues. Although Mendel's ideas of heredity are not discussed directly within Zangwill's play, Mendel is suggested by the Yiddish name of David's uncle, Mendel Quixano. In his 1914 afterword to the play, however, Zangwill explicitly raises Mendelian notions of dominant and recessive traits. He states here that "negroid hair and complexion [are], in Mendelian language, 'dominant,'" while "Jews are, unlike negroes, a 'recessive' type whose physical traits tend to disappear in the blended offspring."[81] His assertion of the dominance of Negro features would have suggested to many that the race would not be desirable in the mix. And, indeed, for an author who boldly threw "black and yellow" into the melting pot, including them in the new American race in his play, in his afterword Zangwill seems to close the lid on the Negro with disturbing language.[82] Still, he argues, eventually black and white will unite in the crucible, and the American race will be darkened as a result of the dominance of Negroid traits preserved in its "hybrid posterity."[83]

Zangwill suggests, then, that, for better or for worse, the physical features of the children of the melting pot will be determined by the mathematics of genetic dominance. Zangwill's understanding of Mendelianism, like that of his contemporaries, is unsophisticated. He does not yet recognize the potential for recessive traits to reemerge in a population. Rather, he implies that the fusion of all races within the crucible will produce a new race bearing the traits dominant in each. And by combining the strongest traits of each of its components, this new race will mark the coming of the superman.

By asserting the recessiveness of Jewish physiognomy, which to many Americans would have seemed as undesirable as blackness, Zangwill neuters the racial threat of Jewish immigrants. He insists that Jewishness will be rendered invisible in the melting pot. There is no need for native-born Americans to overcome repulsion of the Jewish face, as they must to the Negro, for it will be lost in the mix in no time, the afterword suggests. And in all the early runs of the *Melting Pot*, non-Jewish actors played the role of David Quixano, perhaps so that there was never any risk onstage of the intermarrying Jew spoiling the phenotypic stew.

But Zangwill perhaps inadvertently pushed the issue of Jewish physiognomy to the forefront of his play in the controversial scene that closes act 2. Immediately after David declares to Mendel his intention to leave home and marry Vera, we find the Quixano family and their Irish maid celebrating the festival of Purim. This holiday commemorates the survival of the Jewish people in the Persian Empire thanks to the intervention of the Jewish queen Esther, who, by virtue of her marriage to the king of Persia, was able to save her people from massacre. Because she reversed the deadly decree, the day is celebrated through masquerade, the loosening and reversal of all norms; its theme is *venahafokh hu*, topsy-turvy. In *The Melting Pot*, the entire family, including Kathleen but excepting David, wear "grotesque noses" and dance to the music of David's fiddle. The holiday epitomizes and makes light of the central conflict between David and Mendel in this act over the responsibility of the individual Jew to his race. It recognizes the potentially positive impact of intermarriage while simultaneously and contradictorily celebrating the perpetuation of the Jews as a distinct and separate minority within the Diaspora. And the sight of the family in their grotesque noses provides comic relief from the tension between these polar opposites.

Kathleen (E. Noland O'Connor) searches for the Purim nose with Vera (Grace Lane), Herr Pappelmeister (Clifton Alderson), and Quincy Davenport (P. Percival Clark) looking on in *The Melting Pot*. London production, 1914. (Central Zionist Archive A120/163, Jerusalem, Israel).

Despite the fact that, as Zangwill insisted, such masks were traditional Purim-wear ("in case you have any doubt on the subject I refer you to the Jewish encyclopaedia . . . and a picture on page 275 of Vol. X," he wrote to one shocked reviewer),[84] the exaggerated noses, purchased on Hester Street by the elderly Frau Quixano and her Irish companion, threaten to undermine the promise of Zangwill's melting pot and the desirability of the Jew within. The sight of Kathleen in what would undoubtedly be seen as a "Jewish nose," worn, as she says, "Bekaz we're Hebrews! . . . It's our Carnival to-day. Purim," confronts the audience with the Schultzian image of the future American as a grotesque mongrel—an Irish woman with a Jewish nose speaking a combination of Yiddish, Irish brogue, and American slang and honoring a bizarre mix of Jewish and Catholic faiths.[85] It is not surprising that this scene horrified Gentile reviewers.[86] Instead of suggesting the recessiveness and presumed erasability of Jewish traits, it embodied their worst fears about the blending of races in the melting pot, "one's sense of the 'chill,'" as Henry James called it, at even contemplating the results of the combination of "elements in the cauldron."[87] Jewish American reviewers were similarly distressed, fearing precisely this reaction on the part of their Gentile colleagues.[88]

The anxiety provoked by this scene is unmistakable, but it does not seem to have been Zangwill's intent. Nor did he consciously wish to destabilize race by showing that it is simply a matter of performance, as one critic suggests,[89] for he unshakably believed in the biological reality of race. For Zangwill, assimilation is mere performance, but amalgamation is a very real and genetically determined mixing of bloodlines. As suggested by a speech on Jewish territorialism, given at the same time in which he was working on *The Melting Pot*, Zangwill may have wanted the Purim mask to represent the problem of assimilation, not the problems of amalgamation:

> The Russian or Roumanian Jew, when he shakes off the blood-stained dust of his native land, has shaken off his Russian or Roumanian nationality. He has *no* nationality. When he buys his steamer-ticket he is choosing a new nationality. Unless he is criminal or unhealthy, he can become a Briton or a Dutchman, a Canadian or a Mexican, or whatever he pleases. He is like a child buying a *Purim* mask. He can have any mask he likes—French or German, Persian or Turkish. But suppose the emigrant says, No, I will have nothing to do with masks. I will wear my own face—the Jewish face. I will go out and build up a nationality of my own. How dare you give him anything but sympathy.[90]

Here Zangwill represents choosing a nationality other than the one that corresponds to one's race as selecting a Purim mask, describing this choice as a performance, an act of imitation, in the same way in which he talks about assimilation. It is a choice to appear and to behave other than as oneself. The only alternative presented here to the wandering Jews' life of acting and masking their essential nature is building up a national land where they can "wear [their] own face" and develop according to their own hereditary inclinations. Within the world of Zangwill's *Melting Pot*, this nationalist idea is alluded to, but the primary alternative to masking within the play is wearing one's own face into marriage with an other wherein that face will be remolded in succeeding generations. It is the characters who remain outside the melting pot who don the Purim mask: Kathleen, who accommodates to the Jewish atmosphere in which she lives; Mendel, who while preserving love for Jewishness in his heart, is desperate to appear American to the world; and Frau Quixano, who tenaciously clings to Jewish customs. They end up making a grotesque mockery of Jewishness in America, the scene suggests. David, having chosen to marry Vera, is the only member of the Quixano household not to wear the Purim mask. He will be the only one to lose the markers of his Jewishness by losing its recessive physical traits through Mendelian means.

But though Jewish features may disappear, Zangwill believes that Jewish ethos will dominate.[91] While he considers the Jew a recessive physical type, he deems the Jewish sense of justice—which he understands as a racial, sociobiological trait—to be the dominant and most powerful of ethical forces. "It is precisely in the Old Testament that is reached the highest ethical note ever yet sounded, not only by Judaism but by man," he argues,[92] describing this philosophical development in evolutionary terms by claiming that "whatever its scientific explanation, the Jews had . . . reached this phase of evolution centuries before the rest of the world."[93] And Zangwill insists that this "spiritual originality" has "the strength to survive in the struggle and the interaction of the races."[94] The essence of Jewish ideals and character will thus be preserved in the struggle between and intermixture of the races.

As the land of the melting pot, merging all races and throwing the Jew into the mix, America will become the new Zion,[95] with its hybrid race spreading the Jewish ethic of justice to the world. It was on this ethic that America was founded, Zangwill insists, and to this ethic that its Jewish immigrants will return it, through both their example and their blood. As can be imagined, Roosevelt's notion of the crucible differed dramatically from Zangwill's.

Roosevelt's "American Mould"

For Roosevelt, the new American race was not new at all. Even with the addition of millions of new immigrants from new countries, the future American, Roosevelt insisted, would not be much different from the past. "Here in this country," he wrote, the representatives of many Old World races are being fused together into a new type, a type the main features of which are already determined, and were determined at the time of the Revolutionary War; for the crucible in which all the new types are melted into one was shaped from 1776 to 1789, and our nationality was definitely fixed in all its essentials by the men of Washington's day.[96]

In a deliberate move to ground American nationality in presumably immutable race, Roosevelt collapsed the political and the biological, dating the establishment of the American racial type as simultaneous with the birth of the nation. He argued that though new (white) elements may be added, the essentials of the American race have not changed from the time of the Revolution; the "new type" is already old. New immigrants have little or no impact on the physical or national characteristics of the American. As he would say even more strongly during World War I, "The crucible does not do its work unless it turns out those cast into it in one national mould; and that must be the mould established by Washington and his fellows when they made us into a nation."[97] Roosevelt did not allow for a free and unregulated flow of materials within the melting pot. In the face of tremendous pressure, he did keep the door open to new immigrants of eastern and southern Europe, but he demanded that they recast themselves in the "American mould," and he trusted that they then could be absorbed into the American race without significantly changing it. On what did he base his faith?

Acquiring a New Race

As has been well established by historian Thomas Dyer, Roosevelt was a neo-Lamarckian.[98] Even in the face of mounting empirical evidence to the contrary, Roosevelt maintained that individuals acquire new characteristics in response to changes in their environments and that they transmit these new traits through their reproductive materials to their offspring, a principle known as the "inheritance of acquired characteristics." This means that an organism might alter its behavior and body structure involuntarily, in response to a change in the environment (growing longer hair in a colder climate, for example), or by exercising its body in a new way to adjust to new conditions (such as stretching its neck to reach a higher food—the classic Lamarckian explanation for the gradual lengthening of a giraffe's neck). The alterations made in the body and behavior of adult organisms are embedded in their reproductive materials and passed down to their children. A steady accumulation of minute changes over the generations directs the evolution of the species toward higher civilization.[99]

A sickly child who transformed his body and image through rigorous exercise, Roosevelt embraced Lamarckism largely because it suggests that heredity can be modified by environmental change and individual activity.[100] He rejected the deterministic notion—embraced by up-and-coming geneticists and eugenicists—that physical characteristics are immutable, passed unchanged from parent to child, leaving some fit and others hopelessly unfit for survival.[101] Like his friend Jacob Riis and other progressive reformers, Roosevelt believed that the American people could be shaped through the manipulation of their environment. Good homes, for instance, would literally create good bodies, good characters, and good citizens, improving the biological and moral future of generations to come.

It is precisely this physical, inheritable influence of the environment on bodies that Roosevelt believed would transform all white European immigrants into people of the American type—and do so without significantly altering the type itself. Roosevelt explicated this idea most fully in his Oxford University Romanes Lecture, "Biological Analogies in History" (1910). First drafted in 1908,[102] this speech enables us to pinpoint what the president thought about race, nation, and evolutionary science at the very moment in which he endorsed Zangwill's *Melting Pot*. In this speech, he draws an analogy between the American situation and that of the Germanic invasion of Rome. He insists that the migration or invasion of one European race into the territory of another has no lasting effect on the established racial composition of the land. Though the invaders might appear at first to alter and dominate the physical makeup of the populace, there is ultimately a reversion to the original type.

Why this reversion happens, Roosevelt cannot explain definitively, but he does offer several possibilities, virtually all of which involve the pressures of environment on the genetic makeup (genotype) and/or physical appearance (phenotype) of the people who dwell therein. He does suggest that it is possible that the invading race failed to breed sufficiently and was swamped out of existence by the native residents who bred at far greater speeds—an early example of "race suicide," which Roosevelt warned members of the white world would happen to them if they did not keep pace with the birthrates of nonwhites. But Roosevelt is far more taken here with environmental explanations:

> As the blood [of the invaders] is mixed with the ancient blood, has there been a change, part reversion and part assimilation, to the ancient type in its old surroundings? Do tint of skin, eyes, and hair, shape of skull, and stature change in the new environment, so as to be like those of the older people who dwelt in this environment? Do the intrusive races, without change of blood, tend under the pressure of their new surroundings to change in type so as to resemble the ancient peoples of the land? Or, as the strains mingled, has the new strain dwindled and vanished, from causes as yet obscure? . . . We cannot say.[103]

He suggests that it is possible that the blood and/or the physical traits of the "intrusive race" alter as a result of the "pressure of the new surroundings" with or without intermixture with the blood of the original inhabitants of the land.

Roosevelt is not confident in any explanation of the phenomenon of the maintenance of original types. Throughout his lecture he remains hesitant about stating any theory of evolution with surety. He recognizes that scientific knowledge is in a moment of crisis.[104] "As our knowledge increases our wisdom is often turned into foolishness, and many of the phenomena of evolution which seemed clearly explicable . . . to us nowadays seem far less satisfactorily explained," he acknowledges.[105]

Realizing that his long-held scientific worldview is now being shaken, Roosevelt is reluctant to speak authoritatively when discussing the forces of evolution. But his tentative suggestions are nonetheless significant for what they reveal about the conceptual framework in which he continues, albeit hesitantly, to operate. He believes that "the persistence of the old type in its old home"[106] is an observable fact, and that the pressures of the environment will force newcomers to acquire the necessary characteristics to survive in that place, making them indistinguishable from the original type on the land within only a few generations.

Applying these historical and scientific principles to the context of the United States, Roosevelt was able to claim that the mixed race that established itself in America and built a nation in the late eighteenth century had proven itself fittest for the American environment. Immigrants who enter the land must adapt to it in order to survive. They do so by acquiring the characteristics of the descendants of the founding fathers and transmitting them bodily to their offspring. Through this mechanism—what we might consider cultural assimilation, but which for Roosevelt was a sociobiological process—immigrants would be absorbed into the nation while leaving its basic characteristics intact. They would be recast in the "American mould."

Implied in Roosevelt's science of assimilation was that only certain peoples could rapidly acquire the traits necessary for American racial identity. He believed in the equipotentiality of all races, that all peoples have the capacity to progress from savagery, to barbarism, to civilization and increased social efficiency by slowly acquiring and passing on the right characteristics.[107] But Roosevelt, like the vast majority of his white European and American contemporaries, placed races on a hierarchical scale. He believed, for instance, that the black race as a whole was not yet fully civilized. However, it had the potential to evolve further and further until meeting the highest standards of civilization. Roosevelt insisted that some rare individuals, including his trusted adviser on race matters, Booker T. Washington, had already achieved this level of development.[108] Such individuals should be treated as equals to white Americans and granted equal civic and employment opportunities. But until the black race as a whole had evolved sufficiently, it could not participate completely in American citizenship.[109]

Immigrants from "insufficiently evolved" racial groups also could not be expected to rapidly acquire the traits necessary to become Americans. For this reason, Roosevelt considered it dangerous to allow them to enter the United States. "It is urgently necessary to check and regulate our immigration, by much more drastic laws than now exist . . . to keep out races which do not assimilate readily into our own," he wrote, often referring to the Chinese with this phrase.[110] Peoples from highly evolved racial groups that were vastly different from the American race also needed to be shut out, for they had developed too far in other directions to alter their course and acquire Americanness. Such was the case with the Japanese, Roosevelt believed, so that "an effort to mix together . . . the peoples representing the culminating points of two such lines of divergent cultural development would be fraught with peril; and this . . . because the two are different, not because either is inferior to the other."[111]

For those immigrants from assimilable races, among whom Roosevelt controversially included all Europeans, the proper environments needed to be provided to facilitate the acquisition of American characteristics. For this reason, Roosevelt promoted the public school, the popular magazine, and reform of cities and homes. Speaking of the public school, he wrote, "Our task here has been in large measure to amalgamate many different race stocks, to fuse them into a common American citizenship. With adult immigrants this is a task of great difficulty. But children are pliable, and it is children whom it is best worth while to turn in the right direction."[112] He saw the school not simply as an agent of assimilation but as a mechanism of amalgamation, of fusing the American race not by interbreeding but by influencing the development of children.

Provide capable European immigrants with the right American environment and they will transform mentally, ideologically, and bodily into Americans indistinguishable from the founding fathers. This was Roosevelt's idea of the melting pot.

Fusing Over the Melting Pot

The difference between the American futures imagined and yearned for by Zangwill and Roosevelt reflects their larger aims and concerns. Zangwill was worried about the 1907 push in the U.S. Congress for greater restriction of immigration, similar to what had been enacted in Britain. He therefore insisted that the essence of the American people is an ever-changing admixture of races from all over the world, and that by closing off immigration, the nation would never have the opportunity to reach its full potential. Roosevelt was much more ambivalent about immigration. He was receptive to "assimilable" races entering the United States but anxious to preserve the essence of the America he knew. He therefore was most comfortable with scientific theories that assured him that the American race would remain virtually unchanged by a controlled influx of immigrants capable of acquiring American characteristics.

Despite the drastic differences in their theories and goals, Zangwill and Roosevelt united over *The Melting Pot*. They used each other's language and quoted each other's words, even though their meanings diverged. Zangwill's motives are simple to understand. He undoubtedly desired

Roosevelt's support to promote his career and his causes. And with Roosevelt endorsing his play, Zangwill could pack the house with theatergoers whom he would assail with visions for an American race far more radical than they might have expected.

Roosevelt's goals are more inscrutable. "The 'Melting Pot' . . . has been in my mind continually, and on my lips very often, during the last three years," he wrote to Zangwill in 1912. "It not merely dealt with the 'melting pot,' with the fusing of all foreign nationalities into an American nationality, but it also dealt with the great ideals" of America.[113] Roosevelt invoked the play as a way to talk about both racial fusion and Americanism, even though he believed that these processes occur and end very differently than Zangwill did. The play's popularity across the country allowed him to make reference to its central image without explanation. A shrewd politician, he may well have wanted to keep Zangwill's theories and his own ambiguous in the minds of his audience, so that they could imagine that he supported whatever it was that they believed in.

Ultimately, the power of *The Melting Pot* lay in its ability to popularize a metaphor that was broad enough to include Roosevelt's and Zangwill's disparate notions of the development of an American race. Both visions would leave legacies as the discussion of Americanness shifted from race to culture later in the century, with some using the "melting pot" to describe the fusion of all cultures into a new and superior American culture and others using the same term to describe the melting away of difference into a homogeneous preexisting American culture.[114] Still, the trope of the melting pot accommodated both views, just as it did Zangwill's and Roosevelt's. Through its emphasis on the blending of immigrants with each other and with the native-born American, it offered the assurance that all Europeans, if not others, would ultimately become part of America. This promise proved more important to many than the question of how. Once newcomers were invited into the nation under the shared vocabulary of "the melting pot," however, new voices became empowered to debate the nature and future of American identity, creating more complex notions of what it meant to be an American.

CHAPTER 2

Two Flags to Love

Jacob Riis and the Transnational American at the Turn of the Twentieth Century

> Happy he who has a flag to love. Twice blest he who has two.
> —Jacob Riis, *The Making of an American*, 1901[1]

> He did not come to this country until he was almost a young man; but if I were asked to name a fellow-man who came nearest to being the ideal American citizen, I should name Jacob Riis.
> —Theodore Roosevelt, introduction to *The Making of an American*, 1914[2]

"[The immigrant] must take pride in the things we can all take pride in. He must revere only our flag; not only must it come first, but no other flag should even come second," declared Theodore Roosevelt in his 1894 speech and article "True Americanism."[3] As seen in the previous chapter, Roosevelt was theoretically confident that the masses of European immigrants arriving at this time would ultimately fuse bodily into the "American mould." However, he, like the majority of his contemporaries, feared for the emotional and political allegiances of the new arrivals. These qualms only intensified over time, reaching their peak with World War I, which strained the loyalties of new Americans and tested the limits of the nation's tolerance. "There is no such thing as a hyphenated American who is a good American. The only man who is a good American is the man who is American and nothing else," Roosevelt insisted in 1915 before a gathering of the Catholic Knights of Columbus.[4] "As for the hyphenated Americans, among the very many lessons taught by the last year has been the lesson that the effort to combine fealty to the flag of an immigrant's natal land with fealty to the flag of his adopted land, in practice means not merely disregard of, but hostility to, the flag of the United States."[5] One nation, one flag, Roosevelt insisted in this era as previously. Hyphenated identities would not be tolerated, it seemed.

Until recently, few have questioned whether such demands were heeded by the immigrants at whom they were directed. Accepting the myth that émigrés to the United States at the turn of the twentieth century were eager to feel at home in America, scholars, suggests historian Rebecca Kobrin, have typically read immigrant history and literature of this period in terms of adaptation and Americanization rather than exile or transnationalism.[6] Transnationalism, the continued connectivity of peoples beyond national borders, has generally been understood as a late twentieth-century phenomenon, facilitated by globalization, advances in travel and telecommunications, and in the United States by the replacement of the melting-pot model of Americanization with multiculturalism.[7] But despite official narratives to the contrary, transnational practices and identities have always been a part of American immigrant life, and imaginative connections to home and homeland are a constant in immigrant writings, even by the most Americanized.

"Happy he who has a flag to love. Twice blest he who has two," declared the Danish immigrant and famed U.S. reformer Jacob Riis in his autobiography *The Making of an American* (1901).[8] Best known for his groundbreaking exposé *How the Other Half Lives*, Riis made no secret of his dual loyalties. In his autobiography, Riis, who took regular trips back and forth to Denmark, expressed not only nostalgic yearning for the land of his birth but militant nationalism. This nationalism took political form throughout Riis's life in his attempts to enlist in the army to liberate his home region of Slesvig, his work on behalf the diasporic Danish community, and his advocacy for the Danish crown with U.S. officials. Beyond his personal commitments, Riis promoted and defended hyphenated Americanism for all immigrants and their children. "The immigrant America wants and needs is he who brings the best of the old home to the new, not he who threw it overboard on the voyage," he proclaimed in his collection *Hero Tales of the Far North* (1910). Immigrants must record and preserve their own national and nationalist narratives and "cherish them with the memories of the mother land."[9]

Even with its overt calls for hyphenated identity and dual nationalism, Riis dedicated *Hero Tales* to "my living hero, Theodore Roosevelt,"[10] and Roosevelt in turn wrote the introduction to the second edition of Riis's autobiography reprinted after the author's death in 1914. "He did not come to this country until he was almost a young man; but if I were asked to name a fellow-man who came nearest to being the ideal American citizen, I should name Jacob Riis," Roosevelt proclaimed.[11] This interaction between the flag-waving president and the man of two flags offers a unique opportunity to examine not only the nationalist practices and loyalties of the immigrant but also the realities behind the rhetoric of the native born.

Roosevelt knew full well that Riis considered and conducted himself as a "hyphenated American." Jake and the Colonel, as they preferred to call each other,[12] had been close friends, political allies, and mutual promoters from the mythic moment that Roosevelt read Riis's reform tract *How the Other Half Lives* and went to the reporter's office at the *Evening Sun*, leaving his card with a note on the back saying, "I have read your book, and I have come to help."[13] Roosevelt read Riis's autobiographical writings as well and was often the object of his appeals on behalf of Denmark and Danish Americans. Roosevelt recognized Riis's dual loyalties; he even hyphenated Riis himself: "By the way, I was a good deal touched in San-Francisco," the president wrote to his friend in 1903. "I happened to mention you in one of my speeches, and certainly half a dozen different men and women of Danish birth came at different times to call upon me and say how proud they were of you as a Danish-American."[14] Before mailing the letter, Roosevelt lightly crossed out "a Danish-American," and deliberately changed it to simply "an American." Nonetheless, in conflict with his long held demands for 100 percent Americanism, Roosevelt clearly acknowledged Riis's continued Danishness and his status within a distinct diasporic community. Yet despite Riis's overt dual loyalties, Theodore Roosevelt declared over and over again that Jacob Riis epitomized the "ideal American citizen." Roosevelt dubbed Riis so privately in his extensive correspondence with the Riis family and in letters of introduction to powerful friends on Riis's behalf,[15] and he held Riis out as a model of citizenship for the nation in his introduction to the reformer's autobiography, in his own autobiography, and in many popular essays and speeches, including the one cited earlier in which he decried "hyphenated Americanism."[16]

The story here lies in the very lack of a story, the absence of conflict between the official narrative of 100 percent Americanism and an immigrant's officially praised life and tale of dual nationalism. The contradictions do not simply tell of a friendship or demonstrate yet again the personal inconsistencies of public figures. The relationship between Riis and Roosevelt and their public and private expressions and acceptance of hyphenated identity and dual nationalism illustrated in this chapter provide opportunity for a reconsideration of transnationalism during this period from the perspective of both the immigrant and the native-born American. Riis's literary forms, gendered tropes, and racialized language reveal the discourses through which the prospect of dual loyalty was made palatable to the American public, and Roosevelt's responses reveal the extent and terms of acceptance. What emerges from this analysis is a more complex and flexible, if fraught, picture of American identity, citizenship, nationalism, and narrative at work during this period, an Americanness whose contours were shaped by a constant process of negotiation between immigrant and native-born American.

Discovering the Other Half: Riis, Roosevelt, and Reform

> Long ago it was said that "one half of the world does not know how the other half lives." . . . It did not know because it did not care. The half that was on top cared little for the struggles, and less for the fate of those who were underneath, so long as it was able to hold them there and keep its own seat. There came a time when the discomfort and crowding below were so great, and the consequent upheavals so violent, that

it was no longer an easy thing to do, and then the upper half fell to inquiring what was the matter . . . and the whole world has had its hands full answering for its old ignorance.[17]

Thus began Jacob Riis's exposé *How the Other Half Lives* (1890). Confronting the nation with verbal, pictorial, and photographic depictions of its "other half," Riis in effect created the popular image of America's urban immigrant poor at the turn of the twentieth century. Of greatest concern to him were the conditions in which they lived, "because they are the hot-beds of the epidemics that carry death to rich and poor alike; the nurseries of pauperism and crime that fill our jails and police courts; that throw off a scum of forty thousand human wrecks to the island asylums and workhouses year by year; . . . because, above all, they touch the family life with deadly moral contagion."[18] The living spaces of the urban poor had become a threat to the physical, economic, and moral health and stability of the entire nation. The "sea of a mighty population, held in galling fetters, heaves uneasily in the tenements," Riis warned.[19] A neo-Lamarckian like Roosevelt, he trembled at the impact of such environments on the bodies and characters of the youth in particular. "The young are naturally neither vicious nor hardened, simply weak and undeveloped, except by the bad influences of the street," he insisted.[20] But "be it remembered, these children with the training they receive—or do not receive—with the instincts they inherit and absorb in their growing up are to be our future rulers."[21] Turning to his readers, he demanded, "What are you going to do about it?"[22]

Among those who responded, one man in particular would become Riis's most steadfast and powerful ally, and he, of course, was Theodore Roosevelt. Writing to Riis seven years later from his new post as assistant secretary of the navy, Roosevelt recalled: "When I went to the Police Department it was on your book that I had built, and it was on you yourself that I continued to build. Whatever I did there was done because I was trying, with much stumbling and ill success, but with genuine effort, to put into practice the principles you had set forth, and to live up to the standard you had established."[23] Riis's book had indeed shaped Roosevelt's sense of urgency and direction. Brought in in the spring of 1895 to clean up the New York City Police Department, still reeling from the Lexow Committee's exposure of extensive police graft and corruption,[24] Roosevelt had already made something of a name for himself as a reformer. In his years as a New York State legislator

(1882–84), he had demanded the investigation and impeachment of corrupt officials, called for the dissolution of the Manhattan Elevated Railroad Company, spearheaded the statewide push for civil service reform, and supported a bill banning cigar making in tenement sweatshops, saying, much like Riis, that "these conditions rendered it impossible for the families of the tenement house workers to live so that their children might grow up fitted for the exacting duties of American citizenship."[25] Roosevelt's reform work as an assemblyman led to his appointment as federal Civil Service commissioner, a position he held from 1889 to 1895, during which time he established the foundations of a new merit system.

Now seeking to reform New York City's notoriously corrupt police force as one member of its three-man police board, Roosevelt turned immediately to Jacob Riis, then a city reporter for the *New York Sun*. According to fellow journalist Lincoln Steffens, on Roosevelt's first day on the job:

> T.R. seized Riis, who introduced me, and still running, he asked questions: "Where are our offices? Where is the board room? What do we do first?" Out of the half-heard answers he gathered the way to the board room, where the old commissioners waited. . . . He introduced himself, his colleagues, with hand-shakes and then called a meeting of the new commissioners; had himself elected president, . . . and then adjourned to pull Riis and me with him into his office.
> "Now, then, what'll we do?"[26]

Roosevelt depended on Riis in particular to help him set his agenda, navigate city politics, accomplish meaningful reform, and at the same time, cement his reputation.

The power of the New York City Police Board was limited, and Roosevelt's efficacy and standing depended largely on public perception. Recalling these days in his *Autobiography*, Roosevelt writes:

> The then government of the Police Department was so devised as to render it most difficult to accomplish anything good. . . . Nevertheless, an astounding quantity of work was done in reforming the force. We had a good deal of power anyhow; we exercised it to the full; and we accomplished some things by assuming the appearance of a power which we did not really possess.[27]

Jacob Riis and Theodore Roosevelt survey the streets of lower Manhattan. Original illustration from *The Making of an American,* Macmillan, 1904.

The press was essential to Roosevelt's creation of the "appearance of power" at this moment as throughout his career.[28] As the *World* put it, the key to the commissioner's policy was "publicity, publicity, publicity," and the crusading immigrant reporter helped provide just that.[29]

Some of the most widely publicized acts by Commissioner Roosevelt were his legendary nighttime rambles through the seamier areas of New York City guided by Riis, the apparent expert on this other half.[30] Beginning at 2:00 AM on June 7, 1895, Riis led Roosevelt southeast from Forty-second Street, acquainting him firsthand with the late-night life of the city's saloons and brothels and providing him with the opportunity to check up on beat cops and roundsmen. Finding the vast majority away from or sleeping at their posts, the next day Roosevelt reprimanded the guilty and gave stern warning to the entire force. His dramatic gesture was all over the papers, imbuing in the New York City police force a sense of fear and discipline and instilling awe and confidence in people nationwide. Despite his actual limited powers, Roosevelt was perceived by the police as the official truly in charge and by the country as a man to be remembered.[31] Indeed, even the illustration accompanying the account of the tour in Riis's autobiography puts Roosevelt in front of his guide, establishing his dominance and authority.

During their walks, Riis gave the commissioner tours of the districts through which he had figuratively guided his readers in *How the Other Half Lives*, shaping Roosevelt's understanding of the situation and suggesting concrete proposals for its amelioration.[32] As president of the Police Board, Roosevelt was also an ex officio member of the New York Health Board, giving him the authority to propose housing, labor, and health reform, and both Roosevelt and Riis took advantage of this position. "I felt that with Jacob Riis's guidance, I would be able to put a goodly number of his principles into actual effect. . . . Our ideals and principles and purposes, and our beliefs as to the methods necessary to realize them were alike," he recalls in his *Autobiography*.[33] Their alliance led to the investigation and destruction of some of the worst tenements in the city, the demolition of the Tombs prison, and the permanent closing of the police lodging houses, which Riis had opposed since his own horrifying experience there as a destitute young immigrant. The motives and impact of these efforts on behalf of the poor have long been disputed,[34] but the reputation they created for both men is certain.

The mutually beneficial relationship between the two continued well beyond Roosevelt's stint as police commissioner. Once elected governor of New York in 1899, Roosevelt called on Riis again to take him through the tenements. He also asked Riis's assistance in writing speeches on the slum, and he turned to the reformer for advice on bills reforming labor and housing laws.[35] Riis, in turn, looked to Roosevelt to aid him in his causes and brought other reformers, including the Hull House settlement founder, Jane Addams, to meet and petition the governor. Riis continued to make requests of Roosevelt even once he became president, calling upon him to lend support to projects such as the Sea Breeze Hospital for crippled children and the Public Schools Athletic League, which aimed to improve the physical and moral health of children by altering their environment and their interactions with it. And as president, Roosevelt continued to call frequently upon Riis to speak, write, and in one instance, testify in court on his behalf.[36] He supported Riis's dedication of several books to him, and encouraged Riis's authorship of the hagiographic campaign biography *Theodore Roosevelt the Citizen* (1904).[37] Though each man constantly apologized to the other for imposing, their alliance clearly served and delighted them both.[38] "As regards any amount of what I have done," Roosevelt wrote to Riis in August 1900, "it has really been your work and not mine, but I have had the privilege of pulling the handle, so to speak, and starting the machinery which you arranged along the line of which you spoke."[39] Roosevelt viewed his reforms of the physical environment and material conditions of the poor, the foreigner, and the child as the fulfillment of Riis's work and "tried to live up to the doctrines that you have preached and practiced."[40] Riis, in turn, viewed Roosevelt as the power that "made my dreams real."[41]

But at the same time that he worked tirelessly with Roosevelt to improve conditions in the United States so as to make better Americans, Riis positioned himself as a spokesman for Denmark and the Danish American émigré community, urging the president to personal and public action and engaging in precisely the hyphenated politics that Roosevelt feared.

Two Flags to Love: Jacob Riis's Hyphenated Politics

Jacob Riis was always an ardent Danish nationalist. Born in Ribe, Denmark, in 1849, Riis came to the United States at the age of twenty-one, a penniless émigré seeking to escape his painful rejection by Elisabeth Gjortz, the beautiful, wealthy young niece of his erstwhile employer. The son of a poor schoolmaster and a carpenter himself, Jacob exiled himself to America, hoping he might there acquire the means to win Elisabeth's hand. But Riis found it impossible to secure steady work in the post–Civil War Northeast and spent four years tramping around New York, New Jersey, and Pennsylvania picking up jobs where he could, mining coal, making bricks, sawing lumber, trapping, and peddling. He slept in barns and woods in the countryside, church doorways and police lodging houses in New York City, until finally he landed a job as a reporter with a Brooklyn newspaper, finding security and his lifework. It may not have been his American semisuccesses as much as Elisabeth's Danish failures in love that enabled him to win her hand after all, and seven years after leaving Denmark, he returned to marry Elisabeth and bring her back to Richmond Hill, New York, where they made their life together until her death in 1905.[42] But Denmark was never far from their thoughts. Their home combined elements of both worlds.[43] Danish music, foods, and religious customs were important elements of the Riis family's life;[44] the older children could speak Danish, and the parents regretted not teaching the younger ones.[45] And with the means acquired through Jacob's American accomplishments, they made frequent return trips to their homeland.

Riis candidly declared his love of Denmark and the Danish crown in his personal life as well as in his writings. In one instance, in flagrant contradiction to Roosevelt's demand that "the immigrant must learn to celebrate Washington's Birthday rather than that of the Queen or Kaiser, and the Fourth of July instead of St. Patrick's Day," Riis conspicuously wore the Cross of Dannebrog to the Roosevelt White House on the Danish king's birthday only to discover that not even foreign diplomats wore any sort of decoration there.[46] It was because of Riis's good works in America, not Denmark, that King Christian had bestowed the cross upon him, declaring Riis an exemplary Dane in exile.[47] And Riis asserted this transnational identity within Roosevelt's inner sanctum. "I wear the cross proudly for the love I bear the flag under which I was born and the good king who gave it to me," he stated.[48]

But more than symbolic ethnicity or symbolic nationalism, Riis repeatedly acted to influence the political situation of his homeland and to shape American attitudes toward it.[49] In his early years in the United States, he attempted several times to enlist in the Franco-Prussian War, to "take revenge [on Prussia] for the great robbery of 1864" when Bismarck won the Danish region of Slesvig (German, Schleswig), which bordered Riis's hometown, for the German Confederation of States.[50] "All the hot blood of youth was surging through me," he recalled in his autobiography of 1901. "I remembered the defeat, the humiliation of the flag I loved,—aye! and love yet, for there is no flag like the flag of my fathers, save only that of my children and of my manhood."[51] While carefully insisting on his love for the United States, Riis asserts an equal and undying love for the land of his fathers, again contradicting Roosevelt's demand that the immigrant "must revere only our flag; not only must it come first, but no other flag should even come second."[52]

In later years, Riis continued to join Denmark's nationalist struggles, if not through arms then through words directed at both the American public at large and Roosevelt in particular. "I was a boy when they planted the black post at the line and watered it with the blood of my countrymen. Gray-haired and with old roots in foreign soil, I dream with them yet of the day that shall see it pulled up and hurled over the river where my fathers beat back the southern tide a thousand years," he wrote in *The Making of an American*.[53] And Riis indirectly petitioned Roosevelt to make this happen. In one of several letters to the president in which he sought favors on behalf of Danish immigrants,[54] Riis enclosed a letter from a Mr. Jacobsen, formerly of Slesvig, which explains how the writer and his brothers came to the United States "on account of being Danes from principle" and being unable to live as such in the German-controlled territory: "The children there are not allowed at all, not even in private school to study danish [*sic*] and consequently I have a sister who cannot write to me in our mother tongue," Jacobsen wrote.[55] In his cover letter, Riis told Roosevelt, this "is so typical of the people of that sundered part of Denmark from which he came and tells so graphically of the hardships imposed upon them by the German conqueror—who will *never* conquer them," subtly urging the vice president to take up the Danish struggle for national rights in this region. Roosevelt's reaction indicates that he clearly understood the subtext of Riis's letter.[56] In addition to praising the "sturdy stock" and "self-respecting and upright manhood" of southern Danes, which might give hope that he sympathized with them, Roosevelt added the following anecdote:

> The other day a couple of German and Irish friends called on me to say they thought we ought to interfere for the Boers, or at any rate express our sympathy for them. I asked them where we should stop if we once went into that business, and said that I took it for granted that they would both sympathize keenly with our including an appeal for the Danes in Schleswig against the Germans, or for the Finns against the Russians. Inasmuch as their feeling was really much less friendship for the Boers than hostility to England, this was rather turning the tables on them.[57]

Though Roosevelt makes it seem as if he is telling Riis this story to show how he cunningly disarmed a German and Irishman who sought U.S. support for the Boers purely out of anti-British sentiment, the point of his anecdote is clear. Despite all the rhetoric of national rights he employed in promoting U.S. involvement in the Cuban Revolution, Roosevelt would not involve the United States in "that business" of national liberation, including for the Danes of Slesvig. But this did not stop Riis from trying to keep Slesvig on Roosevelt's mind through correspondence and conversation with the president throughout the years.

In addition to quietly promoting his own nationalist agenda for Denmark and representing the concerns of Danish Americans to Roosevelt,

Riis served on occasion as unofficial ambassador for the Danish crown to the president of the United States—an even more problematic position as it implies not only continued ethnic ties and nationalist sentiments but actual political intervention on behalf of a foreign country. Several months after returning from their 1904 trip to Denmark, for instance, Elisabeth wrote to Roosevelt, reporting to him "something Crown Prince Frederick then said to me personally and which I am sure he said with the intention of having me tell it to you, Mr. President, and to Americans generally." Elisabeth went on to tell how the prince of Denmark informed her that his sister Dagmar, dowager empress of Russia, suffered greatly during the recent spate of pogroms against its Jews; "she can not help existing conditions; if she could, she would, but she has no influence whatsoever," Elisabeth conveyed on behalf of the prince.[58] Jacob reported the same incident in his second autobiography, *The Old Town* (1909), adding that Prince Frederick said further, "Now, take back with you my warm greeting to your great President, and tell him that we all of us admire him and trust him, and are glad of the prosperity of his people—your people."[59] The message is one of support for the president and exoneration of the Danish royal family from Russian persecution of Jews, which Roosevelt opposed. More striking, however, is the fact that the Riis family was employed as intermediaries between the Danish government and the president of the United States, revealing their internationally recognized status as prominent hyphenated Danish Americans and the political uses to which it was put.

How did Riis justify his open cultural hybridity and political transnationalism? And on what terms did Roosevelt accept and indeed embrace it?

"Is This Going to Be a Love Story, Then?": The Gendered Language of Dual Loyalty

Picking up on the unmistakable strain of dual nationalism in Riis's writings, one reader wrote in 1903 to the famed reformer demanding to know where his loyalties ultimately lay; if there were to be a war between the United States and Denmark, for which country would he fight?[60] Riis's response reveals the subtle language through which he sought to make dual nationalism palatable to an American audience:

> I should always fight for the flag to which I owed my allegiance—if I had to. That was the meaning of the oath I took when I gave up the old. I am profoundly glad I will never have to, both because there can never be any quarrel between Denmark and the United States, both wanting to do right; and also because I am too old. It would break my heart to see my mother and my wife fight. Wouldn't it yours?[61]

Refusing to consider the possibility of conflict between his two allegiances and relieved to be too old to fight should the unthinkable occur, Riis uncomfortably acknowledges that his final responsibility lies with his new country. But he further attempts to justify his emotional connection to both by referring to his two lands as mother and wife.

Riis represents his ties to Danishness and Americanness through metaphors of kinship. As Werner Sollors has suggested, "Americans perceive, feel and conceptualize the harmony or conflict between ethnic and national loyalties" through such tropes.[62] They imagine ethnic identity as natural and immutable, based in blood, ancestry, and descent, and describe it in terms of parents and the past. And, as we saw in the previous chapter, they imagine American identity as volitional and consensual, like romantic love and marriage, which male writers describe in terms of wives, offspring, and the future.[63]

Riis employs these familial metaphors in a distinctly gendered way to authorize the fusion of his Danish and American identities. In one of the most famous passages of *The Making of an American*, he declares:

> Alas! I am afraid that thirty years in the land of my children's birth have left me as much a Dane as ever. I no sooner climb the castle hill than I am fighting tooth and nail the hereditary foes of my people whom it was built high to bar. Yet, would you have it otherwise? What sort of husband is the man going to make who begins by pitching his old mother out of the door to make room for his wife? And what sort of wife would she be to ask or to stand it?[64]

Riis's familial analogy serves as a direct response to and revision of Roosevelt's declaration that "a man who loves another country as much as he does his own is quite as noxious a member of society as a man who loves other women as much as he loves his wife."[65] Zangwill's Quincy

Davenport embodies this idea. But Riis vigorously objects. The other woman in the immigrant's life is none other than his mother, he declares, and no one can expect a man to reject his mother as he embraces his wife. These two loves can and must be held together without rivalry or envy from either, and the male son/husband is obligated to love and protect both. Appealing to his audience's sense of masculine responsibility, Riis insists that America must not demand otherwise. To do so would be cruel and immoral.

Riis embodies his fused identities in the figure of his wife, Elisabeth, born in Denmark, loved in Denmark, but won through American successes and brought to the United States[66] to build for Riis "a blessed, good home" there.[67] Riis turns Elisabeth into the heroine of *The Making of an American*. Beginning the text with his childhood sighting of Elisabeth on the wooden bridge over the Nibs River in Ribe, the narrator asks on behalf of the audience: "And is this going to be a love story, then? Well, I have turned it over and over, and looked at it from every angle, but if I am to tell the truth, as I promised to do, I don't see how it can be helped.... It was all in the way of her that I came here."[68] This combination of sentimentalism and realism—of telling a love story in order to tell the truth— proved a successful strategy in much of Riis's writings. As scholar David Leviatin has argued, Riis sentimentalized the poor throughout *How the Other Half Lives* in an attempt to gain audience sympathy.[69] His melodramatic focus on children in that work as in many of his exposés served the same function.[70] Deliberately straddling the old and new genres of sentimentalism and journalistic realism, Riis succeeded in winning a middle-class audience in the process of shifting its literary expectations. In his autobiography, Riis joins sentimental romance to Americanization narrative. Priscilla Wald argues that "the love story about him and his wife . . . is inseparable from the love story about him and America," because Riis "became an American . . . to escape a Danish identity . . . deemed insufficient by his wife's family."[71] But Riis had no intention of escaping a Danish identity. He did not create an Americanization story to win love. Rather, he told his love story in order to make possible the telling of a particular kind of Americanization tale, one that feminizes and domesticates Danishness in order to bring it safely home to America.[72]

"Every Land Has Its George Washington": Riis's Transnational Narrative of Nationalism

Despite the romance of Danish Americanness neutralizing the potential threat of dual identity for American audiences, the content of Riis's attachments takes nondomestic form, reaching outside his new home and new homeland. The metaphor of the mother and wife together in the immigrant's American household fails to account for the reality that Riis's actual mother remained in Denmark, and she and the land retained a pull on him that hyphenated Americanism could not satisfy. He longs for Denmark, not simply Danishness or Danish Americanism. The place that Riis considers his psychic home shifts constantly throughout *The Making of an American*. "I came home to give you Elisabeth for a daughter," he announces to his mother in Ribe.[73] "It was no easy life to which I brought home my young wife," he says shortly after, referring to America.[74] Seeming to have established a sense of belonging in the United States, he later writes of Richmond Hill and Elisabeth: "It has been . . . a blessed, good home; how could it help being that with her in it?"[75] But toward the end of his autobiography, on a return visit to Denmark, he declares: "Dear old mother! Gray-haired I return, sadly scotched in many a conflict with the world, yet ever thy boy, thy home mine."[76] Riis constantly shifts between calling the house of his birth and the house of his marriage "home," unable and unwilling to bring the two together, despite Elisabeth's double identity as ethnic wife.[77]

Elisabeth herself often claims Ribe as her most beloved home. "How well I remember the days of which my husband has written—our childhood in the old Danish town where to this day, in spite of my love for America, the air seems fresher, the meadows greener, the sea more blue, and where above it all the skylark sings his song clearer, softer, and sweeter than anywhere else in the world!" she writes within her own chapter in her husband's text.[78] But Elisabeth too was often ambivalent about where she felt she belonged. Writing to her daughter Clara from Ribe on a return visit in August 1904, she says: "Indeed we have met much kindness in our old home-country, and seen many friends, but yet—tears come in my eyes when we see the Stars and Stripes and I feel so homesick sometimes."[79]

Writing in the United States, she romanticizes Ribe; writing from Ribe, she longs for the United States. A permanent exile, she never feels entirely at home anywhere. Elisabeth's experience belies her husband's gendering of the male immigrant's fantasy of cultural fusion. She resists Jacob's desire to make her symbolize his continued connection with Danishness or with his ethnic American home. His metaphors fail to account for her reality as much as for his mother's and his own.

The Riises' ambivalence about the location of "home" cannot be dismissed simply as a question of rhetoric. Homes were too important to Jacob, who devoted so much of his life to housing reform. As we have seen, his concern about the quality of housing in the United States stemmed from his neo-Lamarkian belief in the power of environment to shape an organism and its offspring.[80] More specifically, Riis claimed that it is in the home that the next generation of citizens is fashioned; a good home will create good citizens, a bad one will create bad citizens, and a proliferation of tenements and slums will threaten the very existence of the Republic. "American citizenship in the long run, will be, *must be*, what the American home is," he declared.[81]

The link between home and nation was twofold for Riis. "A man cannot live like a pig and vote like a man.... With no home to cherish, how long before love of country would be an empty sound? Life, liberty, pursuit of happiness? Wind! says the slum, and the slum is right if we let it be."[82] Riis believed that slums threaten the nation because their horrific conditions deny life and shake the foundations of the American faith in opportunity. He also believed in an analogical connection between home and nation. If one does not learn to love locally, one cannot love nationally; attachment to one's country is an extension of attachment to one's home.[83] Patriotism depends on the "home feeling."[84] And as will be developed in the next chapter, that home feeling relies on women.

Riis's claim to two homes—one Danish American in New York and one Danish in Ribe—had political ramifications. His love of both homes spawned a love for both nations, and Riis felt and behaved as a man and patriot of each.[85] Indeed, Riis sought to use one nationalism to reinforce the other. During the Spanish-American War, he tried to harness the nationalist fervor in the United States to incite similar emotion and action in Denmark. As Matthew Frye Jacobson has demonstrated in his work *Special Sorrows*, immigrants with nationalist yearnings for their homelands generally supported the Spanish-American War. In doing so, they hoped to gain respect for their ethnic communities in the United States by demonstrating their loyalty and bravery in battle, and they hoped to win American support for the liberationist causes of their homelands.[86] Both were true for Riis, but Riis additionally sought to use American fervor to inspire resistance within Denmark itself. He wrote on the war in Danish for a newspaper in Denmark that ultimately rejected his articles for being "so—er-r—ultra-patriotic, so—er-r—youthful in their enthusiasm," he reports, implicitly criticizing Denmark's failure to exhibit a fraction of this youth and enthusiasm in liberating Slesvig.[87] "[I] thank god that he sent me over the sea to cast in my lot with a country and with a people that do not everlastingly follow worm-eaten precedent, but are young enough and strong enough and daring enough to make it when need be," he goads bitterly, seeking to impose his American idea of manhood and manly military action on behalf of the home onto his motherland.[88]

Riis also attempted the reverse, using Danish national mythology to stir American patriotism. This he did most strikingly in *Hero Tales of the Far North*, his largely unread collection of stories about Christian Scandinavian warriors and two modern Danish scientists who struggled for national independence and glory.[89] Though written in 1910 in English, this work participates in the nineteenth-century Danish literary movement to romanticize the heroic past in order to escape the humiliations of the present.[90] At the same time, it takes part in the genre of diasporic national literatures written for the community in the United States that called for national pride, identification, and heroic action on behalf of the homeland in the present.[91]

But Riis wrote *Hero Tales* for a broader American audience, using it to win American sympathy for the Danish nationalist struggle and for the politics of dual nationalism more generally in the United States. "When a man knocks at Uncle Sam's gate, craving admission to his house, we ask him how much money he brings, lest he become a hindrance instead of a help," the book begins. "If now we were to ask him what he brings, not only in his pocket, but in his mind and in his heart, this stranger, what ideals he owns, what company he kept in the country he left that shaped his hopes and ambitions,—might it not, if the answer were right, be a help to a better mutual understanding between host and guest?"[92] From these questions it seems that Riis will use this work to teach Americans about Danish culture and to prove that Danish ideals and immigrants are of the "right kind."

His own place in this transaction is strikingly unstable: "What we want to know of the man is: were [his native country's] heroes his? This book is an attempt to ask and to answer that question for my own people, in a very small and simple way."[93] On the one hand, Riis positions himself as one of the established Americans, the "we" who must investigate the immigrant; on the other, he identifies himself with the immigrant group, "my own people," seeking acceptance and understanding in the United States.

Holding both identifications in tension here as always, Riis insists on the merit and indeed the advantage of immigrants who are patriots of their homelands:

> The *Mayflower* did not hold all who in this world have battled for freedom of home, of hope and of conscience. The struggle is bigger than that. Every land has its George Washington, its Kosciusko, its William Tell, its Garibaldi, its Kossuth, if there is but one that has a Joan d'Arc. What we want to know of the man is: were its heroes his.
>
> . . . I should like to see some Swede write of the heroes of his noble, chivalrous people. . . . I should like to hear the epic of United Italy, of proud and freedom loving Hungary, the swan-song of unhappy Poland, chanted to young America again and again, to help us understand that we are kin in the things that really count and help us pull together as we must if we are to make the most of our common country.[94]

Though his examples are purely European, his heroes almost exclusively male, and his focus entirely on nationalist struggles for independence, Riis calls for the sharing of national narratives in the United States. He believed this would foster mutual understanding because it would show that all (read: Christian Europeans) share what Americans mistakenly see as their exclusive love of freedom and independence.[95]

Even more than telling their heroic struggles for freedom to Americans, Riis wanted European immigrants to hold on to their national heroes. "These were my—our—heroes, then," he writes:

> Every lad of Northern blood, whose heart is in the right place, loves them. And he need make no excuses for them. Nor has he need of bartering them for the great of his new home; they go very well together. It is partly for his sake that I have set their stories down here. All too

quickly he lets go of them on the new shore. Let him keep them and cherish them with the memories of the mother land. The immigrant America wants and needs is he who brings the best of the old home to the new, not he who threw it overboard on the voyage. In the great melting-pot it will tell its story for the good of us all.[96]

In Riis's concept of the melting pot, so different from Zangwill's and Roosevelt's transformative ones, immigrants must maintain not only their national cultures but even more radically their nationalist yearnings for their native lands, and they must contribute their heroes and histories to a larger, transnational narrative of nationalism, manhood, and independence. It is not that Riis believed that America should become a cosmopolitan meeting place of European cultures, along the lines imagined by Randolph Bourne, who called for a "wholly novel international nation."[97] Rather, Riis believed that the distinctive nationalism of the United States could be reinforced and reinvigorated by the nationalist expressions of those of other countries. And he too called his distinct vision the "melting pot."

In response to those like Roosevelt who feared that continued loyalty to one's native land would conflict with and undermine loyalty to America, Riis deflected political concerns, focusing instead on the *sentiment* of nationalism. He argued that nationalism is a transferable feeling that is simultaneously specific to each political context and transcendent of national boundaries. A nationalist in the "old home" will be a patriot in the new, for the feeling and values are identical. Perhaps playing on fears of anarchism, Riis argued that dual nationalism is in fact a benefit to the nation, for the most desirable new Americans, and particularly new American men, are those who know what it means to love and struggle for country.[98]

Riis suggests further, however, that even if immigrants wished to "thr[o]w overboard" their connections to and feelings for their homelands and histories, this would be impossible, for such ties are embedded in their physical being.

"How Little We Have the Making of Ourselves": Race and Diasporic Nationalism

Frequently, as he states in the passage on the castle hill, Riis experienced his connection to Denmark as a yearning to fight "tooth and nail against the hereditary foes of my people." Werner Sollors concludes from this that Riis's Danishness is an oppositional identity, pitted against Germany,[99] and perhaps for this reason, increasingly acceptable in the years leading up to World War I. Even more, however, using the language of Darwin, Spencer, and Tennyson, Riis claims a hereditary tie to Denmark and Danishness, one that is inborn, inherited, and uneradicable.

Riis's conceptualization of an unalterable blood inheritance is somewhat surprising given his insistence in his reform work that environment is what shapes the individual. But throughout his writings, he relinquishes his environmentalism when talking about national characteristics, returning instead to the language of race. This switch is particularly striking in *How the Other Half Lives*, where Riis claims, against accepted wisdom, that lack of opportunities, not biological limitations or sinful sloth, makes people poor.[100] He further argues that it is environment that corrupts the character of the poor; thus, if they were only provided with better housing, they would become better citizens. At the same time, however, Riis makes endless essentialist claims in *The Other Half* about the unalterable racial characteristics and depravities of the immigrant poor: "As scholars, the children of the most ignorant Polish Jews keep fairly abreast of their more favored playmates, until it comes to mental arithmetic, when they leave them behind with a bound. It is surprising to see how strong the *instinct* of dollars and cents is in them."[101] The Italian immigrant, he states further, "promptly reproduces conditions of destitution and disorder, which set in the framework of Mediterranean exuberance, are the delight of the artist, but in a matter-of-fact American community becomes a danger and a reproach. . . . [H]e soon reduces what he does find to his own level, if allowed to follow his *natural bent*."[102] And of the Chinese he writes, "He is *by nature* as clean as the cat, which he resembles in his traits of cruel cunning and savage fury when aroused."[103] It is this contradiction between environmentalism and essentialism that makes Riis so frustrating to the modern reader.

Riis was aware of this contradiction in his thought, particularly as it applied to his sense of himself. Again describing his emotions upon returning to the landscape of his youth, he writes in *The Making of an American*:

> The moor was ever most to my liking. I was born on the edge of it, and once its majesty has sunk into a human soul, that soul is forever after attuned to it. How little we have the making of ourselves. And how

much greater the need that we should make of that little the most. All my days I have been preaching against heredity as the arch-enemy of hope and effort, and here is mine holding me fast. When I see, rising out of the dark moor, the lonely cairn that sheltered the bones of my fathers before the White Christ preached peace to their land, a great yearning comes over me. There I want to lay mine. There I want to sleep, under the heather where the bees hum drowsily. . . . Half heathen yet, am I? Yes, if to yearn for the soil whence you sprang is to be heathen, heathen am I, not half, but whole, and will be all my days.

But not so. He is the heathen who loves not his native land.[104]

In this remarkable passage, Riis on the one hand offers an environmental explanation for his attachment to the Danish moor: "I was born on the edge of it, and once its majesty has sunk into a human soul, that soul is forever attuned to it." Because the moor constituted the setting for his childhood, he will always retain his connection to it. But Riis quickly qualifies this explanation, turning instead to claim a bond to the land through ancestral blood and heredity. As on the castle hill, he again describes this connection as an uncontrollable, atavistic desire, which he explains biologically rather than environmentally. He Christianizes this impulse to make it more acceptable, claiming that it would be heathenish not to love his native land, just as earlier he claimed it would be immoral to throw out his old mother, but he clearly views this love as an inborn, hereditary drive that cannot be eradicated.

Riis uses race as a means of explaining to his readers why it would be impossible for him to deny his links to heritage and homeland, and foolish for them to require such a break. Of course this claim was rendered nonthreatening by the fact that Riis was a white, male, Protestant northern European. There was little to fear in the hereditary ties and propensities of the Danish immigrant. In the founding mythology of many native-born Americans, including Roosevelt, Danes were part of the original mixed white northern blood that created the United States, set its race "mould," and established its ideals. In the opening pages of his epic *The Winning of the West*, Roosevelt writes:

The modern Englishman is descended from a Low-Dutch stock, which, when it went to Britain, received into itself an enormous infusion of

Celtic, a much smaller infusion of Norse and Danish, and also a certain infusion of Norman-French blood. When this new English stock came to America, it mingled with and absorbed into itself immigrants from many European lands, and the process has gone on ever since. It is to be noted that of the new blood thus acquired, the greatest proportion has come from Dutch and German sources, and the next greatest from Irish, while the Scandinavian element comes third, and the only other of much consequence is French Huguenot. Thus it appears that no new element of importance has been added to the blood. Additions have been made to the elemental race-strains in much the same proportion as these were originally combined.[105]

In this text, which places the conquest of the American West into a larger narrative of the inevitable and justifiable "spread of the English-speaking peoples over the world's waste spaces,"[106] Roosevelt claims that American blood is identical in its chemistry to the mixed blood of England, albeit altered and improved upon by the rugged North American environment. Both consisted, and continue to consist, primarily of a Low Dutch, Germanic strain combined with Irish, Scandinavian, and French Protestant elements. These northern peoples, who "by the time the Revolution had broken out . . . had begun to fuse together" in the United States and establish the American racial type,[107] have a peculiar, inherited characteristic that suits them for self-rule and for world mastery. Speaking of the founding fathers in his 1888 biography of Gouverneur Morris, Roosevelt wrote:

> The men who predominated in and shaped the actions of the [Constitutional Convention] belonged to a type not uncommonly brought forth by a people already accustomed to freedom at a crisis in the struggle to preserve or extend its liberties. During the past few centuries, this type had appeared many times among the liberty-loving nations who dwelt on the shores of the Baltic and the North Sea; and our forefathers represented it in its highest and most perfect shapes. It is a type only to be found among men already trained to govern themselves as well as others.[108]

Roosevelt views the founders as the epitome of the freedom-loving racial type that supposedly emerged originally in the North Sea and Baltic Sea regions. Because of their blood inheritance, they were able to create a republican government suited for "a proud, liberty-loving, and essentially democratic race"—the new American race.[109] Roosevelt also frequently describes America's frontiersmen as Vikings, using the analogy to both rationalize and celebrate American expansionism.[110] As an immigrant from precisely the region that gave Americans their instinct for democracy and conquest, Riis was not a threat to America, but a reinfusion of that same "northern blood" that Roosevelt says "strengthened" and "sprang anew to vigorous life" the blood of the peoples with which it blended.[111]

Well aware of these racialized narratives of northern blood, Riis uses them deliberately to stake out a place for himself as a Dane in the United States. He emphasizes the congruencies between the Danish "race" and the American, creating what Orm Øverland terms a "home-making myth" that authorizes the perpetuation of Danishness in the United States.[112] Riis resolves his potentially conflicting identities as a Dane and an American by tracing the origins of American democracy back to his homeland. In a letter to his son-in-law during a 1904 trip to Denmark, Riis writes:

> I am spending the last days of our stay digging about in old churches and mausoleums, interring [?] dead kings—dead 800 years and more—and having a bully good time of it. . . . [T]hey have much more to do with our history in our great republic than most of us think of. . . . Thence the sturdy love of freedom that, transplanted by the Viking to England and Normandy left its mark forever on democracy in England and eventually in America, in Australia, in New Zealand, wherever the English tongue is spoken. A people may die or a nation; its spirit, if it have any, never dies.[113]

If the Danish Viking is the true source of American democracy, then returning to Denmark and poking among the ruins of Ribe become American activities, and American citizenship can be rendered a continuation of rather than a break from the spirit of Denmark. In his public writing as well, Riis attempts to make this connection between Danish and U.S. history and types clear to American readers. Describing the codification of Danish law in 1241 by King Valdemar II, for instance, Riis writes:

> "With law shall land be built," begins his code. "The law," it says, "must be honest, just, reasonable, and according to the ways of the people. It must meet their needs and speak plainly so that all men may know and

understand what the law is. It is not to be made in anyone's favor...."
That tells the story of Valdemar's day and of the people who are so near kin with ourselves. They were not sovereign and subjects; they were a chosen king and a free people, working together "with law land to build."[114]

Riis uses the medieval Juttish code of law to insist that Danes are politically "so near kin with ourselves" (including himself here among Americans), while simultaneously emphasizing the democratic nature of the Danish monarchy he still adores.

In all his descriptions of his homeland and its people, Riis consistently emphasizes the Danish "instinct" for freedom and individual rights: "The Danish people ... are essentially honest, intolerant of pretense, stubbornly democratic, and withal good-natured to a degree," he informs American readers.[115] "Stick up for your rights at any cost. These secure, go to any length to oblige a neighbor," he claims as the Danish motto.[116] Yes, Danishness is a racial identity that cannot be expunged, he argues, but how wonderful this is for America. As Zangwill's Jew is already American, so Riis's Dane is simultaneously acceptably Danish and undoubtedly American.

Yet, on one occasion, in the final scene of *The Making of an American*, Riis seems to disclaim all ties with his past, claiming a complete transformation into an American at last.

American Made? Jacob Riis and the Immigrant Conversion Narrative

"I have just told the story of the making of an American. There remains to tell how I found that he was finished at last." So begins the final scene of *The Making of an American*. Riis proceeds to tell of falling seriously ill in Denmark and lying in bed in a village just outside of Elsinore "sick and discouraged and sore—I hardly knew why myself." This mood continues until

> all at once there sailed past, close inshore, a ship flying at the top the flag of freedom, blown out on a breeze till every star in it shone bright and clear. That moment I knew. Gone were illness, discouragement, and gloom. Forgotten weakness and suffering, the cautions of doctor and

"That moment... I knew that I also had become an American in truth." Original illustration of the final scene of *The Making of an American,* Macmillan, 1904.

nurse. I sat up in bed and shouted, laughed and cried by turns, waving my handkerchief to the flag out there. They thought I had lost my head, but I told them no, thank God! I had found it, and my heart too, at last. I knew then that it was my flag; that my children's home was mine, indeed; that I also had become an American in truth. And I thanked God, and, like unto the man sick of palsy, arose from my bed and went home healed.[117]

This passage reads like a disavowal of all that has come before. It is, as Priscilla Wald describes, a conversion scene, with the American flag having Christlike powers to heal the sufferer.[118] What was wrong with Riis that the flag could cure? In reality, he was suffering from malaria, but he omits this information, making it appear instead that the cause of his anguish was a crisis of identity, an uncertainty about the location of home, that only the sight of the American flag could resolve.[119] Read in this way, this scene provides a climactic resolution to Riis's questions of home and belonging and negates all his previous claims to dual identity. Riis seems to proclaim here with finality that he is an American made.

This is the scene that has shaped virtually all readings of Riis's American identity. Many accept Riis's depiction of complete conversion to Americanism at face value. At the end of Enok Mortensen's Danish American novel *Saaledes blev jeg hjemlos* (Thus I Became Homeless; 1934), for instance, the protagonist, who struggles over whether he belongs in New York or Denmark, feeling home to be "whatever lies on the other side of the sea," at least temporarily resolves his conflict by reading *The Making of an American*. He attempts to use Riis's work as the text of his own conversion, as he seeks to become wholly American like Riis.[120] Other readers of *The Making of an American* have suggested that though Riis wanted desperately to claim an entirely American identity here, he inadvertently failed.[121] Despite the fact that Riis's notion of race and identity was in reality much like that of Horace Kallen, who famously declared that one cannot change one's grandfather, Kallen viewed Riis as the first of a series of immigrant authors who futilely tried to negate their ancestral ties. "The Riises and Steiners and Antins protest too much, they are too self-conscious and self-centered, their 'Americanization' appears too much like an achievement, a *tour de force,* too little like a growth," Kallen declared in 1915.[122] Reading the tension beneath the surface of the passage, Priscilla Wald argues further that Riis's sudden reference to himself in the third person ("I have told the story of the making of an American. There remains to tell how I found out that *he* was made and finished at last") is an unconscious expression of his estrangement from himself at the very moment of his proclaimed self-discovery.[123] Like Kallen, she see Riis desiring complete transformation into an American, but unintentionally revealing a repressed ambivalence and insecurity about his success.

An examination of the manuscript of *The Making of an American*, however, reveals Riis in complete control of his rhetoric here. He deliberated over how to depict his Americanism and consciously debated over whether to make his continued attachment to Denmark explicit even in this final statement of Americanization. Riis struggled with the opening of the paragraph, crossing out phrases with, what is for him, unusual frequency: "I have told the story of the making of an American. There remains to tell how I found out that ~~in me~~ he was made ~~at last, and finished the task completed at last and finished~~ and finished at last. It was when I went ~~my roots dug deep in the Danish soil. They burrow there yet after thirty years~~ back to see my mother once more."[124]

In crafting this testimonial, Riis considered how unilateral an American identity to claim publicly for himself. He ultimately decided to conclude his autobiography with an unambiguous proclamation of patriotism and Americanness. Once he made this choice, he pushed full steam ahead, with few hesitations in the rest of the paragraph, though it must be noted that the overt religious symbolism is clearly a later addition. The original ending read: "And I thanked God and took the next steamer for home." In a different pen, Riis crossed out "and took the next steamer for home" and added "like unto the man sick ~~with~~ of palsy, arose from my bed and went home, healed." This striking revision both sanctifies the moment of rebirth and depersonalizes it by turning it into an archetypal conversion scene, rather than a realistic personal narrative. Still, there are far fewer changes in the rest of the paragraph than in its first two sentences. Riis made a deliberate decision about how to represent himself in the final pages of his autobiography and carefully excised his Danishness from its climactic conclusion.

The conclusion of *The Making of an American* provides its audience with a parting snapshot of an immigrant who has successfully fulfilled Roosevelt's demand that "newcomers . . . throw themselves heartily into our national life, cease to be Europeans, and become Americans like the rest of us."[125] Indeed, Riis seems to have written this passage with Roosevelt in mind. Roosevelt held an extremely prominent place in Riis's imagined audience. "I have just sent the 7th chapter of my story to the Outlook," Riis wrote to the then vice president in April 1901, while working on the serialized version of his autobiography. "When that is published, I want you to tell me in all sincerity, such as you will, and also from Mrs. Roosevelt, whether I have overstepped the line or not. I hope not. It is about my wife."[126] Riis asked the Roosevelts' approval after publication of the chapter written by Elisabeth in *The Making of an American*.[127] The postpublication query served no practical purpose, as the response could have no

Manuscript page from the final scene of Jacob Riis's *The Making of an American*. (Jacob Riis Papers, Manuscripts and Archives Division, The New York Public Library, Astor, Lenox and Tilden Foundations).

impact, at least upon the serialized version of the text. However, Riis's letter strikingly reveals his concern over Roosevelt's reception of his writing. He clearly had his powerful friend in mind when writing *The Making of an American*.

More specifically, Riis connected the final scene of his 1901 autobiography with Roosevelt. On July 15, 1904, Riis wrote from Denmark to Roosevelt: "We fled to this little fishing village where I lay sick in 1899 and saw the vision of the flag borne past on a steamer—I am writing this before the very window through which I saw it."[128] Riis believed that this incident, which he ambiguously identifies as a vision here, held great meaning for Roosevelt. And he was correct. Roosevelt responds: "As you know, I think the incident of your seeing the flag through the window while you were lying sick was to me one of the most striking I know, and I am [tou]ched that you should be writing me, seated in front of the same window."[129] Roosevelt loved this patriotic scene. He found it significant and moving, and he was pleased to be linked to it through Riis's letter.

The expectations Riis perceived of his audience—Roosevelt included—appear to have shaped the conclusion of his narrative and, indeed, of his audience's understanding of Riis's cultural and political identity for generations to come. Failing to recognize it as a deliberate and controlled performance, readers seize upon this final scene to confirm their belief that the "ideal American citizen" had in fact properly given up, or at least wished to give up, all ties to another nation or identity. Furthermore, the rhetorical strategy of Riis's conclusion and the structuring of his story as an Americanization tale would impact the genre of immigrant autobiography for the near future, with Mary Antin, Edward Steiner, Edward Bok, and Elizabeth Stern, among many others, attempting to testify to similar conversions.[130] But though he seemed to capitulate to audience expectation and excise Danishness entirely from the final pages of his autobiography, Riis made no attempt to dig up assertions of his Danish roots or continued Danish nationalism from the rest of this text, from his other writings, or from himself.

The focus on the final scene of *The Making of an American* has obscured what we have seen to be Riis's regular declarations of dual loyalty and acts of hyphenated Americanism before and after he wrote this text. But despite the impression it made, the conclusion of *The Making of an American* actually does not have the rhetorical power to negate the narrative's previous claims to dual loyalty, for they were written not as descriptions of how Riis once felt, but as prescriptions for the proper conduct of all immigrants. Statements such as "twice blest he who has two" flags to love, or "he is the heathen who loves not his native land" are pronouncements that cannot be overturned.

Just as this scene cannot erase what Riis has already said of his continued dual loyalties, it also does not function as a definitive closing statement establishing his 100 percent Americanization for the future. In fact, the passage is not definitive at all, for Riis revisits it several times. In his 1909 book *The Old Town*, Riis rewrote the entire episode, giving it a very different spin:

> I am not likely to forget one [autumn] that found me stranded there [in Denmark], sick and desolate just as the century was closing; the long, wakeful nights I lay listening to the storm shaking my window and whistling through the cracks as if it were mocking my helplessness, with four thousand miles of tempestuous sea between me and home. I sailed them all in those nightwatches, with never a rift in the pitiless gray skies, till I saw at last a coast lying golden in the sunset, and knew it from the way my heart leaped within me for the Blessed Isles where home was. It was then I learned that I, too, belonged here where my children were born.[131]

Unlike in the earlier rendition, this time there is no real boat and no American flag at all. It is a hallucinatory vision. Stuck in Denmark, Riis traverses the distance between himself and "home" in his imagination. He envisions the golden coast, recognizes it as "the Blessed Isles where home was," and realizes that he belongs in the land where his children were born. This is in no way a conversion scene. There is no icon, no healing, and no reference to Christ. And though he states that he learns he belongs "where my children were born," Riis never claims here to have discovered that the American flag is his true flag or that he had become "an American in truth." Even what he calls home here is ambiguous. What are those "Blessed Isles where home was"? Long Island? They actually sound more like Denmark or even like heaven, which elsewhere Riis explicitly imagines looking exactly like Ribe.[132] It is quite plausible that the hazy vision of home that he has on his sickbed is not related to America at all this time. Even if it is, however, this version of the episode lacks the drama of the first. Rather than ending the book here, or returning with finality to America in his narrative at this point, Riis goes on to describe the "beautiful summer" he and Elisabeth spent in Denmark in 1904. Though he makes clear his ties to America, Denmark clearly retained its draw, and Riis refused to excise it from the telling and retelling of his life story or from his life.

Good Citizenship: The Truest Americanism

Though the final scene of *The Making of an American* may have been written with Roosevelt's notion of Americanization in mind, as a reader of all of Riis's books, the recipient of Riis's pleas for Danish immigrants, and the object of his political interventions on behalf of the Danish crown, Roosevelt knew well of Riis's cultural hyphenation and political dual loyalties. Yet he accepted them. Even during World War I, when Roosevelt insisted most strongly on the need for 100 percent Americanism, he continued to evoke the now deceased Jacob Riis as the "ideal American citizen." What made Riis's Danish Americanness and dual nationalism acceptable to Roosevelt, and what does this reveal about the limits of Roosevelt's tolerance?

Riis's narration of his hyphenated identity proved particularly effective for the ways in which it meshed with Roosevelt's notions of race, nationalism, home, and masculinity. As we have seen, the linkages Riis made between Denmark and democracy, Denmark and expansion, correspond to Roosevelt's notion of the value of white northern blood and its place in founding of the American race, nation, and ideals. Had Riis been a Russian nationalist or a Chinese one, it is doubtful that his dual loyalties would have met the same reception. The anti-German content of his Danish nationalism also corresponded well with Roosevelt's increasing desire to bring the United States into war with Germany. And Riis's carefully rendered presentation of his feelings and responsibilities to his feminized home of Denmark played on Roosevelt's assumptions about male duty.

The genuine friendship between the two men also undoubtedly accounted for the tolerance shown to Riis. The language of their friendship is striking. During Roosevelt's presidency, Riis, though intensely proud of his friend's office, frequently expressed regret at the physical and psychological distance it placed between them. In 1902 he wrote to Roosevelt, admitting, "Sometimes I wish I were a secret service man and could be where you are always,"[133] and after an evening with the Roosevelts shortly after the president's final term in office, he wrote: "It seemed as if you had come back to me after all these years, and as though we should have some good times again. . . . I am so glad that everything is to be as you told me and that we can work together again. Life is worth living after all."[134] One review of Riis's *Theodore Roosevelt the Citizen* comments explicitly on the author's declarations of love for the president, finding them odd and somewhat unseemly. "Men are not in the habit in these days of going about declaring their love for other men, but Mr. Riis does not hesitate to say that he loves Mr. Roosevelt. If Mr. Riis were an American he would not talk in this enthusiastic manner, but he is a foreigner, a Dane, with poetic ideas and absolute frankness in expressing them."[135] In attempting to explain away Riis's apparent breach of conventional male relationships and etiquette, this critic emphasizes Riis's foreignness, turning his expressions of love for another man into an un-American cultural phenomenon. But Roosevelt's letters to Riis are similarly intense. In May 1897, shortly after he left the New York Police Department to become assistant secretary of the navy, Roosevelt wrote passionately to his friend: "I think of you every day and long for the sight of your face and the touch of your kindly hand."[136] Though Roosevelt was not as close with Riis as with some of his other friends,[137] their personal relationship granted Riis more leeway than the generalized immigrant masses Roosevelt referred to in his speeches or the abstract immigrants he knew only through their writing.

Roosevelt made use of his friend's connections to the Danish immigrant community and to Denmark itself. Despite his villainization of ethnic politics in the United States, he employed such techniques when they served his purpose.[138] And Riis proved his best link to the Scandinavian émigré community in the United States. In a telegram to Danish immigrants in Chicago immediately after the 1904 presidential election, Roosevelt wrote: "I send the heartiest greetings for the success of all the undertakings of my fellow-Americans of Danish birth or origin, and I am proud to send it through the man whom I regard as the ideal of what a good American should be—you, my dear friend, Jacob Riis."[139] Though Roosevelt is careful to call them "fellow-Americans of Danish birth or origin" rather than hyphenated Danish Americans, it is clear that despite his insistence that there be no ethnic vote in the United States, he appeals to this constituency through Riis on precisely such grounds. Roosevelt also turned to Riis in his international dealings with Denmark. When negotiating the purchase of the Danish West Indies by the United States, Roosevelt wrote to Riis: "Before I decide in the Danish Islands business of course I shall consult you at length. I thought if I could get you down there, even though you only intended to stay a few months, and give you some fellow whom you could trust underneath, it would be a good thing all around."[140] Riis was not interested in the position, but he understood the kind of man Roosevelt wanted for the job. "I had my-self been thinking that if you could lay hold of a capable Dane, well-thought-of by his old countrymen and yet a thorough American, it might be a way of letting the islands slide over easily into the new allegiance."[141] It is precisely because he saw Riis as both a Dane plus a "thorough American" that Roosevelt tapped him for the post, attempting, like Prince Frederick of Denmark, to put Riis's hyphenated identity to his own political uses.

But it was Riis's work in the United States that most potently countered any potential threat of his retained sentimental, cultural, and political ties to his homeland and its leaders. While Riis insisted on retaining his Danish identity, spoke publicly of his loyalty to the Danish crown, and dreamed nationalist dreams for his homeland, his work on behalf of the American home and city demonstrated irrefutably to Roosevelt that he was a true and great citizen of the United States. "Grave perils are yet to be encountered in the stormy course of the Republic," Roosevelt warned as early as 1893, "perils from political corruption, perils from individual laziness, indolence and timidity, perils springing from the greed of the unscrupulous rich, and from the anarchic violence of the thriftless and turbulent poor. There is every reason why we should recognize them, but there is no reason why we should fear them . . . if only each will, according to the measure of his ability, do his full duty, and endeavor so to live as to deserve the high praise of being called a good American citizen."[142] It was precisely the "high praise of being called a good American citizen" that Roosevelt bestowed upon Riis. "The most useful citizen in the land," "the ideal American citizen," he hailed Riis. With only few exceptions, he almost never called Riis an ideal "American," though, and the one time he writes that he is "tempted to call [Jacob Riis] the best American I ever knew," he never actually does.[143]

Roosevelt's notions of a "true American" and of an "ideal American citizen" are not identical. For an immigrant to become a "true American" required giving up all other national and cultural ties while assimilating entirely into the nationalist "spirit, conviction, and purpose" of America.[144] But to become an "ideal American citizen" the naturalized immigrant had to become an active participant in the Republic, on behalf of the Republic. "The first duty of an American citizen is . . . that he shall work in politics; his second duty is that he shall do that work in a practical manner; and his third duty is that it shall be done in accord with the highest principles of justice," said Roosevelt, laying out his rules for civic responsibility.[145] For Roosevelt, Riis met these requirements to a T. Not only did Riis dedicate himself to the "principles of justice," but his campaigns for municipal, housing, and educational reform aimed at creating future good citizens. He preached that "from the people's home proceeds citizen virtue and nowhere else does it live,"[146] that "the public school [is] the door to a house of citizenship in which we shall all dwell together in full understanding."[147] He worked to establish institutions that would create "true citizens" out of the poor by constructing homes and parks to foster feelings of love for their country, "true citizens" out of immigrants by instructing them in democratic ideals, and "true citizens" out of the comfortable American born by spurring them to take responsibility for the others. "The millennium of municipal politics . . . will come when every citizen does his whole duty as a citizen, not before," Riis declared.[148] And it was toward this millennium that Riis worked, doing his "whole duty as a citizen," even as he insisted on remaining a hyphenated American.

Indeed, despite its title and its final scene, Riis's *Making of an American* is not so much about the making of an American as it is about the making of an American citizen. "The work . . . justifies the writing of these pages," he claims, and he describes this work as "what I thought citizenship ought to be."[149] It was his work and his desire for others to imitate it that Riis believed gave him the right to present his life story to the American public. Indeed, the climax of this story is not his discovery of himself as "an American in truth" proclaimed at the very end of the text, but his discovery of his mission as a reformer. "In a Methodist revival . . . I had fallen under the spell of the preacher's fiery eloquence," he writes.

> Brother Simmons was of the old circuit-riders' stock, albeit their day was long past in our staid community. He had all their power, for the spirit burned within him; and he brought me to the altar quickly, though in my own case conversion refused to work the prescribed amount of

agony.... In fact, with the heat of the convert, I decided upon the spot to throw up my editorial work and take to preaching. But Brother Simmons would not hear of it.

"No, no, Jacob," he said; "not that. We have preachers enough. What the world needs is consecrated pens."

Then and there I consecrated mine. I wish I could honestly say that it has always come up to the high ideal set it then. I can say, though, that it has ever striven toward it, and that scarce a day has passed since that I have not thought of the charge laid upon it and upon me.[150]

It was his transformation from a drifter and sometimes journalist into a literary crusader that Riis identifies as the true conversion moment in this text. And it was during his serious first attempt to use his consecrated pen on behalf of the "other half" that Riis most dramatically experiences the alienation from self that Priscilla Wald claims conversion produces. He walks off the podium while lecturing on the slum feeling that "it all seemed a long way off and in no way related to me."[151] He forgets his own name when asked by a maid whom she should say is calling: "Until I actually read my name on my card it was as utterly gone as if I had never heard it."[152] In the process of testifying to his conversion into a "consecrated pen," Riis experiences a crisis of identity that does not abate until he proves his transformation through the success of *How the Other Half Lives*, which won him early acknowledgment as a most useful American citizen.

Despite the perpetuation of Riis's cultural and political ties to his homeland, Roosevelt wished to be associated with his "consecrated pen." At a time when many immigrants were seen as preferring the politics of the boss system, which provided for their immediate needs,[153] it was important for Roosevelt to be able to hold up his immigrant reformer friend as a model of civic responsibility. At a time when his Americanization demands seemed too liberal to those who wished to curtail immigration and exclude immigrants from national life and too conservative to others who hoped for fewer hurdles to acceptance, it was useful for Roosevelt to point to Riis as an example of the benefit of the right immigrant to the nation and of the need for a "square deal" for any immigrant who so contributes. And at a time when Roosevelt sought to prove and publicize his own credentials as a progressive reformer working for justice and the public interest, it was useful to keep his name linked with that of Riis.[154] When in

1902 Riis revised his book *A Ten Year's War* and was about to republish it under the title *The Battle with the Slum*, Riis wrote to Roosevelt: "My dear Mr. President, I send you today a copy of my new book—or my made-over book. Will you accept it with my love? I meant to have dedicated it to you and if you had been Theodore Roosevelt plain and simple I should have done it. But it is better so."[155] Five days later, the president wrote in response to this veiled request:

> Is it too late to put in such a dedication in a second edition, or in the copies printed hereafter? I should have been glad and proud to have had such a dedication if I was not President, but even more glad and proud now, for I should like my children to know that after over a year of the Presidency you still thought I had tried to live up to the doctrines that you have preached and practiced, and that I have at least tried to preach and practice.[156]

Riis immediately stopped the presses and inserted a page, proud to display and profit from his relationship with the president.[157] But the desire was clearly mutual. Using his children's judgment as a metaphor for public appraisal, Roosevelt believed that his relationship with the reformer would impact his moral and historical standing, not to mention his political cachet.[158]

It was on his work and image as an ideal American citizen that the Danish American reformer created his identity and won Roosevelt's love. Jacob Riis was not an "ideal American," in Roosevelt's sense of the term, but he was an "ideal American citizen." When it came to Riis, Roosevelt could separate out the political requirements of exclusive loyalty to the nation and the civic requirements of service to the state. And in the calculus of "true Americanism," the demands of good citizenship could supersede the demands for assimilation, at least for a white northern European male. In promoting this dual nationalist as the ideal American citizen, however, Roosevelt created an opening for a new kind of hyphenated politics and identity within the American landscape.

CHAPTER 3

Making American Homes and America Home

Theodore Roosevelt and Elizabeth Stern in the Pages of the *Ladies' Home Journal*

> The nation is in a bad way if there is no real home.
> —Theodore Roosevelt, "The Woman and the Home," 1905[1]

> For the first time mother saw me as that which I had always wished to be, an American woman at the head of an American home. But our home is a home, which try as I may, we can not make home to mother.
> —Elizabeth Stern, "My Mother and I," 1916[2]

"For the first time, mother saw me as that which I had always wished to be, an American woman at the head of an American home."[3] Carefully connecting womanhood and domesticity to newly acquired American identity, these lines first appeared in an anonymous piece entitled "My Mother and I: The Story of How I Became an American Woman," published in the *Ladies' Home Journal* of October 1916. As one of very few stories printed in the popular magazine written from the perspective of an ethnic woman, this first-person narrative about the Americanization of an eastern European Jewish immigrant girl was noteworthy in itself. But even more remarkable was the laudatory preface by former president Theodore Roosevelt "most cordially commend[ing] this story."[4] One year later, when Macmillan published an expanded book edition of the piece, naming E. G. Stern as its author and reprinting Roosevelt's introduction, the reviewer for the *Nation* posed the pressing question: "How does one get a 'pull' with Mr. Roosevelt?"[5] How did this young, obscure author get the former president to write the introduction to her work?[6]

In reality, the yet unknown writer and social worker Elizabeth Gertrude Levin Stern had no "pull" at all with Mr. Roosevelt. Whereas his relationship with Riis and others helped shape his response to their work, Roosevelt had no personal relationship with Stern. It was Edward Bok, editor in chief from 1889 to 1919 of the *Ladies' Home Journal*, the most widely circulated magazine in the nation,[7] who sent the manuscript to Roosevelt.[8] Stern had submitted her full-length book, *My Mother and I*, to the *Journal* in the hopes of having it serialized. Bok rejected the manuscript in that format, but he advised the author to edit it down into a short story for the magazine and to send off the longer text to Macmillan for potential publication as a book.[9] Upon receiving Stern's abridged story and possibly editing it further himself, Bok mailed the manuscript to Roosevelt.

As would be revealed only after his death, for years Roosevelt had secretly played a role in determining the ideological content of this highly influential women's mass-market magazine.[10] In addition to writing signed and anonymous columns, the former president served as a regular reader and editor for the *Journal*, deciding which feature articles should be included in its pages.[11] Just how long Roosevelt acted in this capacity is unclear, but it is certain that his word held tremendous weight with the editor.[12] The relationship here was between two men formulating and disseminating ideas of domesticity and womanhood for the nation. Through Bok's *Ladies' Home Journal*, Theodore Roosevelt helped determine what written materials would enter nearly two million American homes. And he selected Stern's story as one such text, using it as another opportunity

Roosevelt's reader's report on *My Mother and I* for the *Ladies' Home Journal,* reprinted in Bok's *Americanization of Edward Bok.*

to popularize his ideologies through ethnic writers, but this time to a predominantly female audience.[13]

Roosevelt understood well the need to include women in his national narrative, even as they remained excluded from the full rights of citizenship. As seen in the previous chapters, divergent conceptualizations of the American race relied upon the bodies of women; multiple formulations of nationalist and transnationalist sentiment found justification in the gendered notions of mother love and home; and the fate of the nation was said to rest on the home environment created by mothers. Such rhetoric placed an immense burden on the lives of real women to create and sustain the nation and its citizens according to particular dictates. Class played a central, if unstated, role in formulations of Americanness, gender, and domesticity, with the middle class as the standard for all three. American women and their households had to be of the "right type," and immigrant women were told to make themselves and their homes over in this image.

Roosevelt's patronage of Elizabeth Stern's story provides a crucial link between his simultaneous desires to remake the American woman and home and to Americanize the foreigner. This chapter traces his campaign, and the centrality of the *Ladies' Home Journal* in it, to fortify the nation by reforming its homes. It also examines the concurrent campaign to bring working-class immigrant households in line with the new progressive middle-class standards for the home. The overlap of these two agendas reveals the uses of domestic space to, in Amy Kaplan's terms, "domesticate the foreign" within the nation, making foreigners part of the homeland through their homes.[14] And while Stern never interacted with Roosevelt directly, her story reveals the impact of these intersecting policies on the lives and narratives of immigrant mothers and their daughters.

"My Mother and I" seems to fit neatly into the image of progressive American womanhood promoted by the *Journal* and by Roosevelt. Undoubtedly it was published for this very reason. However, Stern's later writings of the 1920s and 1930s explicitly question the values of middle-class American domesticity, marriage, womanhood, and identity, seeming to overturn everything that "My Mother and I" idolizes.[15] Critics who recognize this shift see it both as a signal of Stern's personal maturation and as a sign of the times. They believe that she was able to write in a new mode because of the rise of feminism in the 1920s, allowing her to question the presumed gender role of bourgeois women, and the simultaneous increase in nativism, forcing her to reevaluate the possibility of complete assimilation.[16]

In fact, however, the problems of middle-class American domesticity and womanhood were not later discoveries for Stern. Already in the book edition of *My Mother and I*, she can be found undercutting the assumptions of the progressive womanhood she seems to champion. These moments are highlighted when the *Journal* version of "My Mother and I" is juxtaposed to the book-length Macmillan text. Though it is not known why Bok asked Stern to reduce the length of her manuscript or whether he insisted that particular scenes be eliminated, the omissions follow a clear pattern. An unknown writer seeking to publish her work in the tremendously popular *Ladies' Home Journal*, Stern had to meet the expectations of its editor, Bok, and reader, Roosevelt. In tailoring her text for the *Journal*, she eliminated overt, though not subtle, challenges to the tenets of the magazine; however, when publishing her unabridged story, she subverted the ideologies of her patron and editor far more than previously realized. And yet Roosevelt's introduction remains before her text, testifying to the ways in which Stern negotiated her place within progressive middle-class American womanhood and one of its favorite magazines only to call its whole narrative of American home, gender, and identity into question.

Progressive Domesticity and the Refashioning of Middle-Class American Womanhood

According to Edward Bok, one evening in 1905, as the editor sat talking with the president, Roosevelt turned to him suddenly and pronounced:

> "Bok, I envy your power with your public."
> The editor was frankly puzzled.
> "That's a strange remark from the President of the United States," he replied.
> "You may think so," was the rejoinder. "But listen. When do I get the ear of the public? In its busiest moments. My messages are printed in the newspapers and read hurriedly, mostly by men in trolleys or railroad-cars. Women hardly ever read them. Now you are read every evening by the fireside or under the lamp, when the day's work is over and the mind is at rest from other things and receptive to what you offer. Don't you see where you have it on me?"[17]

This revealing, though perhaps apocryphal, plaint demonstrates Roosevelt's keen awareness of the power of popular literature and the monthly magazine in particular to shape America. Even more dramatically, it reveals the president's recognition, well before women's suffrage, of the vital social and political import of women and writings tailored to them. Roosevelt suggests that women's reading, far more than that of their distracted husbands, has profound effects upon the nation.

At the same time, Roosevelt, like many native-born Americans, feared for the future of that very home by whose fire and lamp he imagined the American woman. Internal and external threats seemed to collide: a weak military and civilian population dangerously unprepared to take its part in the world; a massive foreign presence within the nation with its different customs, its working women and children, and horrifying home conditions; an increasing urban poor population, laboring for a pittance, crowding in slums, growing in dissatisfaction, and threatening upheaval; an emergent feminist movement calling for the release of women from lives centered around the home; and a "decadent" wealthy class, materialistic and self-indulgent, seeking personal pleasure and failing to lead or breed adequately. "The home duties are the vital duties," Roosevelt repeated again and again to multiple audiences, revealing the degree to which he feared they were being neglected.[18] "The nation is in a bad way if there is no real home, if the family is not of the right kind; if the man is not a good husband and father, if he is brutal or cowardly or selfish, if the woman has lost her sense of duty, if she is sunk in vapid self-indulgence or has let her nature be twisted so that she prefers a sterile pseudo-intellectuality to that great and beautiful development of character which comes only to those whose lives know the fullness of duty done."[19] Seeking a national revival of order, strength, and duty, Roosevelt, like many progressive reformers, called for a reimagining and revitalization of the home.

As we have already begun to see, these reformers viewed the home as more than a symbol, believing instead that its character, architecture, and environs literally shaped the nature of its inhabitants. As Jacob Riis proclaimed in his book *The Peril and Preservation of the Home* (1903), "American citizenship in the long run, will be, *must be*, what the American home is."[20] This is in part because the home is, according to Riis, the "greatest factor of all in the training of the young," with the habits learned there transferred later, for better or for worse, into the public arena.[21] But even greater than the impact of the lessons of the home was the perceived influence of its environment on the body and character of future generations. As we have seen, in accordance with the neo-Lamarckian principles that provided the scientific underpinnings for progressive reform, heredity is shaped not solely by one's physical legacy but by physical responses to the environment that become embedded in one's biological makeup and transmitted to one's offspring. Good surroundings can thereby literally create good bodies, good characters, and good citizens, improving the biological and moral future of generations to come, whereas negative surroundings produce the opposite results with devastating ramifications. The power attributed to the environment suggested clear-cut solutions to complex sets of problems and fears produced by industrialization, corporate capitalism, urbanization and the concurrent increase in foreign presence in the United States. It was believed that a healthy, self-restrained, harmonious American citizenry could be produced and sustained by manipulating the environment, and especially that most formative environment, the family and its home.[22]

For progressive reformers like Riis, Bok, and Roosevelt, the ideal family environment was based on a middle-class model, headed by a hardworking male breadwinner, managed by a nurturing, well-organized wife and mother, and complete with healthy, clean, well-behaved children who, as Roosevelt put it, must be "sound in body, mind, and character, and numerous enough so that the race shall increase and not decrease."[23] Such households could be created and sustained in part, they believed, through legislation limiting female and child labor, addressing male desertion and nonsupport, and promoting temperance, tenement reform, and industrial, food, and drug safety standards, all seen as central to the health of the family. But legislation alone could not reform the day-to-day internal functioning of the household. It could not provide the "effective management of duties" Roosevelt and others called for as, to use Robert Wiebe's term, they "searched for order" in a changing nation.[24] Other approaches were needed to bring to bear upon the home the lessons and methods devised by the newly professionalized middle class, with its scientific management, streamlined organization, and emphasis on skill—all motivated by this desire for order, efficiency, and control.[25] Such values and methods needed to be modeled and promoted in order to proliferate.

Fortifying, modernizing, and promoting progressive middle-class domestic life and its embodiment in the home was precisely how Edward Bok perceived the mission of his *Ladies' Home Journal*. Other progressive magazines preached similar values, but with its target audience of households earning between $1,200 and $2,500 per year and a record-breaking circulation of more than one million by 1904 and two million by 1919,[26] Bok's

Journal reached unprecedented numbers of middle-class women.[27] And as advertisers, retailers, and scholars alike have attested, it influenced the way they lived and the way they consumed culture and products.[28] "Women buy perfume and scented toilet soap for one of two reasons," said a Charlotte, North Carolina, drugstore owner. "One: they see it advertised in the Ladies' Home Journal.... Two: They hear that some other woman is using it."[29] But seeing himself not just as a businessman but as a reformer,[30] Bok wanted his *Journal* to do even more to shape the lives of its readers and the nation.

Edward Bok used the *Ladies' Home Journal* very deliberately as a means of reforming the structure and function of the middle-class home and of promoting the proliferation of such spaces across the United States. The editor aimed to set new norms for American taste and behavior by vividly portraying and stridently dictating standards for every aspect of American home life. His *Journal* offered professional advice on home design, decor, management, child rearing, and more, providing visual models and written instructions and cajoling readers into imitating them. Bok was appalled, for instance, by the "wretched architecture of small houses" throughout the United States, which he found "repellently ornate."[31] Just as squalid tenements signaled to reformers a disorderly, unrestrained citizenry threatening to undermine American society from below, so the architecturally unrestrained homes of the upper classes and their imitators seemed to embody and foster the decadence and decline in spirit of the nation's more prosperous inhabitants.[32] Advocating a "simple life" of comfort and contentment over want and luxury, order and usefulness over laxity and self-indulgence, Bok sought to promote these values and to implant them in the physical environment of the nation.[33] To this end, he hired architects to plan simple, affordable houses, and he printed and sold their plans. These model homes generally disposed of private nooks and showpiece parlors, centering instead around an open living room that would increase family contact by uniting the family in a single social space.[34] Though the designs varied widely, adaptations of the Colonial, with its geometric regularity, simplicity, and historic overtones, were frequently published and praised for representing traditional American values.[35] Bok's goal was for these homes to cover the American landscape, shaping its surroundings and thereby the bodies and minds of its future citizenry.[36] With *Ladies' Home Journal* houses springing up across the country, Theodore Roosevelt himself would note: "Bok is the only man I ever heard of who changed, for the better, the architecture of an entire nation, and he did it so quickly and yet so effectively that we didn't know it was begun before it was finished."[37]

Home design and decor were given moral significance in the *Journal*, where the way in which a house was furnished was seen as a mark of proper living and good citizenship. Bok railed against the plush furniture, ornate moldings, heavy drapery, and abundant bric-a-brac of the Victorian age, which he believed to be useless, unhealthful dust collectors that detract from the essential therapeutic function of the home as a hygienic, well-ordered haven from the chaotic modern world.[38] The *Journal* transmitted his progressive middle-class domestic aesthetic through a barrage of visual images aimed at persuading readers to refurnish their homes accordingly.[39] Believing that women are most strongly influenced by the taste of their peers and social competitors, Bok attempted to convince readers to conform to his ideals by depicting how they had been actualized in "the most carefully furnished homes in America" through a long-running series entitled, at various points in time, "Inside 100 Homes," "In Other People's Homes," and "Inside Other Women's Homes."[40] In 1906, he began a "Good Taste and Bad Taste" column, focusing each month on a different home furnishing and providing two columns of photos—one of, say, lamps or window curtains in good taste (simple and straight) and the other in bad taste (ornate and impractical)— and educating readers to choose correctly.[41]

The *Ladies' Home Journal* also provided constant professional advice to the housewife on how to manage the nation's homes and raise its future citizens.[42] In doing so, it combined the values of republican domesticity of an earlier age with the needs and methods of the new industrial economy and the principles of its reformers. Information on child rearing, for instance, was provided by Dr. Emelyn L. Coolidge, who portrayed motherhood as a science requiring careful training, rigorous methods, strict schedules, and set rules for raising children to become healthy and productive citizens in the new economy.[43] The *Journal* similarly professionalized housekeeping, running articles from leading home economists that taught women both the urgent need and practical methods for maintaining a clean, germ-free, orderly, and efficient household. In a highly influential series by the renowned domestic scientist Christine Frederick, women were instructed on how to run their homes, and particularly their bright, new laboratory-like kitchens, as scientifically managed factories that "work like a clock," with every step of every task carefully planned to ensure efficiency.[44]

Such methods were meant not only to improve the home and the bodies and characters of its inhabitants but also to satisfy women with the role of housekeeper by making them managers of their own domains. "If housework is 'drudgery' to a woman it is only because that woman refuses to avail herself of the improved equipment and efficient methods offered her on every hand. Certainly baking a cake or bathing a baby is not a whit as much 'drudgery' as monotonously addressing envelopes or pounding a typewriter," Frederick declared.[45] With production taken out of the household in the new urban industrial economy, potentially freeing women from housework and enabling them to enter the work force in new ways, Frederick, Coolidge, and Bok insisted that there was far more stimulating and important work requiring greater organization, scientific knowledge, and management skills to be done at home.

The *Journal* encouraged women to view their households expansively, applying their skills to help make their larger communities reflect the same ideals as their homes, a principle of "national housekeeping" that some women were using to justify their call for suffrage, but which the antisuffrage crusader Bok believed to be part of a woman's extended domestic responsibility to the nation. The *Journal* led campaigns to get rid of obtrusive outdoor advertising,[46] dirty streets, ramshackle buildings,[47] and heavy drapery in Pullman cars.[48] Bok also spearheaded campaigns against public drinking cups[49] and patent medicines[50] and for sex education.[51] All these reforms were moderate in nature, advocating the proliferation of progressive middle-class values, methods, and aesthetics rather than radical changes in the economic and social structure of the nation.[52] But in promoting public spaces that mirrored the forms and ideals of the progressive middle-class home, *Journal* women could impact the moral and physical health of the nation. In the process, they would "Americanize" themselves.

Though Bok's *Journal* was not aimed at immigrant women—many of whom read similar magazines in their native languages[53]—it did have a distinct Americanizing mission.[54] Bok himself was not American born. Some have read the Dutch immigrant's attempt to dictate the contours of the American home as stemming from a desire to prove himself more American than the Americans.[55] But, having emigrated from Holland as a child, he argued, against Roosevelt's demands, that "when a man is born in one country and adopts another, he always is and remains a man of two countries. . . . A man always remains what he was born! Not in feeling or in spirit, perhaps, but in fact."[56] Yet Bok and the president bonded over their shared Dutch origins. "We must work for the same ends," Roosevelt said to Bok. "You and I can each become good Americans by giving our best to make America better. With the Dutch stock there is in both of us, there's no limit to what we can do. Let's go to it," again revealing the tension between Roosevelt's notions of civic practice and racial advantage.[57] Bok understood his own Dutchness as a privileged point from which to critique America, claiming in the tradition of de Tocqueville that the foreigner can see "distinct lacks" that "loom large" in the United States that native-born Americans cannot perceive.[58] In his Pulitzer Prize–winning autobiography, *The Americanization of Edward Bok* (1920), he criticizes Americans for lack of thrift, thoroughness, obedience to the law, respect for authority, and informed suffrage—all considered hallmarks of middle-class life in a republic. He insists, "There are thousands of American-born who need Americanization just as much as do the foreign born."[59] For, as he writes at the height of post–World War I nativism,

> America in the truest aspect, in the real sense, is not a place on the map only. . . .
> The real America is an ideal—a vision yet to be fulfilled.
> The real American is he who feels that ideal, makes it a part of himself—and does his share and makes his contribution to the attainment of the goal and the clear realization of the ideal, whether he be born in the US or thousands of miles from its borders. . . .
> Again, how many of us, born here or elsewhere, could qualify as a "hundred per cent American?" Scarcely one, because, in truth, there is no such American.[60]

Bok defines Americanization as the process through which all Americans, wherever they were born, improve themselves and their country by living up to its ideals. In depicting class and domestic standards as part of the civic ideals of the nation, his *Journal* turned the acts of redecorating, cooking, cleaning, and child rearing into means by which the American woman could Americanize her home and herself, a message Elizabeth Stern would clearly understand.

"Foreign Missions at Home"

At the same time that Bok and, as will soon become apparent, Roosevelt were using the *Ladies' Home Journal* to reconstruct American domestic life on a progressive middle-class model, reformers focusing on the working class, and particularly the immigrant working class, sought to bring them and their homes in line with these same ideals. At stake here was not simply the orderliness of the tenement kitchen or the manners of its children. Beneath the surface was the fear that, as Riis put it, "A man cannot live like a pig and vote like a man. . . . With no home to cherish, how long before love of country would be an empty sound?"[61] Alongside this fear, however, was the persistent hope that if immigrants could establish clean, well-ordered homes, they would no longer threaten the nation with upheaval, disloyalty, or even foreignness. Instead, they would be satisfied and contained within their homes, absorbed into the boundaries of the homeland, and joined with native-born Americans in opposition to the foreigners outside the gates.[62]

Foreignness was associated with the working class, which seemed to threaten proletarian revolution, not only in the political or economic sphere but in standards and ways of life. Part of the solution, then, was to alter the class mentality, if not the actual class status, of the new immigrants. By transforming their dwellings into middle-class spaces and converting their habits and ways of thought to middle-class norms, the masses would be rendered harmless and American.

Multiple private and public programs developed aimed at creating a healthier, ordered citizenry in safe homes and homeland. Public schools began to offer classes in hygiene and home economics, providing models for children to relay to their parents so as to "carry the reform home."[63] Settlement houses took form as islands of progressive American domesticity in the midst of the foreign sea. Describing the area around the Hull House settlement in Chicago, the evangelical reformer Isabelle Horton wrote in 1904: "Narrow streets and alleys branching off on either side afford vistas of wretchedness. There are sooty tenements, tumble-down sheds, and foul stables. Dirty children in all sorts of demi-toilet swarm everywhere." In contrast to the swarming children, dirt, and disarray stands the settlement house, a beacon of propriety, taste, class, and Americanness. "A few steps and you are standing before the porticoed front of an old but dignified looking red brick house set well back from the sidewalk," Horton continued. "The little court thus formed is well paved and clean, and benches invite rest. You recognize instinctively that this is not a house thrown together by the exigencies of trade, but that it is a place with a history and a purpose." Inside this house, "everywhere there is evidence of cultivated taste. Furniture is handsome and genuine; no cheap or tawdry imitations are permitted. On the walls hang photographs from the masters of art."[64] Such spaces were, as Horton referred to them, "foreign missions at home," preaching simplicity, order, and class values by their very design and decor, identifying these as American, and encouraging foreigners to uplift themselves through imitation.[65] In the face of such examples, Horton reports one immigrant girl, "surveying a neatly-arranged table, perhaps for the first time in her life," saying, "Huh, my dad 'ud think I was crazy if I set a table like that to home." "Nevertheless," the reformer states with pride, "she put in a plea at home for a table-cloth, and, being accustomed to her own way, she succeeded in obtaining one, . . . and little by little there have been introduced into that home 'gentler manners' if not 'purer laws.'"[66] Tablecloths, furnishings, manners, and other symbolic markers of taste and class were deemed signs of progress and Americanization. "It is not the acquisition of facts but the cultivation that the foreign girls need for their future happiness and usefulness," wrote one settlement house leader.[67]

It was hoped that upon marrying, properly trained immigrant girls would establish "truly American homes" in which to raise new American children. Describing immigrant brides as "eager to have the homes which they were about to establish better organized and more intelligently conducted than those from which they had come," Lillian Wald established housekeeping centers designed with "intelligence and taste" at the Henry Street Settlement to teach "housekeeping in its every detail." Providing instruction in "cleaning, disinfecting, actual purchasing of supplies, . . . household accounts, nursing, all the elements of homekeeping,"[68] these centers taught immigrant girls the scientific and managerial skills required for progressive housekeeping and held out the promise of "healthful, happy homes" for them and their future families.[69]

Modeling domesticity in ways that their "mothers have neither time nor ability to teach them," the teacher and social worker replaced the ethnic mother, urging mimesis of American middle-class womanhood over ethnic working-class models.⁷⁰ Jane Addams, the founder of Hull House, was sensitive to the generational tensions created by this dynamic, as well as by the "premature dependence of the older and wiser upon the young and foolish" wrought by Americanization.⁷¹ She created opportunities within her settlement house for parents to exhibit their "old-world" talents and skills, restoring, if only for a short while, their position as knowledge-bearers and teachers. The Hull-House Labor Museum, for instance, included demonstrations by Syrian, Greek, Italian, Russian, and Irish women of their different methods of spinning, enabling the young people to see that "the complicated machinery of the factory had been evolved from simple tools" like those once used by their mothers. But while such displays helped "bring together the old life and the new, a respect for the older cultivation, and not quite so much assurance that the new was the best," the contrast between what Addams calls the "charm of woman's primitive activities" and the "large and pleasant rooms" of the settlement house in which they were displayed undoubtedly suggested which was worthy of imitation in the modern age.⁷²

For these reformers, as for Bok and, as shall become clear, for Roosevelt and Elizabeth Stern, becoming American meant becoming middle-class. As Andrew Heinze has argued, through changes in their home organization, manners, and habits of consumption, immigrant women were offered a safe, relatively simple, symbolic mode of displaying their Americanization that did not require the arduous tasks of language change or participation in American public life, yet granted status within the immigrant community and approval by visitors to it.⁷³ These women could demonstrate their Americanness by reorganizing their dwellings, whatever their size or locale, into homes that appeared middle class. In doing so, they held out the promise for the creation of a nation as neatly organized, carefully regulated, and beautifully tranquil as the pages of the *Ladies' Home Journal*.

"The Largest Opportunity for Strenuous Living": Roosevelt's Domestication of the Strenuous Life

Both the questions of American domesticity and of domesticating the foreigner were of grave concern to Theodore Roosevelt. The very future of the nation lay at stake for him. As he pronounced of immigration "whether the good or the evil shall predominate depends mainly on whether these newcomers do or do not throw themselves heartily into our national life, cease to be Europeans, and become Americans like the rest of us."[74] But who the "rest of us" are often seemed up for grabs. One thing was clear to Roosevelt, though: the future American would be determined in greatest measure by the average American home. "No artistic or scientific development, no material prosperity, no commercial expansion will count . . . unless the foundation of society—which is the home—is made sound," he declared in 1906.[75] "We cannot have good citizenship in the present unless the average man and the average woman do their duty in their home; we cannot have good citizenship in the future unless in the average home the average boy and girl are brought up that in the future they will be American men and women of the right type, able and anxious to meet all the exacting demands that American citizenship now makes," he added five years later.[76] The home, he believed, was the source of the two most essential duties of the citizen to the nation—"perpetuat[ing] its own life, its own blood," and "the building up of . . . character."[77] To ensure the perpetuation and character of American blood, Roosevelt looked to the home and worked to reshape the gendered obligations of both women and men to it.

Roosevelt used any opportunity possible to bolster national commitment to "home values"—to procreation, to establishing a progressive home environment, and to raising vigorous children into good citizens. To the amusement of many, he called frequently for families to have more children. He turned his own family into exemplars of how these children should be raised, and he and his wife, Edith, redecorated the Executive Mansion, making it, as he said, "literally the ideal house for the head of a great democratic republic," a model on the grandest scale of the taste and values of the Progressive Era.[78] He renamed it "the White House," emphasizing its place as the nation's leading home. And he invited in photographers to publicize the activities of the first family: Edith and Theodore's daily horseback rides together, the antics of the children, and the father's famous romps and pillow fights. The household, Roosevelt recalled, embodied "just the proper mixture of freedom and control in the management of the children. They were never allowed to be disobedient or to shirk lessons or work; and they were encouraged to have all the fun possible."[79] With parents acting as guides and companions, providing "advice, example, and the loving friendship that shows trust and understanding,"[80] children raised in this way would undoubtedly "grow up trained and fit . . .

to be both useful and happy," and well equipped to carry on the work of the Republic.[81]

As part of this attempt to sell his domestic ideals to the nation at large, Roosevelt welcomed Edward Bok's offer to become a regular and sometimes secret contributor to the *Ladies' Home Journal*. "Mr. President, I should like to share my power with you," Bok proposed. "You recognize that women do not read your messages; and yet no President's messages ever discussed more ethical questions that women should know about and get straight in their minds.... Have a department in my magazine, and explain your ideas."[82] In 1906–7, the *Journal* ran a column entitled: "The President: A Department in Which Will Be Presented the Attitude of the President on Those National Questions Which Affect the Vital Interests of the Home, by a Writer Intimately Acquainted and in Close Touch with Him." This column, written by Robert L. O'Brien, was based on O'Brien's monthly conversations with the president—allegedly while he was being shaved—and edited by Roosevelt himself.[83] In it the president addressed major issues of progressive reform, including factory laws for women and children, regulation of medicines, modern educational methods, physical education of boys, and "race suicide," all of which fell under the rubric of "national questions that affect the vital interest of the home." Like Bok, Roosevelt defined the home expansively, its "vital interests" including reproduction, education, social reform, and, unlike the editor, suffrage. Ten years later, during World War I and at the same time that Roosevelt was serving as reader for the *Journal*, he and Bok undertook a second project. "Feeling that it would be an interesting experiment to see how far Theodore Roosevelt's ideas could stand unsupported by the authority of his vibrant personality," Bok concocted a plan by which the former president would secretly write the very first Men's page for the *Ladies' Home Journal*.[84] Recognizing the influence of his name and image above the force of his ideas, Roosevelt was hesitant.[85] But with Bok's urging, Roosevelt took the challenge of ghostwriting the column "Men: In Answer to the Oft-Asked Question: Why Do You Not Have Just One Page for Men in the Home Journal?"[86]

In order to rally women and men to their domestic duties, Roosevelt's column for women expanded the home to the larger national domestic sphere, while his unsigned column for men—certainly read by the magazine's target female audience as well—concentrated more narrowly on male duty to the family home, an issue that concerned him far more than scholars have realized.[87]

"More strenuous lives, in the President's opinion, may be found than anywhere else in the homes of America, exhibited by patient mothers who see to it, as each Saturday night rolls around, that the week's work is done, that the children's stockings are mended, and that numberless details of housekeeping have been intelligently performed," readers of the first "The President" column of the *Ladies' Home Journal* were informed in May 1906.[88] Having originally coined and popularized the term the "strenuous life" in his 1899 speech to the all-male Hamilton Club in Chicago, Roosevelt used it then to demand vigorous manhood, national strength, and triumphant imperialism and to bind the three together. "I wish to preach not the doctrine of ignoble ease, but the doctrine of the strenuous life, the life of toil and effort, of labor and strife," he said to the men of the Hamilton Club.[89] In this speech, Roosevelt used individual duty to the home as a model for individual engagement in the nation and national engagement in the world:

> In the last analysis a healthy state can exist only when the men and women who make it up lead clean, vigorous, healthy lives; when the children are so trained that they shall endeavor, not to shirk difficulties, but to overcome them; not to seek ease, but to know how to wrest triumph from toil and risk. The man must be glad to do a man's work, to dare and endure and to labor; to keep himself, and to keep those dependent upon him. The woman must be the housewife, the helpmeet of the homemaker, the wise and fearless mother of many healthy children.
>
> As it is with the individual, so it is with the nation. . . . Far better it is to dare mighty things, to win glorious triumphs, even though checkered by failure, than to take rank with those poor spirits who neither enjoy much nor suffer much, because they live in the gray twilight that knows not victory nor defeat.[90]

"As it is with the individual, so it is with the nation," Roosevelt said in his address, but in the *Ladies' Home Journal*, Roosevelt turns this analogy around, calling upon the popular associations between the term "strenuous life" and the vigorous outdoorsmanship, aggressive politics, and interventionist internationalism of the Rough Rider and turning them back home. Applying this rallying language within the pages of the *Ladies' Home Journal* to the daily domestic chores of mothers, Roosevelt brings women and their labor into the work of the American nation and empire.

For women, the work of the nation meant, first and most important, producing and rearing its children. The first article of his presidential series for women (February 1906) focuses on the problem of "race suicide." In it Roosevelt demands (through the column's author, Robert L. O'Brien) that Americans sacrifice comfort and ease and have at least four children per family, in order to prevent what he expected to be the imminent extinction of the "sturdy, vigorous American people" due to low birthrates.[91] He blames the ominous decline largely on the "emancipation of women." While it is a positive advance in social justice,[92] he argues that "this new freedom has been twisted into wrong where it has been taken to mean a relief from all those duties and obligations which though burdensome in the extreme, women cannot expect to escape. While no one believes that it is the sole duty of the women who are married to rear children, any more than it is the sole duty of the men to be the bread winners of the family, in the main each of the sexes must do this part so long as time lasts."[93] The essential function of the American woman is procreation and housewifery, and the essential duty of the American man is breadwinning. Though Roosevelt insists on the naturalness and ahistoricism of these roles, he clearly fears that nature will be abrogated and history overcome by selfish men, who value personal pleasure over family responsibility, or by twisted women, who choose a life of ease or work outside the home over true maternal duty. His anxiety reveals an underlying awareness of the changing reality of gender roles as well as a corresponding concern over the future of the "sturdy, vigorous" "American race."

Within the pages of the *Journal*, Roosevelt defines the American race in terms of both color and class. The columnist tells his readers that Roosevelt's real concern is the perpetuation of white America, for "what would happen to our Caucasian civilization . . . if the Southern whites should drop to the families of the size of the New Englanders of English stock, and the colored population of the section were to increase as fast as it has done since the war?"[94] But more specifically, Roosevelt wishes to stimulate the reproduction of the white middle class, "the so called 'better classes' of the community."[95] He does not want an increase in the birthrate of paupers or even of the idle rich from whom, he says in his *Journal* column on divorce, "disregard of responsibility may be expected" and who therefore would not make vigorous Americans.[96] What he desires is the reproduction of middle-class Americans of European descent—precisely those who read the *Ladies' Home Journal*. Faced with threatening changes in social and economic life, Roosevelt lays the responsibility for the continuation of his America squarely in the lap of his readers. He insists that masses of middle-class, white women—"average Americans"—commit their bodies to the state and their work to the home, and that those who are members of either the upper or working classes transform themselves into such women.

Roosevelt's "sturdy and vigorous" Americans could not simply be genetically reproduced, as eugenicists would argue a few years later; as we have seen, they had to be deliberately molded. For this reason, parenting is of greatest concern to Roosevelt in these columns. Roosevelt glorifies motherhood but not to "reaffirm that good women were not sullied by contact with male sexuality" required for race preservation, as Gail Bederman suggests.[97] He does not focus on the purity of women or the separateness of the domestic sphere. Instead, Roosevelt recognizes the desire of women for a larger social and political role, and he seeks to satisfy and mobilize this desire by rhetorically altering the nature of domestic work, labeling it the true "strenuous life," and thereby connecting it to new national projects.

Situating the home at the center of heroic national aims also enabled Roosevelt to rally men to their home duties. In his Men's pages, Roosevelt elevates breadwinning into a personal and patriotic duty to be carried out by men. While his first Men's page article in the *Journal* defines male success as both earning a living and serving one's community and nation, he focuses in this context much more on breadwinning.[98] In doing so, Roosevelt makes the home central to the gender definition of the middle-class American male as well as female:

> If he is a healthy human being, fit for citizenship in the human commonwealth, [the ordinary man's] ideal must hold as its foundation a home with a happy wife and healthy children; and his first effort must be to realize this ideal by showing that he can provide and maintain this home for himself, for the wife as his partner and helpmate, and for their children. This, and for this object, to earn a man's livelihood, represents the foundation of his success.[99]

Somewhat tautologically, Roosevelt claims that the average male is a success as a man only if he establishes a nuclear family and earns for it a "man's livelihood." Only then is he fit for citizenship in the "human commonwealth" and implicitly in the American Republic. In contrast to the pervasive image of Roosevelt demanding the rugged lifestyle and macho ethic of the cowboy and soldier for American men, he defines American manhood, at least in the pages of the *Ladies' Home Journal*, much more consistently through progressive middle-class ideals of companionate marriage, engaged fatherhood, and honest breadwinning. Here he clearly, though anonymously, advocates a "domestic masculinity," calling for men to be very much involved in the daily workings of the household.[100] One piece instructs them on how to treat their servants, clearly assuming an audience of employers, not employees.[101] Another explains the role of fathers in the lives of their daughters, for whom marriage, not self-sufficiency, is the ultimate aim.[102] Stressed most often is the urgent need for paternal involvement in the lives of boys in order to overcome the potentially softening maternal influence through lessons in virility and self-sufficiency.[103] In this way, Roosevelt's notion of male domesticity may be seen as linked to his "cult of masculinity" and military and imperialist programs, for the job of the father is to train athletic and independent boys, thereby strengthening the mind and body of America's citizenry.[104] At the same time, however, this national work sent men back to the home.

As Amy Kaplan has argued, if we think of domesticity not only as the female hearth in opposition to the male marketplace but as the domestic in contrast to the foreign, the nation becomes home for women and men who are joined in an obligation to domesticate the savage foreigner both outside and within its borders.[105] In the antebellum period that is Kaplan's focus, those foreigners were largely Mexicans, Native Americans, and African Americans residing within the nation's expanding geographic borders. At the turn of the twentieth century, however, the ranks of domestic foreigners swelled largely as a result of voluntary mass immigration.

It is not surprising, then, that in his final Men's page for the *Ladies' Home Journal*, Roosevelt calls upon native-born Americans to work to Americanize the immigrant, nor that he employs the language and methods of imperialism and domesticity together to rally them to this task. "Under the comparatively simple conditions of fifty years ago the earlier German and Irish immigrants were fairly well able to assimilate themselves to their surroundings. They passed through a period of separate shanty-town existence in the neighborhood of brickyards or small railway centers; but they gradually grew into substantial similarity with their neighbors, mingled with them, and frequently intermarried with them," he writes. Roosevelt represents the erstwhile foreignness of the earlier immigrant wave through the class of its houses and neighborhoods and its assimilation into America in terms of integration into middle-class spaces and families. The problem today, he claims, is that "the Poles and Italians . . . , their present-day successors in the rough, unskilled kinds of laborers' work, . . . are more ignorant, and at first find it harder to learn English; they tend to herd together without intimate contact with the rest of the community, and with few or no civilizing or Americanizing influences."[106] Roosevelt's solution for Americanizing these foreigners is to "civilize" them by assimilating them into middle-class domestic American life. He urges the readers of the *Journal* to reach out to these foreigners and bring them into their communities through regular social interaction. Sports, in particular, he argues, "has a most potent effect in both fraternizing and Americanizing the participants."[107] Like the settlement house workers he so admired, Roosevelt believed in the power of cross-cultural socialization and exposure to average American familial and communal life to Americanize immigrants and make the United States their true and only home.

As Bok predicted, Roosevelt found in the *Ladies' Home Journal* a means of reaching female readers and their husbands with his twofold message of obligation to their own homes and to the nation as home to a diverse population in need of domestication. He and Bok helped redefine what made a home "American" in terms of the class affiliation, gender roles, racial identity, and nationalist spirit of its inhabitants and modeled ways in which these could be fostered and demonstrated in the material and functional organization of a household. When the editor and his reader received a story from a newly Americanized young woman seeming to testify to the success of their doctrines, they quickly published and dramatically trumpeted it.

Elizabeth Stern well understood the domestic forms and expectations of Americanization. Both her childhood experience and her later work going door-to-door collecting data in ethnic neighborhoods exposed her to the conditions of immigrant homes and to the imperative that they be brought into accord with progressive middle-class American standards.

Written from the perspective of an ethnic outsider, her story "My Mother and I" seems to idolize the American home precisely as it was imagined and touted by the *Ladies' Home Journal*. It appears to promote middle-class progressive domesticity, to proclaim its centrality to national identity, and to advocate it as the most effective way of safely assimilating female immigrants and of shaping their offspring, the nation's future citizenry. What better way for the editor and the former president to convince their readers of the value of progressive American middle-class domestic life and its utility in domesticating the foreigner?

"To Be an American Woman at the Head of an American Home": Elizabeth Stern's *Journal* Story

In the October 1916 issue of the *Ladies' Home Journal*, just a few pages before the first of Roosevelt's anonymous Men's pages, Elizabeth Stern's abridged story, "My Mother and I," appeared. Filling two pages and spilling over into four additional columns in the back of the magazine, this illustrated piece was published without the author's name but with the leading subtitle "The Story of How I Became an American Woman," directing readers to focus on the "I" of the title rather than her mother and to understand the work in the context of Americanization and, in particular, the experience of Americanization for a woman. Assimilation, it informs its predominantly female readers, is not only about altering national identities but about redefining one's role as a woman within one's new identity.

Also influencing the audience's reading was "an appreciation" by Theodore Roosevelt. The story of the Americanization of an eastern European Jewish immigrant girl sent by Bok to his reader Roosevelt thrilled the former president. After reading the manuscript, he immediately wrote to the editor, commending the text, and when the piece was published in October, Roosevelt's report appeared as its introduction, adding, as Bok said in his thank-you note to Roosevelt, "value to it for the author and ourselves."[108]

Roosevelt's foreword did, of course, attract attention to the story, to that issue of the *Journal*, and to Stern's later book, which it also prefaced. But his words have further significance in how they instruct their audience to read Stern's text. Roosevelt wrote:

Sagamore Hill.

This is a really noteworthy story—a profoundly touching story—of the Americanizing of an immigrant girl, who between babyhood and young womanhood leaps over a space which in all cultural and humanizing essentials is far more important than the distance painfully traversed by her fore-fathers during the preceding thousand years. When we tend to grow disheartened over some of the developments of our American civilization, it is well worth while seeing what this same civilization holds for starved and noble souls who have elsewhere been denied what here we hold to be, as a matter of course, rights free to all—although we do not, as we should do, make these rights accessible to all who are willing with resolute earnestness to strive for them. I most cordially commend this story.

—*Theodore Roosevelt*[109]

Roosevelt tells the predominantly native-born, female audience to read "My Mother and I" in a way that reaffirms their belief in themselves, to learn from it to value their own nation just as outsiders do. Incorporating Stern's story into a narrative of American exceptionalism, he uses it to reinforce American nationalism. He stresses the rights America grants, without specifying them, and seems to open access to these rights to all those who "are willing with resolute earnestness to strive for them," language that recalls the Americanization imperative of "True Americanism." A discussion of rights seems odd as an introduction to Stern's work, which says nothing about human rights, religious freedom, or freedom from persecution, or even about the contrast between the United States and the "old country," as many immigrant narratives do and as we might expect based on Roosevelt's words.[110] What Stern focuses on instead is a young woman's desire for and belief in her right to a truly "American home."

The protagonist's longing for what we will find to be progressive middle-class American domesticity is undoubtedly what attracted Roosevelt and Bok to this story. Stern's work brought together Roosevelt's ideologies of both the American home and Americanization, domesticity and domestication, seeming to exemplify a gendered version of Roosevelt's notion of assimilation. Roosevelt's introduction implicitly tells readers of the *Ladies' Home Journal* that they must grant the right to American womanhood to their immigrant neighbors "who are willing with resolute earnestness to strive for [it]," and it urges potentially rebellious American-born women to esteem their own lives and homes as the immigrant girl of the story does.

As Roosevelt and Bok clearly realized, the single aim of this unnamed girl is "to be an American woman at the head of an American home."[111] This is not to say that unqualified support for such Americanization was the author's goal for "My Mother and I" as well. In the past, the vast majority of readers have seen the unnamed protagonist, narrator, and author as one and the same. Stern's work had been widely accepted as autobiographical until 1993,[112] when Ellen Umansky presented evidence from Stern's son Thomas Noel Stern proclaiming that his mother was not an immigrant at all, but the American-born illegitimate child of a Welsh woman and a married Pittsburgh merchant of German descent who was raised as the foster child of Russian Jewish immigrants.[113] Even according to her son, whose claims about his mother's origins cannot be substantiated,[114] many of the incidents recorded in *My Mother and I* and in Stern's subsequent book *I Am a Woman—and a Jew* are true to her life. But the first-person narrator, who claims to be Jewish by birth and to have emigrated from Russia at the age of two, should not be seen as identical to the author, regardless of the veracity of Thomas Noel Stern's assertions. Like the narrator of any autobiographical or fictional work, she is a deliberately constructed voice and character. Stern's protagonist also should not be judged as identical to the narrator. As critic Kirsten Wasson suggests, in *My Mother and I*, Stern clearly distinguishes between the girl about whom the story is told and the narrator—the girl grown up—who tells her story from the perspective of adulthood.[115] With the advantage of distance, the narrator can say of her child self, "I did not notice how I was leaving behind me not only the ghetto, but its people also."[116] She is now pained by the rift her new life has created in her once-intimate relationship with her mother, saddened by the fact that "our home is a home which, try as I may, we can not make home to mother."[117]

Still, from the unnamed child's perspective, nothing is as desirable as assimilation into an American feminine identity and the creation of what she believes to be a distinctly American domestic life. Much of her story chronicles her struggles with her father to achieve higher education. Her motives are not intellectual, professional, or even based in a desire "to make myself for a person," as they are for Anzia Yezierska's protagonist of the *Bread Givers*, who tells a similar tale.[118] Education for Stern's protagonist is the means by which to understand and achieve progressive American womanhood. Her high school principal convinces her that she must go to college by showing her that through education, "I could make myself an American woman."[119] She sees her greatest success in college as establishing such a mainstream identity. "I entered that little American university, and I was accepted as part of it, and I grew into American womanhood in its friendly white walls," she declares.[120] The protagonist consistently describes the American school as white. She sees it as sanitized and de-ethnicized, clean of the contaminating dirt and culture of the ghetto tenement and street. The white walls of the university become a paradigmatic American home for her in which she is "born anew."[121] The protagonist's desire for further graduate education stems from her need as a newly made American woman "to live my new life according to my new standards," which she feels she cannot do in her parents' ghetto home. She leaves for New York, where, she announces: "I not only studied in an American school, but I lived—lived!—in an American home."[122]

What are the American home and womanhood this child strives so desperately to achieve? As critic Barbara Shollar asserts, *My Mother and I* equates American identity with middle-classness. Becoming an American means becoming bourgeois, and as Shollar puts it, "by textualizing [middle-class] culture in the form of a narrative of Americanization," Stern delineates "the dominant personality of the period" and provides a model whereby all non-bourgeois Americans are to make themselves over as middle-class citizens.[123] The fact, of which Shollar is unaware, that *My Mother and I* was originally published in the *Journal* further supports her argument that the text works to define middle-class culture as the American norm into which all must be assimilated. Even more, however, it provides a model for the middle class to make itself over in a progressive vein, and Bok and Roosevelt embrace this ethnic narrative as a means of further promoting their national domestic ideals.

"Woman in White": An Immigrant Girl's Yearnings for *Journal* Womanhood

In both the magazine and book versions of Stern's text, her protagonist clearly defines the American woman not only by her cultural and national affiliations but by her class and gender role. Her ideal American woman corresponds exactly to the ideal *Ladies' Home Journal* and Rooseveltian woman. Describing her first contact with one such woman, she says: "I could not believe that the woman who opened the door to my timid knock was my schoolmate's mother. A woman in *white*! Why, mothers dressed in brown and in black, *I* always knew. And this mother sang to us, played with us; I had always thought mothers never 'enjoyed,' just worked."[124] As a child, she believes that the difference between this mother and her own is largely one of ethnicity. "There was nothing that seemed to me more wonderful than to have been born of parents that were Americans," she proclaims, with a Freudian desire to exchange her own parents for ones of higher status.[125] But what the immigrant girl admires in this American mother—her whiteness, her leisure, her seemingly carefree manner—are markers of ethnicity, race, and class. Only a woman with money can afford to "enjoy" time with her children and dress in white. She has assistance in the arduous task of laundering, unlike the ghetto mothers who wear practical brown or black symbolizing both their class and otherness.[126] This middle-class white woman, whose model of joyous motherhood corresponds exactly to Roosevelt's prescriptions for parenting, epitomizes American womanhood for the immigrant girl, and the child longs to enter her world.

Stern's protagonist also understands American womanhood in terms of a particular gender role. She embraces the ideals of what she calls "new womanhood" but what more closely approximates "progressive womanhood":

> At college were opened to my eyes windows that framed marvelous and beautiful visions. With my classmates I saw the ideal of the new woman that we, the college girls of this country were to be. I heard of the serene, wise and conscious motherhood, the strong and sane and effective women in professions, and the fine and cultured wives that it was our destiny to become. We were the new womanhood that the great universities were sending out to America.[127]

She identifies American womanhood with the modern woman who is educated and cultured, capable of professional work outside the home, and conscious and deliberate in her childbearing and child-rearing decisions.

She rejects her Orthodox father's traditional Jewish model of womanhood: "He wished me to grow up a pride to our people, quiet, modest, a good home-maker."[128] He fears that college will make her unmarriageable within her ethnic and religious group: "If we let her go to college, it will only draw her away from us forever. . . . Whom could she ever marry, if she becomes so very learned? There would be no one among our own people to suit her. . . . I could not afford a dowry large enough to get her a lawyer or a doctor."[129]

Concern over the fitness of college-educated daughters for marriage was shared by many parents, immigrant and American born, in the early decades of the century.[130] Though the native-born feared more for the femininity of their independent girls than the affordability of outmoded dowries, the generational conflict over gender roles was nonetheless pervasive—so much so that the *Ladies' Home Journal* devoted many pages each month to the topic.[131]

The story of the Americanized "new woman's" separation from her old-world parents plays out the generational conflict experienced by many *Journal* readers in the extreme. With the cultural conflict overlying the generational one, the story allows readers to consider their own experience from a safe distance. Apparently in response to "My Mother and I," the editorial pages of the following month's issue of the *Ladies' Home Journal* were filled with items on just this problem. In one editorial, Bok bemoans girls' negative estimations of their mothers and pleads with daughters to appreciate their mothers.[132] In another, he chastises mothers for not exerting greater control over their daughters. He insists that "the standard of morality does not change with any time; it cannot since the standard of morality is single and alone. And if more freedom is taken with that standard by the daughters it is not due to the times so much as it is due to the mothers."[133] Bok holds mothers responsible for the values and behaviors of their girls and demands that they enforce strict adherence to what he considers eternal moral and gender codes.

Stern's story might suggest to readers a very different way for mothers and daughters to cope with this crisis in their lives. While the father opposes his daughter's educational goals and feminine models, her mother supports her choices even though she recognizes that they will change her forever. "Mammele," as she is referred to throughout the book, becomes a mediator between her husband and child—a role historian

Paula Hyman has suggested was typical of Jewish immigrant women.[134] It is the mother who convinces the father to allow their daughter to attend both high school and college. Though she speaks to her husband in terms of his values, reassuring him that she has been saving for their daughter's trousseau, she also recognizes the girl's desire for a different kind of life. She even suggests that her daughter take piano lessons, consciously preparing her for "the life of an American lady."[135] And when the girl decides she must have a college education, her mother "declared her intention to give me to that strange new womanhood of America, and I registered that fall."[136] This mother negotiates with her husband, supports her daughter's rebellion against her father, and facilitates her entrance into a new lifestyle with competing values. And in the end, her daughter does appreciate her. "But there is one thing we have in common, mother and I," she proclaims at the end of the work. "We have this woman that I am, this woman mother has helped me to become. And I shall always remember that, though my life is now America's, yet, if I am truly an American, it was mother, she who does not understand America, who made me one."[137] Though she narcissistically believes that the existence of her self, of the American woman she hopes she has become, is adequate compensation for the loss of a real relationship with her mother, she nevertheless recognizes the tremendous contribution of her mother to the creation of this self. And like a proper *Journal* girl, she is grateful for her mother's sacrifice and support.

This conclusion might be seen as promoting the role of mother as mediator and advocate for her daughter's increased freedom rather than, as Bok insists, mother as controller and enforcer of eternal standards. But we must not forget what kind of life this daughter chooses, particularly within the pages of the *Ladies' Home Journal*. Though she breaks with the values and gender ideals preached by her father and lived by her mother, she does so to enter a world more akin to that envisioned by Bok.

Despite her demands for "new womanhood," Stern's protagonist and the generational conflict she experiences serve to reinforce more traditional American ideas of womanhood. Particularly within the abridged magazine version of the story, she struggles to be more like a *Ladies' Home Journal* woman than like her rebellious daughter. Her idea of "new womanhood" is based largely in its contrast with her mother's "old-world" womanhood, which she chooses not to imitate.[138] Stern's protagonist views herself as a new woman primarily as a result of her education and her educated and scientific approach to her roles as homemaker and mother.

The new womanhood of the protagonist retains as its center the family and home. Marriage to a man whom she identifies simply as "an American"[139] marks the culmination of her American womanhood, and the household they create together "is that kind of home in which he has always lived."[140] "I have lived . . . according to what I have tried to make the finest ideal of American home and personal and community life," she claims, though only in the *Journal* version of the story.[141] Her simple life of family and civic responsibility epitomizes the progressive middle-class lifestyle advocated by Roosevelt and the *Journal*, proving the immigrant girl properly domesticated on all fronts.

"In a Charming Old Suburb": Building an American Home

The protagonist's idea of the American home in both versions of her text seems at first to correspond precisely to the model advocated by Bok and Roosevelt in the *Ladies' Home Journal*. Opening her story with a description of her present marital home, attained after years of struggle to escape an unnamed urban, ethnic ghetto, the narrator says:

> Our home is unpretentious but pretty, and is situated in a charming old suburb of an American city where attractive modern residences stand by the side of stately old Colonial houses, as if typifying young America in the shadow of old America. . . . I am so happy, so blessed. We live simply, my husband, our boy and I. We have enough to keep us unembittered. Our friends are men and women who are busy with the making of worth-while American homes, with the problems of American politics, and with literature and art.[142]

This description of a harmonious, suburban neighborhood, with traditional Colonial homes beside simple, modest new ones, seems like a photograph from the architecture and planning pages of the *Ladies' Home Journal*. The unpretentiousness of the house and busy contentment of its inhabitants exemplify the simple, strenuous life advocated by Roosevelt and Bok. The narrator's household is constructed and run like an ideal *Journal* home as well, with a white kitchen used only for cooking, a baby's room with a spotless crib and washable rugs, and a well-behaved, self-sufficient child who "has been taught that he must play without demanding help or attention from adults about him."[143] Stern's story illustrates in an entertaining and moving manner the ideal progressive middle-class American home and dramatizes its import by showing how one working-class immigrant girl forfeited her relationship with her beloved mother to achieve such a household.

Cut from the *Ladies' Home Journal* version of the story is any viable alternative vision of home in America. Mammele's household is described in little detail in the *Journal*. It is depicted largely as a squalid, cramped space that must be escaped at all cost. "Best of all I remember the room we called the 'kitchen,'" the narrator recalls. "We called it the 'kitchen' although it was the one and only room in our new 'home.'"[144] She cannot even refer to this single, cellar room, always damp with rain and clothes water, as home without placing the word in quotation marks.

Though the neighbors describe Mammele as "terrubly pertikler" with regard to hygiene, the single depiction in the *Ladies' Home Journal* of her idea of cleanliness is at complete odds with the rules of domestic science that the *Journal* and social workers so vigorously promoted. "It may seem strange," says the narrator to her audience, "but one of [Mother's social obligations] was the lending of the use of our bathtub! Ours was the only one in the street!"[145] The exclamation points at the end of these sentences encourage readers to feel shocked by the image of neighbors standing in line in the kitchen every Friday to use the family bathtub. The girl represents her audience's assumed point of view, quoting from her physiology books and attempting to explain to her parents that "it was unsanitary—a novel word that amused my elders."[146] But Mammele "would hold a public reception as it were. All who came to bathe, first told her their joys, the gossip of the minute, their woes. By the time the bathers had all been washed half our chicken and stuffed fish for the Sabbath, and most of our homemade bread, had been given away by mother to needy bathers."[147] To the mother, lending her bathtub, ear, and food are acts of social responsibility, opening her house to the community, while to her Americanizing daughter, who stands in for the reader here, they are dangerous violations of health and privacy.

In the *Ladies' Home Journal*, illustrations accompanying the text dramatize and elaborate upon its descriptions of the ghetto household. The descriptions of Mammele's own methods of cooking, cleaning, and charity work validate the immigrant woman's ideas of home and community making. The book depicts the weekly cleaning for the Sabbath, at which time "all the furniture was moved, each corner meticulously cleaned and scrubbed, every window-pane polished. The stove was blacked till it gleamed, the copper pots and the brass candle-sticks were polished until they glowed golden red."[151] This is quite a different image from the filthy kitchen depicted in the *Ladies' Home Journal*. The book also describes how Mammele and the immigrant women of the ghetto work to help one another, adapting traditional methods of charity to a new context. Frequently the mother "made a house-to-house canvass in the ghetto" collecting money for poor brides. "Soho thus contributed to the making of a new home in America," the narrator says in the Macmillan edition only.[152] Though her charity work is unscientific and the households it creates would be considered un-American by the *Journal*, settlement house workers, and even her own daughter, the narrator acknowledges here that Mammele and her community of ethnic women contribute to making new, viable homes in America.

When the daughter attempts to impose on her mother the principles of domestic science she has learned in school, in the longer book version of the story, Mammele responds to these dictates with carefully considered arguments that undercut the teachings of Christine Frederick, Dr. Emelyn Coolidge, Lillian Wald, Isabelle Horton, and the *Journal*. When, for instance, the girl informs her mother that "it would be safer for her and much healthier for us . . . if we ate only thrice a day, and at regular intervals," her mother laughs and responds, "As if it matters when food goes in, childie, just so we have, God praise, enough to eat! And if your stomach asks for bread—will you read in a book, and tell it that it must wait?'"[153] In her gentle way, Mammele ridicules the rules advocated by domestic scientists, which demand extreme control of one's own body and rigorous regimentation of family life by the housewife.

As portrayed in the Macmillan version of Stern's story, Mammele adapts at her own pace and in her own way to life in the United States. She willingly alters many of her standards to meet her daughter's, covering her table with a white tablecloth, setting out napkins at every meal, serving dessert, and, as only the unabridged text relates, celebrating Thanksgiving. This ghetto Thanksgiving is very different from the all-American one the girl experiences at the home of a friend. In her mother's household, on the national holiday the immigrant parents recall the great feasts of the old country. The father infuses the meal with Jewish content, telling "many a tale from the Talmud." And when the daughter explains the meaning of Thanksgiving, Mammele "advised me seriously that one must not give thanks only on one day and for one bird!"[154] This family merges the religious and the secular, the Jewish and the American in their Thanksgiving feast, participating in the American holiday while using it to recollect their pre-American experience and to transmit their own values to their children. They are becoming Americans in their own way, a manner that is potentially threatening to Roosevelt's notion of Americanism and that is ultimately rejected by their own daughter. Like the family's prized kitchen clock—mentioned only in Stern's unabridged text—with a painting of the Statue of Liberty on its glass door but with "erratic hour strokes [that] never would conform to the strict rules observed by less original clocks," this family both participates in American life and symbology and sets its own rules.[155]

One of the most striking changes Mammele allows in her home is the rearrangement of space according to the progressive middle-class model. After seeing a sitting room in the home of a teacher who has invited her to visit and imitate, the daughter decides that she must have such a place too, "a room in which one simply sat."[156] When she first saw such a room at her teacher's house, she "could not imagine people coming together to sit in a house without working while they sat."[157] A nonfunctional room is simply unimaginable in an impoverished household. But by insisting on such a room, she attempts to carve out a middle-class space for herself within her parents' working-class home. Her mother helps her fulfill this desire, setting aside a room in the house and helping to decorate it, but Mammele never sits in this room. And whereas once the girl would study at the kitchen table surrounded by parents, siblings, and visitors, always sharing what she learned with her mother, after establishing her sitting room, she would "drop my books on the table of my room, rather than on the kitchen table, as had been my custom," isolating herself from her family and community and turning education into a private affair. The room becomes a symbol of the young girl's simultaneous Americanization and alienation from her family.[158]

The episode of the sitting room cannot be found in the *Ladies' Home Journal* version of "My Mother and I." Its absence is surprising, since the incident seems to endorse the very structure and arrangement of progressive middle-class American domestic space advocated by the *Journal*.¹⁵⁹ Not only is the episode missing from the *Journal* text, but it seems to have been deliberately cut from Stern's manuscript. When describing the mother's reaction to the living room in her daughter's suburban home at the end of both the book and the *Journal* article, the narrator says: "[Mammele] was not accustomed to sitting in rooms. Her life has been a life of toil. And our living room is as strange a place as was, to me, the first 'sitting room' I saw long ago."¹⁶⁰ Her allusion to this first sitting room has no referent in the *Journal* version of the text. It is clearly a vestige of an earlier draft that contained the story of the room.

While the sitting room story seems to support the physical construct of the middle-class home advocated by the *Journal*, it simultaneously undermines it in potentially threatening ways. As Bok emphasized in the architectural plans he commissioned for the *Journal*, the function of the living room, as opposed to the isolating Victorian parlor, was to provide symbolic and actual space for family togetherness. But translated in the immigrant household of Stern's story, the sitting room becomes the sole possession of the Americanizing child, a symbol of separation, not unity, undermining the moral significance of the space.

The family and neighbors continue to congregate in the kitchen. As historian Lizabeth A. Cohen has uncovered in her study of the material culture of working-class homes in this period, the decision to focus family social life in the kitchen marked a deliberate form of resistance to Americanizers.¹⁶¹ Reformers strongly encouraged workers to create a separate living space in their homes, viewing these rooms as a sign of civilization, the assumption of middle-class values, and an increased understanding of the family as an "emotional sentimental unit."¹⁶² But even after establishing such rooms in their homes, many workers continued to congregate in the kitchen, leaving their empty sitting rooms as a mere nod to Americanization, while perpetuating traditional patterns of socialization.¹⁶³ This actual disuse of designated space requires us to rethink Heinze's claim that the reorganization of domestic space was an easy way for immigrants to Americanize; instead, it suggests that such modifications may have been gestures of symbolic Americanization only, rather than signs of real change in modes of living.¹⁶⁴

In the book *My Mother and I*, Stern shows how the imposition of middle-class forms on immigrant and working-class households can have unintended effects. The creation of a sitting room in this home actually destroys the family as an emotional, sentimental unit by taking one member out of the circle of life in the kitchen. Though the child insists on a sitting room, the author questions the universal applicability of progressive middle-class standards of domestic architecture and living, and her immigrant characters reject household reform, making this incident inappropriate for publication in the *Ladies' Home Journal*.

The American Home That "Cannot Be Home to Mother"

Despite the many moments when the narrator praises her mother and her household, even within the book version of Stern's story, the daughter rejects her mother's home outright as an un-American, "foreign spot,"[165] and carefully establishes her own suburban household with her "American" husband, following precisely along the lines of the progressive, white, middle-class home prescribed by social workers and the *Ladies' Home Journal*. In the Macmillan edition of the work, the girl does bring elements of her mother's Jewish household into her marital home. Shortly before the girl's wedding, her mother gives her what she considers the most important items in a Jewish woman's home—her Sabbath candlesticks, her brass mortar and pestle, and her own mother's copper fish pot used to cook fish for Sabbath. But when the mother visits her daughter's home, she finds the candlesticks in the living room and the fish pot holding an arrangement of autumn leaves. "There is no need for mother's pot in my kitchen; it has become an emblem of the past, an ornament in my living room," says the narrator.[166] In the *Ladies' Home Journal* version of the story, the girl makes a cleaner break with her past, taking none of these symbolic items with her. But even in the book, stripped of their utilitarian value, the tools of the Jewish kitchen become fetishized artifacts, signs of a distant past that is exotic and decorative, but entirely unnecessary within the progressive Americanized home.[167]

In both editions of the story, we find that the immigrant mother holds the same status as her fish pot in this household. She too is banished from the kitchen, center of her life and the bustling lives of her family and friends within her own home. "She does not understand my white kitchen, used only for cooking, 'as white as a drug store,' she said in a low voice."[168]

Despite her own gradual Americanization, Mammele is lost in the sterile, scientifically managed kitchen. She also has no place in the "strange white baby world which was her grandson's."[169] When the daughter looks in on her mother and son, she finds:

> Mother was standing, looking dully at the spotless baby cot, the white wicker chairs, the little washable rugs on the floor, the gay pictures on the white walls. . . . Little son had been taught that he must play without demanding help or attention from adults about him, that "son must help himself." In Soho little boys are spanked and scolded and carried and physicked and loved and fed all day and all night. . . . She was afraid to touch the crib, to soil the spotless rugs. Here was her grandchild; they were together it is true. And her grandchild had no need of her. She felt alien and unnecessary.[170]

Within the whitened world of this American home and its generic baby, the immigrant woman, like the tools of her religion and housekeeping, loses her sense of usefulness as a mother, grandmother, homemaker, and cook. Her model of womanhood is finally replaced by that of teachers, settlement house workers, and American friends.

Both versions of *My Mother and I* end tragically with the permanent alienation of mother and daughter. This loss is actually more painfully told in the *Ladies' Home Journal* story, which closes with the utter dejection of the immigrant parent. "There are many men and women who have gone, as I have, far from that place where we started," the narrator reflects.

> When I think of them lecturing on the platform, teaching in schools and colleges, prescribing in offices, pleading before the bar of law, I shall never be able to see them standing alone. I shall always see, behind them, two shadowy figures who will stand with questioning, puzzled eyes, eyes in which there will be love, but not understanding, and always an infinite loneliness.[171]

The *Journal* story ends in "infinite loneliness" and the near invisibility of the older generation in the shadows. But their loneliness appears inevitable in this version of the story, where parents are depicted as incapable of Americanization and children must break from them to achieve American identities. In the Macmillan version of the text, with its more complex descriptions of both Mammele and her household, the breakdown of the filial relationship is less understandable and feels far more deliberate and cruel. To take the edge off, Stern adds one more paragraph to her story. Rather than leaving Mammele and her kind in infinite loneliness, she continues: "For those men and women who are physicians, and lawyers, and teachers, and writers, they are young, and they belong to America. And they who recede into the shadow, they are old and they do not understand America. But they have made their contribution to America—their sons and their daughters."[172] Though the immigrant parents do not understand America and the American children they have produced, the narrator rewards them, giving meaning to their pain by praising their achievement of what is assumed to be the greatest accomplishment of all—the making of Americans.

Roosevelt sees the tragedy of the alienation of mother and daughter in precisely this redemptive way. He rejoices with the young girl over the success of her Americanization. He celebrates as a heroic feat "the Americanizing of an immigrant girl, who between babyhood and young womanhood leaps over a space which in all cultural and humanizing essentials is far more important than the distance painfully traversed by her forefathers during the preceding thousand years."[173] Roosevelt takes it entirely for granted that the culture she has acquired is far more civilized than the "thousand year" legacy of her forefathers. He recognizes the pain in this "profoundly touching story" yet sees it as an unfortunate but unavoidable result of the achievement of that greater goal—the creation of a new American in a new American home.[174]

But as one reviewer asked in 1917 regarding the result of this immigrant girl's Americanization: "Curiosity at this point may be pardoned if it inquires whether the mother is not the better off of the two, since the mother possesses herself and her daughter while the daughter has only herself and her self-satisfaction. The completeness of her break with the ghetto left some precious things behind."[175] This critic attacks the author, whom he believes to be identical to the protagonist and the narrator, for smugly rejoicing in her own Americanization while neglecting to see what she has abandoned in the process. The reviewer fails to realize, however, that the author forces us to ask precisely this question, pushing readers of even the *Ladies' Home*

Journal version of her story to question their assumptions about the value of an American home that "cannot be home to mother."

Stern's construction of voice and interweaving of perspectives work to create ambivalence. Though the protagonist of the story desires Americanization wholeheartedly, the tragic ending and the persistent sadness of the narrator reflecting on her own heartlessness serve to critique the entire project of American homemaking celebrated by her younger self, her literary patron, and the progressive reformer community that she herself joined. Her perspective on her younger life has been achieved not only through time but through her own experience of motherhood. Reflecting on her choice to leave home, the narrator says, "We had come to the point where we could no longer remain together; I cannot state the tragedy of that hour better than in just these words. I did not then realize what it meant to mother to see the diverging point of her life and mine. I had not then a little son of my own."[176] Motherhood enables her to empathize with Mammele in a way in which she was previously incapable. It also calls upon readers who are mothers to sympathize with the foreign woman. The narrator does not regret her decision to leave her mother's home, but she does rue her own insensitivity and the completeness of her break with her family that her desire for American identity seemed to demand.

The inclusion of Mammele's reactions toward her daughter's increasing alienation adds further to the ultimate ambiguity of Stern's stance on total assimilation and rejection of the past.[177] Possibly through the urgings of Bok or Roosevelt, the *Journal* story attempts to blunt the mother's perspective, telling its readers immediately through the subtitle that this is "The Story of How I Became an American Woman." The Macmillan book omits this subtitle, however, maintaining a balance between the views of "my mother" and "I" and refusing to label the text as a successful Americanization tale. But even in the *Journal* edition, with its leading subtitle, Mammele's perspective, as understood by the newly aware narrator and the mother's own quiet comments, remains. By including the mother's feelings in this first-person Americanization tale and by splitting the text's "I" into two—the girl longing for Americanization and the narrator commenting with ambivalence on these longings—Stern is able to win the approval of Bok and Roosevelt for her overt story while simultaneously embedding other viewpoints in her text.

"The Mere Writing . . . Is a Chain, Slight But Never to Be Broken"

Something else was missed by Roosevelt and Bok. The text itself functions as a means through which to reconnect, in a way that the girl herself cannot, to her mother and to her past. "The mere writing of this account is a chain, slight but never to be broken; one that will always bind me to that from which I had thought myself forever cut off," she declares in the opening lines of the book.[178] Writing about her childhood "open[s] the door closed upon the past"; it reunites her with the ghetto world she thought she had left behind.[179] This motive is very different from that of another famed eastern European Jewish immigrant autobiographer of the time, Mary Antin, who "longs to forget" and like "the Ancient Mariner, who told his tale in order to be rid of it," tells her tale so as "never [to] hark back any more," but to "write a bold 'Finis' at the end, and shut the book with a bang!" Instead, Stern's narrator tells her story to open the book on her past, to remember and to reconnect.

While Roosevelt believed that this work was intended for American-born readers and served to illustrate the value of their middle-class lives and homes, Stern perceived her audience and purpose in an entirely different way. She carefully targeted an audience composed of both second-generation Americans and readers with a longer history in the United States. "I am writing to those sons and daughters of immigrant parents who are now in America, to those who will come after this devastating war with their parents to America, and to those who will receive them," she states explicitly in both the magazine and the book.[180] And her goal was not to cheer disheartened Americans by showing them, as Roosevelt put it, "what this same civilization holds for starved and noble souls," but "to remind myself and those who are, like me, foster children of this land of ours, who it was that opened the bright gates of this beautiful land of freedom to us, and on whose tumuli of gray and weary years of struggle, we rose to opportunities."[181] Regardless of whether Stern was an immigrant herself, her narrator urges the Americanized children of immigrants, now *Journal* women themselves, to remember that it was their parents, who may not understand their present lives and values, who had the vision to bring them to the United States and who enabled them to take advantage of its many opportunities. Her text is both a personal act of remembering and a public call to remember.[182]

The book version of *My Mother and I* takes this notion of writing as a chain linking the narrator back to her ethnic past even further than the magazine story. In this edition, the young woman provides a lengthy discussion of her development as a writer that is entirely omitted from the *Ladies' Home Journal*. In it, as Kirsten Wasson notes, she tells how she first discovered writing as an expression of herself and her ties to her mother.[183] As a child she is asked to serve as the scribe for the community, penning letters for illiterate immigrants to their families back in Europe. She "wrote the best Yiddish letter composed by a female of any age in Soho," her mother would declare with pride.[184] However, the child needs her mother to interpret the codes and outlook of the immigrant and to explain the expectations of the old-world audience before she can compose her letters. "Shall I tell her mother that the little grandchild is dead of the children's sickness?" she asks Mammele in one situation. "No. Death casts a far shadow," her mother replies.[185] More intimately aware of the ethnic culture, the mother understands how the news will be received. Mammele the interpreter and her daughter the writer must create these compositions together, uniting their experiences, perspectives, and talents in each letter.

Extending Wasson's idea of writing as a tie between mother and daughter, we find that the act of letter writing links the Americanizing girl to an even larger female community. Writing letters for "Polish Anna," for instance, joins her to a transnational, multiethnic network of women. Anna, a former resident of the mother's hometown, speaks only Polish. When she wants to send a letter to her family in Europe, she must first tell Mammele what she wants to say in Polish. The mother translates these ideas into Yiddish for her daughter, who then writes the letter in Yiddish. The text is sent to Mammele's own mother in Poland, who then translates the Yiddish letter into Polish for Anna's mother. In this instance, letter writing becomes a series of translations of oral and written texts, each linking generations of women across cultural and geographic boundaries. In doing so, writing resists the limitations of the domestic realms of both home and homeland foisted upon new American women.

Significantly, all this literary activity takes place within the confines of Mammele's small kitchen. It is in this damp, cramped room, where her mother sews piecework while rocking the youngest baby and neighbors cram to air their collective griefs—this ethnic, working-class, feminine space, so unlike the white, orderly, sterile kitchens of the *Ladies' Home Journal* and settlement house— where the young Americanizing girl discovers her creative potential and its capacity to bridge the gap between generations and nations. "From our kitchen table went letters to the far corners of the world," she recalls.[186] "For it was as if all the life of Soho streamed through our little kitchen, through mother's life and mine, by way of the letters which I wrote for our neighbors."[187]

Although she writes letters for men as well as women, writing for men takes place outside of her mother's kitchen. The men are ashamed of their illiteracy and are unwilling to have their letters written in their neighbor's apartment. The child does not enjoy writing for men nearly as much as for women. She depicts male writing as conformist and formulaic. "The men merely desired me to tell the state of their health, to write how much they had 'been raised' in the store or factory, and to end with 'I hope we'll be together soon.' That was all," she recalls.[188] "Best of all I loved to write for the women."[189]

Women's writing represents creativity, artistry, and community for the girl. For women, letter writing is part of a vibrant female culture that thrives in Mammele's kitchen. The immigrant women enter the kitchen, babies in hand. They sit down, tell her mother of their problems with their landlords, and talk at length about the Americanization of their sons, the courtships of their daughters, the state of their own health, and the depths of their dreams. Only after "all aspects of health, economic situations, and hopes had been considered," would they ask the child to write. "Mother would draw closer to the table, the neighbour would quiet her children, and I would begin to write," she recalls.[190] As she writes, she becomes absorbed into this community of ethnic women in the kitchen. Unlike their menfolk, these women "desired beyond all else . . . to have their letters beautiful, the script clear, 'like print,' and the pages full of flowing idioms so that their missives would be read with admiration."[191] These letters, created through the joint efforts of the girl, her mother, and the illiterate immigrant women, are both literary and visual "work[s] of art."[192]

By representing art as the creation of ethnic women in the kitchen, Stern creates an ethnic female tradition, one that her narrator as writer figure can claim as her own. She rejects her father's Judaism in favor of Americanism. She leaves the world of the urban ghetto for the comforts of a suburban

American home. But at the same time that her text announces her successful Americanization and her final break from the world of her parents, the very act of writing declares her part of the creative multigenerational and transnational heritage of Jewish women. Writing is an ethnic female act in this text, and it is through narrative that she can reforge the broken bonds between "my mother and I," through words alone that the narrator can return to the nourishing kitchen that she has traded in for Americanism.

It is not surprising, then, that this episode, so integral to the book *My Mother and I*, is virtually absent from the *Ladies' Home Journal* story, reduced to only three sentences and an illustration of the girl writing for a stereotypical-looking Jewish man.[193] While again it is unknown whether the segment was deliberately cut by Bok, omitted by Stern, or written later as an addition to her book manuscript, this section clearly undermines everything that the *Journal* stands for and that Roosevelt believed this story is about. By suggesting that the dirty, chaotic, packed kitchen is the site of warmth, community, and art, it highlights the cold sterility of the progressive middle-class American home, where furniture and children are too white to touch and daily living is conducted in a room where one may only sit. While the narrator certainly does not reject her suburban home in favor of the ghetto tenement, she feels nostalgia for the richness of its life and taps into it as the source of her creativity, subtly revealing that the home of her ethnic, working-class mother has more "culture and humanity" than Roosevelt can imagine.

In her later writings, Stern would further examine ideologies of Americanization and the American home side by side in order to understand the expectations placed on ethnic women in the United States and to provide a specifically gendered critique of bourgeois cultural norms. In these later texts, written under the pseudonyms Leah or Eleanor Morton, Stern would attack these ideologies in far more explicit and caustic ways.[194] But it was "My Mother and I" that set the stage for these later analyses. *Journal* exposure and particularly Roosevelt's introduction had granted Stern a place as a writer by engulfing her story into the larger national narrative of immigrant transformation and progressive womanhood even as she quietly critiqued it.

CHAPTER 4

"Threatin' Him as a Akel"

Finley Peter Dunne's Ethnic Critique of "True Americanism"

> Above all we must stand shoulder to shoulder, not asking as to the ancestry or creed of our comrades, but only demanding that they be in very truth American, and that we all work together, heart, hand, and head, for the honor and the greatness of our common country.
> —Theodore Roosevelt, "True Americanism," 1894[1]

> "On th' thransport goi'n to Cubia I wud stand beside wan iv these r-rough men threatin' him as a akel, which he was in ivrything but birth, education, rank an' courage."
> —Mr. Dooley, "quoting" Tiddy Rosenfelt in "A Book Review," 1899[2]

In November 1899, the fictional Chicago Irish saloonkeeper Mr. Martin Dooley, whose biting wit had become known nationwide during the Spanish-American War, turned his tongue on then governor of New York, Theodore Roosevelt. Dooley described

Roosevelt's new book, *The Rough Riders*, to Mr. Hennessy, the straight man at his bar: "'Tis 'Th' Biography iv a Hero be Wan who Knows.' 'Tis 'Th' Darin' Exploits iv a Brave Man be an Actual Eye Witness.' 'Tis 'Th' Account iv th' Desthruction iv Spanish Power in th' Ant Hills,' as it fell fr'm the lips iv Tiddy Rosenfelt an' was took down be his own hands." In this book, according to Dooley, Roosevelt claims to debate, declare, and fight the war entirely on his own, winning it with just one shot from his small .32 that manages to hit its initial target and then pass through the entire line of Spanish soldiers before "fin'lly imbeddin' itself in th' abdomen iv th' Ar-rchbishop iv Santiago eight miles away." As Dooley pronounces, "If Tiddy done it all he ought to say so an' relieve th' suspinse. But if I was him I'd call th' book 'Alone in Cubia.'"[3]

The country chuckled heartily at this send-up of the obstreperous Rough Rider. The colonel laughed too and immediately contacted Dooley's creator, Chicago columnist Finley Peter Dunne. "My dear Mr. Dunne," he wrote: "I regret to state that my family and intimate friends are delighted with your review of my book. Now I think you owe me one; and I shall exact that when you next come east you pay me a visit. I have long wanted the chance of making your acquaintance."[4] Dunne responded one and a half months later:

> I admit it is at least one on me and I shall be very happy to call on you the next time I go to New York. At the same time the way you [talk of] Mr Dooley is a little discouraging. The number of persons who are worth while firing at is so small that as a matter of business I must regret the loss of one of them. Still if in losing a target I have, perhaps, gained a friend, I am in after all.[5]

These letters mark the beginning of a relationship between the politician and the satirist strikingly different from any other examined here. The child of middle-class Irish immigrants, Dunne was more comfortable in America than either Riis or Stern ever became. A journalistic sensation seeking no political or literary favors, he was more independent than even Zangwill. And cloaked beneath satire and a voice completely other than his own, Dunne proved far more securely able to criticize the powerful. Instead of desiring Roosevelt's backing, he eschewed it, at least initially seeking to keep his distance in order to maintain his critical perspective. Roosevelt, on the other hand, initiated the contact and pursued the relationship, and he did so despite, or perhaps because of, Dunne's sardonic lampoons, seeking to take the sting out of the swipe through laughter, to temper future attacks through friendship, and to put the column to his own use.

The media-savvy Roosevelt quickly realized what Mr. Dooley offered him. The nationally syndicated column put him again on center stage before an incredibly diverse national audience. Its folkloric use of extreme hyperbole and embellishment highlighted, even as it mocked, the image of force and manhood that Roosevelt sought to produce. And its presentation of Roosevelt as one who at least claimed to stand and fight alone, rather than as part of a tired, entrenched system, heralded the arrival of a new kind of reform politician. In the voice of a common man, and an Irish immigrant at that, who laughed at, yet simultaneously admired the colonel, Roosevelt found backhanded but powerful support for his image and agenda as an independent-minded, masculine, progressive reformer working on behalf of the people and for a better, more inclusive America.[6]

At the same time, however, Dunne's column brazenly exposed the silences and failures of Roosevelt's rhetoric. It uncovered and problematized its violent masculinity. It branded its imperializing nationalism undemocratic and un-American. It exposed the political impact of its racial imagination. And it revealed the ways in which Roosevelt's production of his own image elided the realities of his privileged position and failed to empower many of the people and communities on whose support it relied. Even in this first seemingly good-natured spoof of the politician's self-aggrandizement, Dooley cut to the heart of Roosevelt's self-produced myth. As historians Gary Gerstle and Richard Slotkin have argued, Roosevelt hand-selected his Rough Riders to enact in microcosm the process of the crucible forging white men of diverse backgrounds into a single, cohesive unit on the battlefield.[7] Roosevelt insisted further that the social interactions of his men, as modeled by himself, their colonel, epitomized the egalitarian civic ethic of true Americanism:

> We had the Northerner and the Southerner, the Easterner and the Westerner . . . ; we had men in it who worshipped their Creator some according to one creed, some according to another. . . . We had men who had been born abroad and men who were born here, whose ancestors came to what is now the United States at the time of the landing of the first

colonists. . . . We had men of every grade socially; men who worked with their heads; men who worked with their hands; men of all the types that our country produces; but each of them glad to get in on his worth as a man only, and content to be judged purely by what he could show himself to be.[8]

Roosevelt suggested that men of all backgrounds are made equal by their participation in national, and particularly military, endeavors.[9] But Mr. Dooley questions the sincerity of Roosevelt's rhetoric. His Roosevelt recalls with greater honesty than he intends: "'On th' transport goi'n to Cubia . . . I wud stand beside wan iv these r-rough men threatin' him as a akel, which he was in ivrything but birth, education, rank an' courage, an' together we wud look up at th' admirable stars iv that tolerable southern sky an' quote th' bible fr'm Walt Whitman.'"[10] From the perspective of the barely middle-class, Irish-born Dooley, the patrician politician's eager claims of egalitarianism resonate as false, condescending, and undoubtedly politically motivated, and Dooley punctures them with a smile.

As seen in the previous chapters, Roosevelt's Americanism was constructed on claims of race, nationalism, and gender, and it created expectations in all these areas for those who wished to join the nation. He used writings by and about new Americans to buttress and publicize his vision, even as Zangwill, Riis, and Stern subtly posited alternatives. But though Roosevelt hoped to fold Mr. Dooley similarly into his personal and national narrative, Finley Peter Dunne brazenly exploited ethnicity to destabilize the very foundations, authority, and intent of that narrative. A member of the second generation, distanced from the experience of immigration and Americanization, and part of an ethnic group that had come to hold distinct political power, Dunne was able to embrace Irish Americanness and find in it a perspective and voice for critiquing Roosevelt's America. This chapter establishes the ethnic nature of Dunne's critique and examines its function in both the creation and the deflation of Roosevelt's image and Americanism.

Dooley's assertions are not unlike Roosevelt's; he claims to speak for the people against special interest, corruption, and exclusivity, and for opportunity, egalitarianism, and civic responsibility—a rhetoric that political historian James Connolly argues defines "Progressivism."[11] But in his very proclamation of these values, Dooley questions Roosevelt's agenda and indeed his right to speak "for the people." Replacing the voice of the nationally powerful with the accented one of the lower-middle-class, midwestern, Irish-born Mr. Dooley suggests the superior legitimacy of the ethnic American to serve as spokesman for the people and guardian of true American ideals.[12]

"Is he Irish at all?": Mr. Dooley's Ethnicity

Before examining the content and nature of Dunne's critique, the issue of whether the Dooley columns should be considered ethnic at all must be resolved. Many critics have questioned the authenticity of the ethnic in Dunne's work, raising the long-standing issue of what makes writing "ethnic": the author's background, the audience, the subject matter, the language, the sensibility? "Is he Irish at all?" asks Grace Eckley about both Dunne and Dooley.[13]

Dunne's own life is frequently taken as the starting point for such debates. Peter Dunne, as he was baptized in 1867,[14] was born and raised in a middle-class Irish neighborhood in Chicago. The child of Irish immigrants who came to North America when they were quite young, he was raised nominally within the Catholic Church but squarely within a tradition of diasporic Irish nationalism and Irish American Democratic politics. After the national success and syndication of the Dooley columns during the Spanish-American War, he left Chicago for New York. He married the daughter of a Boston Brahmin,[15] and he sent one of his sons to Groton (a decision he rued upon learning of its strong Church of England identity) and two sons to Harvard. He joined the most elite clubs in New York City and spent much of his time conversing, drinking, and golfing with upper-class friends in Southampton, New York. Photographs and portraits of Dunne from the early twentieth century emphasize his status and success. If, as suggested in the previous chapter, class ascension is associated with Americanization, then Dunne's wealth and privilege seem to take him outside the "ethnic" and into the realm of the "American." And indeed, Dunne's life experience and class status left many later questioning his Irish American credentials.

Many critics have seen the Irishness of Mr. Dooley's voice as a rhetorical contrivance, devoid of authentic ethnic content. Finley Peter Dunne's own

Portrayal of Finley Peter Dunne, reprinted in *Mr. Dooley Remembers*, 1963.

account of the invention of his famed character has contributed to this view. Dooley's original purpose was to provide a progressive critique of local politics, not to comment on the experience of the ethnic community per se. According to Dunne, he created Mr. Dooley in 1893 to expose the corruption of the most powerful men in Chicago city politics without fear of legal or financial repercussions: "It occurred to me that while it might be dangerous to call an alderman a thief in English no one could sue if a comic Irishman denounced the statesman as a thief."[16] So Dunne created the Irish American dialect-speaking saloonkeeper, first named Colonel McNeery and later changed to Mr. Dooley.[17] Under the guise of this fictitious, distinctly Irish American character, Dunne could speak without fear, knowing that he could easily explain the columns' attacks as the views of Mr. Dooley rather than himself.

Mr. Dooley was quite unlike his creator. Born in County Roscommon, he apparently emigrated to the United States during the Great Famine. By October 7, 1893, the day on which he was first introduced to the public, he had already worked his way up to become a fairly successful pub owner in the working-class Chicago neighborhood of Bridgeport. Dooley was a confirmed bachelor and Democrat, and he identified most decidedly as Irish American. Readers clearly perceived him as such, and illustrators across the country highlighted his Irishness by depicting him with stereotypical features. He fervently supported the cause of Irish national liberation, though not the institutions built up around it, and he chastised the Irish American community for insufficient diasporic political activism: "Be hivins," says Dooley. "[I]f Ireland cud be freed be a picnic, it 'd not on'y be free to-day, but an impire, begorra."[18] But because Dunne created Dooley as a progressive tool by which to reform urban municipal politics, Dooley and his dialect have been seen as inauthentically Irish, "merely . . . a device," as Barbara Schaaf put it.[19]

The most striking of these discreditations came from none other than Dunne's son, Philip, whose republication of his father's work attempted to de-ethnicize his father, his father's writing, and, by extension, himself. Introducing Finley Peter Dunne's autobiographical essay "On the Irish," in *Mr. Dooley Remembers*, Philip writes:

> He was proud of his Irish blood, but he disliked being described as an Irishman. In his own view, he was simply an American whose ancestors happened to have been Irish. And his view was entirely correct. His Dooley articles, though written in the brogue, are humor in an essentially American tradition. They are concerned with American politics and America's position in the world. He saw the world through his American eyes and set down what he saw with his American pen. Remove the brogue, rewrite the articles in plain English, and there is little of Ireland left in them.[20]

Overlooking the complexity of American "eyes" and "pen," perspective and literature, Philip Dunne insists that the columns, like his father, were always 100 percent American. To support this claim, the Harvard-educated son attempts literally to rewrite his father's work so as to remove all traces of ethnicity. In an appendix to *Mr. Dooley Remembers*, which is a collection of the elder Dunne's fragmentary memoirs along with commentary by the son, Philip provides a selection of Dooley columns "translated" into "plain English."[21] He insists that these pieces must be translated in order to enable "modern lay reader[s]" to overcome the "insurmountable hurdle" of Dooley's dialect, and other editors of Dunne's work have agreed.[22] But audience proved only one of Philip Dunne's concerns. Years later, he would argue: "Mr. D's identity as an Irishman was the *least* important of his attributes. My father's choice of an Irishman as his mouthpiece to express his own political analyses was entirely incidental. . . . Eliminate the brogue and the pieces stand out as what they were: pure Americana."[23] Yet his father's "choice of an Irishman as his mouthpiece" was not incidental, inconsequential, or un-American.

While it is certainly true that Finley Peter Dunne created Mr. Dooley for the purpose of progressive municipal reform, his progressivism was of a particularly ethnic stripe. At a time when native-born middle-class reformers often directed their attack on corruption against the "boss-immigrant machine" as a way of delegitimizing ethnic power,[24] the voice of Mr. Dooley provided satirical critique from the inside. As Dunne recalls:

> The crooks were ridiculed by their friends who delighted in reading these articles aloud in public places, and, as they were nearly all natural Irish comedians, doing it well. If I had written the same thing in English I would inevitably have been pistolled or slugged, as other critics were. But my victims did not dare to complain. They felt bound to smile and treat these highly libelous articles as Powers would say. "But why don't you take a crack at Mann, or Judah or Madden. (Three highly respectably representatives of big business). Ye notice they always vote with us when we need them." So I did, and was treated with sour looks from the author of the Mann act (in later days) but received heartfelt thanks from the Hon. John Powers and his fellow sufferers.[25]

Rooted within Irish American Chicago, Mr. Dooley became a force of communal censure. Although published in a general paper, Dooley's brogue appeared to keep his criticisms within the family, less threatening perhaps, but more effective because of local mechanisms for enforcing ethical codes. Read and quoted within the community, his words pressured

Portrayals of Mr. Dooley, reprinted in *Mr. Dooley Remembers*, 1963.

corrupt men to acknowledge through laughter their own misdoings, to expose others who had acted similarly, and possibly to alter their behaviors in order to prevent Mr. Dooley from making them the laughingstock again. Using an Irish American voice to attack the corruption of Irish American municipal politicians also suggested that reform was not the sole possession of native-born Americans and did not require the return to power of native-born politicians. Irish Americans could recognize and censure corruption themselves, putting the city's best interest first.

While acknowledging the Irish American nature of Dunne's Chicago columns, other critics have argued, however, that once Dunne turned to the national scene, his work lost its ethnic character. As critic Charles Fanning documents, the early Dooley columns, written between 1893 and 1898, were deeply rooted in the local community, using Dooley's voice to represent the struggles of impoverished Irish immigrants and their children in Chicago.[26] These pieces, written for a local and largely Irish American audience, dealt explicitly with the ethnic community and its concerns. Indeed, the very language of the column came out of this local experience. Describing the brogues of Bridgeport, Chicago, in the preface to the first collection of Dooley columns, Finley Peter Dunne explains that "in this community you can hear all the various accents of Ireland, from the awkward brogue of the 'far downer' to the mild and aisy Elizabethan English of the southern Irishman, and all the exquisite variations to be heard between Armaugh and Bantry Bay, with the difference that would naturally arise from substituting cinders and sulphuretted hydrogen for soft misty air and peat smoke."[27] Without sentimentalizing Ireland or idealizing America, Dunne attempts to display in the very language of his characters the ways in which their lives and ways have been "modified and darkened by American usage,"[28] and the columns provide an ethnic critique of the conditions that produced these changes.

In his Americanized brogue, Dooley comments in the early columns with wit and compassion on the christenings and deaths, courtships and disputes, social advancement and grinding poverty of his community. He depicts the proud refusal of the Callaghan family to accept charity from the haughty, well-to-do Irish of the St. Vincent de Paul Society,[29] and he describes the fight between Hogan and his wife over the name of their tenth child (Hogan wants Michael or Bridget, while his Americanizing wife insists on Augustus).[30] He discusses the reaction of the community to Molly Donahue's scandalous bicycle ride in her "divided skirt,"[31] and to the heroism of their firemen.[32] Social and political commentary always remain close to the surface in these pieces as well as those on subjects such as the Pullman strike,[33] the distribution of graft and spoils in Chicago,[34] and the implications of tensions between Germany and Britain for the Irish.[35] Often, though not always, when dealing with national or international politics, Dooley brings his observations back home with an anecdote about a friend or acquaintance that illuminates the heart of the issue or reveals its effects on ordinary people.[36]

With their local interests, focus on adaptation, and Irish American audience, these columns have been taken by some to be Dunne's "real" Irish American pieces, while his later nationally syndicated columns have been deemed nonethnic. The trajectory of Dunne's personal life has fostered this view. To many observers, his move to New York City in 1900 marked a move into "respectability" and out of a genuine satiric perspective.[37] Joining the social world he once ridiculed, Dunne could not maintain an ironic posture, they argue. Furthermore, concerned about maintaining the interest of a national audience for the syndicated columns, Dunne turned Dooley's focus in these later pieces away from Bridgeport and the lives of its residents almost exclusively onto national and international affairs. The shift in Dooley from local commentator to "national sage" has been seen as a decontextualization and de-ethnicization of his character. He "joined the 'cash raygisther' crowd along with other successful Irishmen," write Joseph Boskin and Joseph Dorinson.[38] All that remained of the original Dooley was a "disembodied national voice," says Fanning.[39]

But while it is true that after syndication, Mr. Dooley and Mr. Dunne rarely concerned themselves with the Irish American community of Bridgeport, the language, form, structure, and content of the columns continued to provide a particularly ethnic critique of American politics and America, now on a national scale.[40]

Dialect and the Literary Forms of Ethnic Critique

In selecting the genre, language, and form of his column, Finley Peter Dunne played on the borders of what literary critic Gavin Roger Jones has identified as both the nostalgic and the menacing in vernacular literature.[41] Dunne created a character in the tradition of Petroleum V. Nasby,

Josh Billings, and Artemus Ward—a "crackerbox philosopher," a simple, down-to-earth, uneducated, dialect-speaking man of the people whose instinctive common sense gives him unusual insight into American life.[42] This was, as Philip Dunne said, "humor in an essentially American tradition." But his father, Finley Peter Dunne, transposed the time-honored, rural humorist onto the urban immigrant scene, placing him in a tavern within nose reach of Chicago's infamous stockyards.[43]

The effect of the ethnicization of the "crackerbox philosopher" was, on the one hand, reassuring. Inserting the urban immigrant into the form of the simple, amusing, vernacular country sage made him familiar. It Americanized the Irishman, turned Chicago into a small town,[44] and enabled audiences to hear Mr. Dooley out even as he spoke in his strange, foreign English. Dooley did not promote socialism, anarchism, or any other of the terrifying political impieties suspected of the immigrant. Instead, he embodied staid American values. Dunne made Dooley even less threatening by portraying him as the antithesis of the stereotypical Irishman. He was a saloonkeeper who rarely drank or brawled, a business owner who never cheated, a former precinct captain who despised corruption. Furthermore, as an aging bachelor, Dooley cast no seed into the seething melting pot, posing no threat to the racial composition of the nation.[45] And when Dooley attacked the United States and its leaders, he did so in a nonaggressive fashion. He did not rouse himself or others to action. He did not even confront America directly. Instead, he spoke his criticisms to his customer and friend Malachi Hennessy and invited America to eavesdrop on the humorous conversations between these two middle-aged men who were rarely seen outside the pub.[46]

At the same time, however, Dunne purposely passed the "crackerbox" to a Chicago Irishman, claiming him to be the new and preferred repository of traditional American values. Dooley supplants the Yankee, who has failed to keep the nation on the path of true democracy. His urban ethnic dialect replaces the rural native's vernacular. Not unlike David Quixano, the protagonist of Zangwill's *Melting Pot*, Mr. Dooley claims to understand and uphold American ideals far better than the native born. He seems to be another example of the trustworthy immigrant with whom Roosevelt threw in his lot.[47] But instead of celebrating the nation, as Quixano does, Dooley pointedly exposes its failures and fallacies.

Dooley's tale of his own Americanization, for instance, brings together the rhetoric of national myth and the tropes of immigrant autobiography with the realities of American experience, in order to collapse and rewrite the preferred national narrative. Recalling his arrival to the United States in a 1901 column, Mr. Dooley claims: "Th' stars an' sthripes whispered a welcome in th' breeze an' a shovel was thrust into me hand an' I was pushed into a sthreet excyvatin' as though I'd been born here." Conditions were so bad that he figured there must be "a hole in th' breakwather iv th' haven iv refuge an' some iv th' wash iv th' seas iv opprission had got through."[48] Dooley's phrasing is hard to resist, but the sentiment it expresses challenges the heart of America's self-image. For Dooley, America has failed to live up to its promise. His assimilation is into an America of menial labor, social inequities, corrupt politics, and limited opportunity, which to him are the realities of the United States: "I was afraid I wasn't goin' to assimilate with th' airlyer pilgrim fathers an' th' instichoochions iv th' counthry," he recalls, "but I soon found that a long swing iv th' pick made me as good as another man an' it didn't require a gr-reat intellect, or sometimes anny at all, to vote th' dimmycrat ticket, an' befure I was here a month, I felt enough like a native born American to burn a witch."[49] Would-be European emigrants ought to be more wary of immigration than native-born Americans: "Teach thim all about our instichoochions befure they come" and they will stay home, he proposes, shifting the balance of power.

Part of the problem, Dooley suggests, lies in the failure of native-born Americans to uphold the founding principles of the nation, instead pursuing obscene wealth at home and aristocratic status abroad. He mocks the likes of William Waldorf Astor, who, he claims, stood before the British Royal High Court to confess his crime of being born in New York, begging to be reborn as British nobility:

An' Willum Waldorf Asthor renounced fealty to all foreign sovereigns, princes an' potentates an' especially Mack th' Wanst, or Twict, iv th' United States . . . an' he come out iv th' coort with his hat cocked over his eye, with a step jaunty and high, afther years iv servile freedom, a bondman at last!

So he's a citizen iv Gr-reat Britain now an' a lile subject iv th' Queen like you was Hinnissy befure ye was r-run out.[50]

The American's eagerness to discard his heritage of freedom, even if a problematic one, and to submit himself to the British Crown is unthinkable for Dooley, who would "rather be Dooley iv Chicago than th' Earl iv Peltvule" any day.[51] Dunne represents the expatriate in the same gendered language that Roosevelt employed, calling him "effete," "tired," and without fight. Life in America, according to Dooley, "'tis a gloryous big fight, a rough an' tumble fight, a Donnybrook fair three thousan' miles wide an' a ruction in ivry block," and if you are "a tired la-ad an' wan without much fight in ye, livin' in this counthry is like thryin' to read th' Lives iv th' Saints at a meetin' iv th' Clan-na-Gael. They'se no quiet f'r anybody."[52] Not man enough for the struggle, Astor and those like him leave for Europe, where their dollars buy them comfort and ease. But Hennessy, Dooley, and their likes—Irish immigrants fresh from the Donnybrook fair—are accustomed to and raring for the fight.

Much in the same way that Zangwill employed the decadent native-born American, Quincy Davenport, to highlight the true Americanness of the Jewish immigrant, Dunne used the occasion of Astor's embrace of the British as an opportunity to propose the superiority of Irish immigrants as Americans. The Irish have rejected and been rejected by the British; they value the "servile freedom" of the United States, and they have the gumption to struggle and succeed in America. Their stereotypical pugnacity, derided and worried over by many native-born Americans, is precisely what suits them to the realities of American life to a far greater degree than many of those born to it.[53] However, while the effect of this representation made the immigrant a less menacing figure than imagined, it simultaneously put him forward as a serious challenge to the authority of the native born.

No one could have agreed more than Roosevelt with Dooley's assessment of native-born Americans like Astor, whose social pretense and cultural inferiority complex sent them groveling before the British aristocracy. Such individuals, Roosevelt also argued, exhibited an attitude of "self-deprecation and apologetic servility habitually adopted in relation to their own land,"[54] a "spirit of colonial dependence on, and exaggerated deference to, European opinion."[55] They are "in reality by education and instinct entirely un-American."[56] As we have found, Roosevelt was willing to replace these failed native-born Americans with immigrants of the right spirit: "I for one, would heartily throw in my fate with the men of alien stock who were true to the old American principles rather than with the men of the old American stock who were traitors to the old American principles," he declared.⁵⁷

But Dunne lobbed his attack against "the men of old American stock" who seemed true "old American principles" along with the traitors, and he did so not only through his words but through the very structure of every column. Each piece is constructed as a narrative, sometimes several narratives, within a narrative. Dunne almost never employs the device of a standard English-speaking narrator, which so often framed dialect texts of the period and served to subordinate the linguistically inferior to the grammatically proper, reinstating the cultural hegemony of the white, native, middle and upper classes.⁵⁸ Instead, every one of Dunne's pieces is framed by a brief conversation between Mr. Dooley and one of his loyal customers, most often the reticent Mr. Hennessy, in Dooley's pub. The opening conversation raises the topic to be discussed, and the closing frame comments on the issues, often ending with a final pun or zinger. In between, Dooley describes a situation, generally quoting those involved at length. Because Dooley is the sole narrator and speaker within the central narrative, the words he cites, no matter who he claims spoke them, become accented by his Irish American tongue.

A closer look at a single column reveals the workings of this structure and their rhetorical and political usefulness in articulating an ethnic critique of power and the powerful in the United States. In an early national piece entitled "On a Speech by President McKinley," for example, the opening frame begins as follows:

"I hear-r that Mack's in town," said Mr. Dooley.
"Didn't ye see him?" asked Mr. Hennessy.
"Faith, I did not!" said Mr. Dooley. "If 'tis meetin' me he's afther, all he has to do is to get on a ca-ar an' r-ride out to number nine-double-naught-nine Archey R-road, an, stop whin he sees th' sign iv th' Tipp'rary Boodweiser Brewin' Company. I'm here fr'm eight in the mornin' till midnight. . . . "⁵⁹

This beginning sets up the person and topic to be lampooned as well as Dooley's general attitude toward the primary actor, in this case, McKinley.

The piece goes on to describe the banquet of the "Prospurity Brigade" of Chicago, about which Dooley supposedly "r-read be th' papers," a phrase repeated in many of the columns to indicate Dooley's source of information that he could not have accessed otherwise. Mr. Dooley reports that the banquet opened with "a prayer that Providence might r-remain undher th' protection iv th' administhration,"[60] and continued with speeches by the secretary of the Treasury, General Shafter, and finally McKinley. In his speech, the president asks what to do with the "fruits iv victhry," that is, the liberated islands, now that the war with Spain has been won. Dooley "quotes" McKinley's supposed response at length:[61]

> "Our duty to civilization commands us to be up an' doin'," he says. "We ar-re bound," he says, "to—to re-elize our destiny, whatever it may be," he says. "We can not tur-rn back," he says, "th' hands iv th' clock that, even as I speak," he says, "is r-rushin' through th' hear-rts iv men," he says, 'dashin' its spray against th' star iv liberty an' hope, an' no north, no south, no east, no west, but a steady purpose to do th' best we can, considerin' all th' circumstances iv the case," he says. "I hope I have made th' matther clear to ye,' he says, 'an', with these few remarks," he says, "I will tur-rn th' job over to destiny," he says, "which is sure to lead us iver on an' on, an' back an' forth, a united an' happy people livin'," he says, "undher an administhration that, thanks to our worthy Prisidint an' his cap-ble an' earnest advisers, is second to none," he says.[62]

McKinley, as created by Dooley, obfuscates his message, throwing in fragments of patriotic rhetoric in ways that make no sense and often undermine the impression he is trying to create. He insists that the United States must realize its destiny, but he has no idea what that is—a frightening thought, considering that the president leaves the future up to destiny with no plan of his own for how to lead the nation. Saying that time is dashing its spray against the star of liberty and hope, McKinley ends up mired in a mixed metaphor that suggests that as time goes by, the islanders' hopes for liberty from both Spain and the United States are being dashed. Dooley comments on this prospect in the closing frame. The piece ends back with Dooley and Hennessy in the bar. Hennessy asks, "What do you think ought to be done with th' fruits iv victhry?" to which Dooley responds, "Well, if 'twas up to me, I'd eat what was r-ripe an' give what wasn't r-ripe to me inimy. An' I guess that's what Mack means."[63] Dooley has the final word, and with it he exposes American involvement in the war for what he believes it to be, a play for international land and markets covered up by the meaningless and fraudulent language of political destiny and moral responsibility.

Like many immigrants with national longings for their native lands,[64] Dooley vigorously supported the United States' effort to aid Cuba's nationalist struggle against Spanish domination, but he was horrified at the moment of victory to find his own country assuming the role of the imperialist power.[65] "Was I drunk, during the war?" he asks of himself elsewhere. "Whin I think iv th' gaby I made iv mesilf dancin' ar-round this here bar an' hurooin' whiniver I he-erd iv Rosenfelt's charge again Sandago me blood r-runs cold with shame."[66] The content of his column proves consistently anti-imperialist.

The language of and structure of the column deepens Dooley's critique of the United States and, in this case, its imperialism. Because he is the only speaker, Dooley's accent inflects both his own and McKinley's words. Voicing in brogue the president's assertions of the moral right and religious destiny of the nation to imperial domination immediately problematizes them. The struggles of Ireland against British occupation echo as he speaks, undercutting his claims and raising the specter of oppression and resistance with every word.

The linguistic ethnicization of all of the men he describes constantly raises questions about the inequities of American politics. Throughout the columns, Dooley consistently ethnicizes his subjects via the names he calls them, the dialect he causes them to speak, and the characteristics with which he imbues them. In this column, the Scotch-Irish Presbyterian President McKinley becomes "Mack."[67] In others, Commodore George Dewey becomes "Cousin George"—"Sure, Dewey or Dooley, 'tis all th' same. We dhrop a letter here an' there, except th' haithches,—we niver dhrop thim,—but we're th' same breed iv fightin' men. Georgy has th' thraits iv the fam'ly."[68] Similarly, he proclaims of the U.S. consul general to Cuba, Fitzhugh Lee: "Iv coorse, he's Irish. Th' Fitz-Hughs an' th' McHughs an' th' McKeoughs is not far apart."[69] And Dooley goes on to describe the consul general as a red-faced Irishman with a temper and a complete lack of interest in diplomacy.[70]

This strategy of ethnicization has multiple effects. As with the columns on imperialism, it keeps Irish nationalist concerns in the background, and sometimes the foreground. But more generally, characterizing the military elite as fighting Irishmen, Dunne dismantles Anglo-America's stereotype of

Irish immigrants. He reveals the irony inherent in the way that America's leaders encourage and take pride in the very same belligerent characteristics that they presume and deride in Irish immigrants. Within the Dooley columns, it is the peaceable Irishman behind the bar who distrusts the violent aggressiveness of the native-born American.

Through playful acts of linguistic subversion, Dooley furthermore imagines Irish Catholics in positions of real national power from which they were otherwise excluded.[71] In his discussion of African American vernacular humor, Ralph Ellison puts forth a useful model for understanding the function of such play. Ellison provides the example of a group of black men sitting around a barbershop talking about John D. Rockefeller, Sr. They imagine his harem of women, how much he must spend on their silk underwear, the number of illegitimate children he must have, the whiskey he drinks. "Poor old John D. didn't know it, but they put him through the windmill of their fantasies with gusto," Ellison writes. "What's more, he emerged enhanced in their sight as an even more exceptional man among such exceptional men as themselves, thanks to their having endowed him with a sexual potency and an utter disregard for genteel conduct that would have blown that gentleman's mind." But in making Rockefeller play out their dreams, "they had touched one of the most powerful men of the nation with the tarbrush of their comic imaginations, Afro-Americanized him, and claimed him as one of their very own."[72] Reflecting on this mode of ethnic humor, Ellison remarks, "I suppose such preposterous comedy is an indispensable agency for dealing with American experience precisely because it allows for redeeming perspectives on our rampant incongruities."[73]

When Dooley Irishizes America's elite, he similarly claims them as his own. His audience must have laughed at the incongruity of their leaders speaking brogue. But if, as Ellison argues, laughter "calms the clammy trembling which ensues whenever we pierce the veil of conventions,"[74] laughter enabled readers to imaginatively leap the barriers erected against Irish Catholics. If only momentarily, they could envision an Irishman with national power, as their ambassador, commodore, or even president, thereby exposing and repairing social and political inequities, while at the same time questioning the values and legitimate hold of those with real national power. Through the language and form of his columns, then, Dunne formulated an ethnic critique of America even when addressing apparently "nonethnic," national and international affairs.

The Making of Tiddy Rosenfelt

"Tiddy Rosenfelt" proved somewhat of an exception to Mr. Dooley. Judaized, not Irishized in name only, as he often was in the press, Roosevelt was largely respected by both Dooley and Dunne. Upon McKinley's assassination, Mr. Dooley defended the sudden president against concerns about his youth, saying, "Well, a man is old enough to vote whin he can vote, he 's old enough to wurruk whin he can wurruk. An' he 's old enough to be prisidint whin he becomes prisidint. If he ain't, 't will age him."[75] He defended Roosevelt against the hysteria created by his White House dinner with Booker T. Washington, arguing more broadly against segregation than Roosevelt ever dared:

> They was no mark on th' table clother where his hands rested an' an invintory iv th' spoons after his departure showed that he had used gintlemanly resthraint.... Th' ghost iv th' other Wash'nton didn't appear to break a soop tureen over his head. P'raps where George is he has to assocyate with manny mimbers iv th' Booker branch on terms iv akequality. I don't suppose they have partitions up in th' other wurruld like th' kind they have in th' cars down south. They can't be anny Crow Hivin. I wondher how they keep up race sypreemacy. Maybe they get on without it.[76]

And Roosevelt sought to harness his support.

At first, Dunne kept his distance from the politician. From the time of the publication of "A Book Review" until he became president, Roosevelt tried repeatedly but without success to have Dunne visit him at Oyster Bay.[77] Dunne seems to have been wary at first of Roosevelt's intentions, graciously postponing and declining invitations, perhaps to retain his target and perspective. Once Roosevelt became president, however, Dunne dined with him on several occasions, and the two thoroughly enjoyed each other's witty company. With their friendship solidified, Dunne acknowledged in 1907 that "my firm belief in what you are doing and my knowledge of it sometimes disarm me. Ignorance or the appearance of it is a foundation for fun making."[78] As many critics have argued, Roosevelt may indeed have intended this disarming effect, trying to take the bite out of Dooley's satire by befriending his creator.[79]

Even more, however, Roosevelt desired the production and circulation of the image that Mr. Dooley fostered of him. As Roosevelt wrote to Dunne toward the end of his presidency, "I feel that what you have written about me, with exceptions too trivial to mention, has been written in just the nicest possible style—that what Dooley says shows the good-humored affection that the boys in the army felt for old Grant and the people in Illinois for Lincoln."[80] Roosevelt recognized the fondness beneath Dooley's raillery. Moreover, he appreciated how Dunne disseminated his legend as a masculine leader of men and a grassroots man of the people.

Mr. Dooley fostered Roosevelt's most treasured image—that of the powerful, straight-talking, independent, masculine reformer speaking for and promoting the good of the average American. This image was essential to Roosevelt's identity, popularity, and progressivism. "We know what Wash'nton said to his gin'rals an' what Grant said to Lee an' what Cleveland said to himsilf. They're in th' books. But engraved in th' hearth iv his counthrymen is what Rosenfelt said to th' throlley man" who bumped into him, Mr. Dooley tells Hennesey in a piece entitled "Swearing." Roosevelt, according to Dooley, delivered a "good, honest, American blankety-blank":

'Twas good because 'twas so nachral. Most iv' th' sayin's I've read in books sounds as though they was made be a patent inkybator. They go with a high hat an' a white tie. Ye can hear th' noise iv th' phonygraft. But this here jim of emotion an' thought come sthraight fr'm th' heart an' wint right to th' heart. That's wan reason I think a lot iv us likes Tiddy Rosenfelt that wudden't iver be suspected iv votin' f'r him. Whin he does anny talkin'—which he sometimes does—he talks at th' man in front iv him. Ye don't hear him hollerin' at posterity. Posterity don't begin to vote till afther th' polls close. So whin he wished to convey to th' throlley man th' sintimints iv his bosom, he done it in wurruds suited to th' crisis, as Hogan wud say. They do say his remarks singed th' hair off th' head iv th' unforchnit man.[81]

Roosevelt can be trusted, the sketch implies; he speaks his mind openly, "nachrally," in the language of the common man, only far more forcefully.

At the same time that Dunne created Roosevelt as one of the people, he attributed superhuman powers to the president. In describing Roosevelt's reaction to Upton Sinclair's exposé of the meat industry in *The Jungle*,

Dooley declares: "Suddenly he rose fr'm th' table, an' cryin': 'I'm pizened,' begun throwin' sausages out iv th' window. Th' ninth wan strhuck Sinitor Biv'ridge on th' head an' made him a blond. It bounced off, exploded, an' blew a leg off a secret-service agent, an' th' scatthred fragmints desthroyed a handsome row iv ol' oak-trees."[82] This representation of Roosevelt's impulsive reaction, its physical force, and the absurd chain of events it triggered fed Roosevelt's masculinized cult of personality.

Dooley's emphasis on the violence of Roosevelt's language and behavior helped blend the upper-class politician with the popular images of the western cowboy, the urban tough, and particularly the stereotypically pugnacious Irishman. Describing Roosevelt's verbal attack on those in government who violate his expectations, Mr. Dooley remarks that a "reproof fr'm him is th' same thing as a compound fracture. A wurrud iv caution will lay a man up f'r a week an' a severe riprimand will sind him through life with a wooden leg." Soon the papers will report: "'Rayciption at th' White House. Among th' casualties was so-an'-so. Th' prisidint was in a happy mood. He administhered a stingin' rebuke to th' Chief Justice iv th' Supreme Coort, a left hook to eye. Sinitor Hanna was prisint walkin' with a stick.'"[83]

While he acknowledges the president's sophistication and intellectualism, by wedding these to his physicality and force, Dooley constructs and upholds Roosevelt's populist image. Describing a typical day for the president in his retreat at Oyster Bay, Dooley reports:

> There day be day, th' head iv th' nation thransacts th' nation's business as follows: four A.M., a plunge into th' salt, salt sea an' a swim iv twenty miles; five A.M., horse-back ride, th' prisidint insthructin' his two sons, aged two and four rayspictively, to jump th' first Methodist church without knockin' off th' shingles; six A.M., wrestles with a thrained grizzly bear; sivin A.M., breakfast; eight A.M., Indyan clubs; nine A.M., boxes with Sharkey; tin A.M., bates th' tinnis champeen; iliven A.M., rayceives a band iv rough riders an' person'lly supervises th' sindin' iv th' ambylance to look afther th' injured in th' village.[84]

All of this activity is followed by a noon dinner, attended by a boxer, an Ivy League champion roller skater, a professor of archaeology, a British lord, an Irish nationalist, a badlands scout, the Negro poet "Immanuel Kant Gumbo," a Mexican mine expert, a writer on female suffrage, an Indian chief, the ambassador of France, and a family of jugglers—which, based on descriptions of the famous Roosevelt dinners, may be only a slight embellishment of the typical assemblage.[85] Dooley shows the president's capacity to relate to all of those assembled, conversing about literature, poetry, science, politics, and reform in the same breath as boxing, horse breaking, shooting, mountain lions, the pivot bow, and, of course, his favorite topic, the "campaign in Cubia." His scope and energy encompass all, making him the ideal representative of a diverse nation.

Such descriptions, provided by Mr. Dooley to Hennessy and every American who cared to listen in, did extremely important work for Roosevelt. As Gail Bederman, Arnaldo Testi, and Sarah Watts, among others, have argued, having been portrayed in his early career, along with other upper-class reformers, as an effeminate "Jane Dandy," Roosevelt drew on rhetorical and physical violence to, among other things, establish a place for himself in the male arena of electoral politics.[86] He turned against the "silk stocking" reformers from whom he had descended, calling them "hostile to manliness" with a "vein of physical timidity," "sitting in cloistered—or rather pleasantly upholstered—seclusion, . . . sneering at and lying about men who made them feel uncomfortable."[87] As Roosevelt claims in his *Autobiography* (1913), these armchair reformers told him before he ever entered politics that electoral politics were "low," run by "saloon-keepers, horse-car conductors, and the like," men who were "rough, brutal, and unpleasant to deal with."[88] But seeking to demonstrate his manhood and practical politics particularly to the men outside his class, who were deemed more virile than the upper and middle classes,[89] Roosevelt claims that he went straight to the Republican Association above a saloon, determined to prove that "I [could] hold my own in the rough and tumble."[90] And it was to the "rough and tumble" that he continually sought to appeal through a deliberate masculinization of his rhetoric and exploits.

As a working-class Irish American saloon keeper/crackerbox philosopher deeply invested in Democratic Party politics, yet attracted to Roosevelt, Dooley proved the ideal image maker for the politician. He was the man outside Roosevelt's own caste whom the politician sought to impress. The president was wont to say that the "man he works for," the American whom he keeps before his mind when making decisions, is the "weather-hardened, plainly dressed elderly man, who is poring over his newspaper." He is a man of "plain American common sense," the "hard-headed practical man of the every-day life" who is "working just as hard as he knows how, and doing his duty as he sees it." This ideal American of Roosevelt's imagination "wants certain affairs in the Government improved, not so much because existing conditions are injuring him, but by reason of his inherent love of what is fair and just. . . . He feels for the honor of the flag. He is aroused lest injustices may rot out the moral fibre of the American people."[91] He is the imagined public behind Roosevelt's ideologies and reforms, and Dooley gave him voice.

That Dooley's voice was accented by Americanized brogue only enhanced its effectiveness for Roosevelt. Roosevelt himself played with brogue in his *Autobiography*, precisely at the points where he sought to model himself as a new type of "practical politician."[92] Describing how he was taken under the wing of Joe Murray in his first days with the Republican Association, Roosevelt explains that Joe, a former Democrat whose hard work was met with indifference by the local boss, decided "to vote furdest away from the leader." "I am using the language of Joe's youth," Roosevelt explains, though he did not know Joe then.[93] Joe's words reveal a mode of independent-minded, ethnic reform politics with which Roosevelt sought to be associated. And working-class, immigrant men supported him, Roosevelt claims with pride. Recalling how one Irish American politician came to his defense in the New York legislature, he writes: "I would like you to know, Mr. Cameron, . . . that Mr. Roosevelt knows more law in a wake than you do in a month."[94] These dialect moments in Roosevelt's *Autobiography* provide humor of a Dooleyan sort that Roosevelt appropriates for himself to add to his populist and manly image, even enabling him to play on ethnic politics indirectly. When Dooley speaks of Roosevelt in this same language, and especially when he talks of his physicality and unaffectedness alongside his reforms and intellectualism, he disseminates this image far and wide, rallying a diverse class and ethnic community of male supporters behind the president while creating his legend.

But even as he fosters it, Mr. Dooley does not quite buy Roosevelt's self-representation. Dunne never made this as explicit as in "A Book Review" (1899), yet Dooley's tall-tale, blarney manner of exaggerating Roosevelt's physicality and populism ironizes and problematizes them. His Roosevelt is over-the-top, suggesting a stagy, performative rather than "authentic" manhood and egalitarianism. At the same time that Dunne's humor seems to serve Roosevelt's purpose and reflect Dunne's largely positive attitude toward the president, it often contains a stinging critique that has the potential to undermine all the goodwill it creates. For instance, while the piece "Swearing" suggests that Roosevelt is one of those rare trustworthy politicians who speaks clearly and honestly, the column simultaneously and in no uncertain terms accuses Roosevelt of duplicity. The moment before the president was hit by the trolley car, Dooley claims, Roosevelt was working on a speech on trusts. "'Th' thrusts,' says he to himsilf, 'are heejous monsthers built up be th' inlightened intherprise iv th' men that have done so much to advance pro-gress in our beloved counthry.'"[95] The president's view of large corporations and their barons is schizophrenic; he insists that they are fiends yet believes that they are an essential engine driving American economic progress. Because of this ambivalence, Roosevelt, according to Dunne, refuses to come down decisively against the trusts and on behalf of the people. The supposedly straight-talking, reforming president deliberately obfuscates in order to hide his true feelings about big business from the public. He even goes so far as to attempt to disguise his decision not to "stamp thim undher fut" as concern for the public's well-being. He does not wish to foster feelings of enmity in the nation, he claims, not even hatred of the trusts. "'Betther blue but smilin' lips anny time thin a full coal scuttle an' a sour heart,'" the working-class Dooley understands Roosevelt to say.[96] This piece, which proclaims Roosevelt as one of the people, simultaneously suggests that he cannot be relied upon to protect their interests or to speak honestly to them about his plans.

Similarly, the sketch about the president's hilariously forceful methods for dealing with his opponents implies that intimidation is a key component of Roosevelt's political method:

> F'r th' first time since I've been at it, Ar-rchey road methods has been inthrajooced in naytional polliticks. I knew th' time wud come, Hinnissy. 'Tis th' on'y way. Ye may talk about it as much as ye want, but govermint, me boy, is a case iv me makin' ye do what I want an' if I can't do it with a song, I'll do it with a shovel. Th' ir'n hand in th' velvet glove, th' horseshoe in th' boxin' mit, th' quick right, an' th' heavy boot, that was th' way we r-run polliticks when I was captain iv me precinct.[97]

The corrupt methods of local politics Roosevelt claimed to fight have been introduced on the national level by none other than Roosevelt himself,

Dooley suggests. For Dooley, these methods are not problematic in the least. In fact, they help turn the president into a familiar, knowable figure who follows the rules of ward and street. But the column suggests that Roosevelt is no better than the politicians he made his reputation attacking. He, too, forces compliance and silences dissent.

Yet Roosevelt laughed and laughed out loud. "Let me repeat," the president wrote to the satirist in January 1907, "that Dooley, especially when he writes about Teddy Rosenfelt, has no more interested and amused reader than said Rosenfelt himself."[98] Though genuine, Roosevelt's amusement was also politic. "Let him be careful not to show himself so thin-skinned as to mind [criticism]," Roosevelt warned would-be reformer-politicians, and he deliberately followed his own advice.[99] Laughing at himself with the Irishmen at the bar and their readers across the country, he further promoted the image of himself as one of the men.

But when Mr. Dooley used his ethnic voice to cast doubt upon Roosevelt's commitment to "True Americanism," questioning Roosevelt's motives, revealing the implications of its racialized underpinnings, and exposing his failure to live up to its promise of equality for those who complied with its dictates, Roosevelt could not simply laugh.

"The Anglo-Saxon 'liance" and the Implications of Roosevelt's "American Race"

"Now, ole laughing philosopher, (because you are not only one who laughs, but also a genuine philosopher and because your philosophy has a real effect upon this country)," Roosevelt wrote to Dunne shortly after the president's 1904 election triumph, "I want to enter a strong protest against your very amusing and very wrong-headed article on the 'Anglo-Saxon Triumph.'"[100] What follows is an unprecedented five-page letter by the president defending himself in every possible way against the fictional barkeep. "The Anglo-Saxon Triumph"[101] had attacked the core of Roosevelt's Americanism, and the president could not abide it.

Dunne's piece raged against the popular assertion that Roosevelt's electoral victory was a coup for the Anglo-Saxon race and a mandate for the much-trumpeted alliance between the United States and Britain. "I want to offer my congratulations," wrote Columbia professor Brander Matthews, for instance, in a letter to the newly elected president, "not merely on your election, for that seemed to me inevitable. No,—rather because you are the chief of a people that knows a good man when they see him,—a people compounded now (as ever) from all the other peoples of the world—and yet retaining (or acquiring) the old Anglo-Saxon respect for character and courage and straightforwardness. And I don't want that foreign mission, either!"[102] Matthews's depiction of the American race as mixed yet "retaining or acquiring" the original characteristics of its founders recalls Roosevelt's notion of the workings of the melting pot. Matthews labels those original characteristics "Anglo-Saxon." Roosevelt never did so; in fact, he distinctly disclaimed the existence of an Anglo-Saxon race, arguing instead that even the English are a mixed race. And yet, as we have seen, Roosevelt argued that the same elements "in the same proportion" that constituted the mixed British race also constituted the mixed American race, both of which are "two substantially similar branches of the great English race,"[103] or, as he preferred to call it "the English-speaking race."[104] And it was to this race that all European immigrants were assimilating.[105] Scientifically, as Thomas Dyer put it, the term the "'English-speaking race' provide[s] an effective conceptual substitute for the more traditional Anglo-Saxon idea," which had become outmoded and from which Roosevelt, himself of Dutch and Scotch-Irish descent, was excluded.[106] At the same time, however, it posited a racial connection between the United States and Britain that to Mr. Dooley, and even to Brander Matthews, smelled and functioned just like Anglo-Saxonism.[107]

Well before Roosevelt's election, indeed from the time that he first burst on to the national scene, Dooley derided American Anglo-Saxonism in all its theoretical, social, and political forms. "An Anglo-Saxon, Hinnissy, is a German that's forgot who was his parents," said Dooley in 1898:

> They're a lot iv thim in this counthry. . . . Mack is an Anglo-Saxon. His folks come fr'm th' County Armagh, an' their naytional Anglo-Saxon hymn is "O'Donnell Aboo." Teddy Rosenfelt is another Anglo-Saxon. An' I'm an Anglo-Saxon. I'm wan iv th' hottest Anglo-Saxons that iver come out iv Anglo-Saxony. Th' name iv Dooley has been th' proudest Anglo-Saxon name in th' County of Roscommon f'r many years. . . . I tell ye, whin th' Clan an th' Sons iv Sweden an' th' Banana Club an' the Circle Francaize an' th' Pollacky Benivolent Society an' th' Rooshian Sons of

Dinnymite an' th' Benny Brith an' th' Coffee Clutch that Schwartzmeister r-runs an' th' Tur-rnd'ye-mind an' th' Holland society an' th' Afro-Americans an' th' other Anglo-Saxons begin f'r to raise their Anglo-Saxon battle-cry, it'll be all day with th' eight or nine people in th' wurruld that has the misforture iv not bein' brought up Anglo-Saxons.[108]

Dooley's satire plays on what Matthew Frye Jacobson has identified as the inherent contradiction in American Anglo-Saxonism.[109] Native-born Americans asserted their claims to an Anglo-Saxon identity as a way of excluding European immigrants from full participation in the nation.[110] They created a hierarchy of whiteness, asserting the racial superiority of the Anglo-Saxon over the Celt, Teuton, Slav, Latin, Hebrew, and so on. And they insisted on a natural racial link between the people of the United States and England, working to forge political policies and strategic alliances based on purported racial relatedness. In proclaiming America an Anglo-Saxon nation, however, they simultaneously erased the very racial differences they sought to establish, overlooking the reality of American diversity in claims of a unified Anglo identity. Without questioning the reality of racialized distinctions among nationalities, Dooley contests Anglo-Saxonism by reminding the nation of its multiracial composition.

The problem for Dooley with whitewashing the nation is not, as might be expected, his exclusion from Anglo-Saxon America, but rather his potential inclusion. If America were indeed an Anglo-Saxon nation, or even in Roosevelt's terms an "English" one, then becoming American would mean being Anglicized. "I am a British subjick, Hinnissy," Dooley proclaimed in 1902. "I wan't born wan. I was born in Ireland. But I have a little money put away, an' ivry American that has larned to make wan dollar sthick to another is ex-officio, as Hogan says, a British subjick. We've adopted a foster father."[111] Back in Ireland, where citizens actually are subjects of the Crown, Dooley vehemently rejected Englishness. But in the United States, he finds that once he becomes middle-class, he is automatically constituted as Anglo and expected to proclaim "devotion to th' ol' land from which our fathers sprung or was sprung be th' authorities."[112] Parodying the tired metaphor of immigrant autobiographers who declare America their adopted home and the founding fathers their foster fathers, Dooley suggests that American insistence on relatedness to the English and deferral to British culture turn immigrants into the foster children of England, not the United States. Becoming a middle-class American was beginning to look like becoming an Anglo-American to Dooley, and the pressure to claim closer ties to Englishness in America was reprehensible to the Irish Catholic immigrant.[113]

Dooley finds calls to "cement" a strategic and trade alliance with Britain, naturalized on the basis of race, similarly intolerable. "They've got me so closely knit with Lord Salsb'ry, first be ties iv blood, thin be a common language which we both speak at each other, an' fin'lly a shovelful iv cemint, that I feel like wan iv th' enthries iv a three-legged race at a picnic."[114] Such a union is not at all natural, according to Dooley, and it would psychologically deform the Irish American.

Dooley understands the alliance as an instrument of imperialism. He calls it the "White Man's Burden Thrajeedy Company,—two little Evas, four hundherd millyon Topsies, six hundherd millyon Uncle Toms.... Nawthin' can stop it. Blood is thicker than wather; an' together, ar-rm in ar-rm, we'll spread the light iv civilization fr'm wan end iv th' wurruld to th' other."[115] With the two little Evas of the United States and Britain claiming right and progress on their side, the alliance would subjugate millions. As Dooley has one American businessman, serving as a goodwill ambassador to London on behalf of the alliance, say:

> "We ar-re achooated be a common purpose f'r to march on, ankle to ankle, ceminted so close ye cudden't squeeze a five dollar bill between us, carryin' to th' ends iv th' earth, th' blessin's iv civil an religious liberty an' shootin' thim into th' inhabitants thereof an' teachin' thim th' benfits iv ye'er gloryous thraditions an' our akelly gloryous products, among which is Higgins' Goolden Cremery Butthrine XXX. It melts in th' mouth."[116]

For the sake of expanding international markets, the United States would join with England, forcing itself upon sovereign peoples and masking its intentions beneath the language of racial uplift, the Irish American barkeep discloses.

In terms that grew more and more personal and direct over time, despite their blossoming friendship, Dunne blamed Roosevelt, his expansionist policies, and his administration for promoting the equivalent to theoretical, political, and diplomatic Anglo-Saxonism. Dooley calls Roosevelt's secretary of state, John Hay, "'his majesty's ripresentative in this counthry who is doin' more thin anny other man in th' plastherin' business'" in his attempts to cement the alliance.[117] He depicts the U.S. ambassador to England, Joseph Hodges Choate, drinking enthusiastically to "'His majesty Edward th' Sivinth, iv Gr-reat Britain an' possibly Ireland, iv Inja, Egypt, iv Austhralya, iv South Africa in a sinse, an' iv th' Dominions beyant th' sea, includin' New York, King Definder iv th' Faith. I hope I got it all in.'"[118] And he classes Roosevelt with the British propagandists for Anglo-Saxonism, suggesting in a piece written before Roosevelt's presidency that the colonel would swallow his manly American pride for the sake of an imperialist alliance. "'Ye whelps,' says Lord Char-rles Beresford an' Roodyard Kipling an' Tiddy Rosenfelt, an' th' other Anglo-Saxons," putting down Americans:

> "Foolish an' frivolous people, cheap but thrue-hearted an' insincere cousins," they say. "'Tis little ye know about anything. Ye ar-re a disgrace to humanity. Ye love th' dollar betther thin ye love anything but two dollars. . . . Ye have desthroyed our language. . . . Ye'er morals are loose. . . . Ye ar-re mussy at th' table, an' ye have no religion. . . . But ye ar're whelps iv th' ol' line. . . . Ye annoy us so much ye must be members iv our own fam'ly. . . . So," says they, "come to our ar-ams, an' together we'll go out an conquer th' wurruld."[119]

The thrust of this column is not to critique Roosevelt, but rather to dissuade the nation from allying itself with Britain by portraying the English as untrustworthy allies, lacking respect for the United States and seeking to unify only for the sake of greedy imperialism. As Dooley puts it, "We feel kindly to each other; but it looks to me like, th' first up in th' mornin', th' first away with th' valu'bles."[120]

But in developing his case against the alliance, Dooley makes a surprising observation about Roosevelt. Despite his calls for the United States to assert its power abroad and his vehement exhortations against an American posture of "colonial dependence" on England, Roosevelt's imperialism placed him in just such a dependent position. It made him reliant on the foreign and flawed logic justifying European colonialism and placed him in a deferential position vis-à-vis the British whose complicity and cooperation he sought. "We'll have to set up sthraight an' mind our manners. No tuckin' our napkins down our throats or dhrinkin' out iv th' saucer or kickin' our boots off undher the table. No reachin' f'r anything, but 'Mah, will ye kindly pass th' Ph'lippeens?' or 'No, thank ye, pah, help ye'ersilf first.'"[121] As Dooley sees it, the very act of America's first large-scale assertion of imperial power expresses the nation's continued colonized position. It also exposes its underlying racialized assumptions about the difference between itself and the people it would colonize and the similarities between itself and Britain.

In 1904, immediately after Roosevelt's election, Dunne lodged his most explicit personal attack on the president, his notions of the American race, and their implications. The president "regards his iliction as a great triumph f'r th' Anglo-Saxon race," says Dooley in disbelief:

> So ye see, Hinnissy, 'twas th' Anglo-Saxon vote that did it. I see now what th' Prisidint was up to whin he sint f'r Cassidy iv th' Clan-na-Gael. Th' Clan-na-Gael is wan iv th' sthrongest Anglo-Saxon organyzations we have. Its whole purpose is to improve Anglo-Saxon civilyzation be ilivatin' it. There's on'y wan way to do it, an' that's th' way they do. Th' raison Cassidy an' Kelly an' Murphy an' Burke an' Shea an' all th' boys up an' down th' sthreet voted f'r Rosenfelt was because they ar-re Anglo-Saxons. Th' A.O.H., which, iv coorse, ye know, manes All Ol' H'Englishmen, was f'r Rosenfelt f'r th' same raison. So it was with th' Anglo-Saxon turnvereins an' sangerfests. Me frind Schwartzmeister down th' sthreet voted f'r Rosenfelt because iv his sthrong feelin' in favor iv cimintin' th' alliance between th' two nations. An' he was ilicted, I hear.[122]

Using the same technique of calling things their opposite that he had employed six years earlier to lambaste the notion of an Anglo-Saxon America, Dunne exposes the speciousness of the claim that it was the Anglo-Saxon vote that got Roosevelt elected. On the contrary, Dooley insists; it was the Irish and German ethnic vote that put him back into power. If the president wants to turn around and claim this as an Anglo-Saxon victory, then he must believe that the Irish and the Germans are both Anglos and that the Irish American revolutionary organization, the Clan-na-Gael, must actually be seeking "to improve Anglo-Saxon civilization by ilivatin' it" with dynamite. Dooley's outrageous assertions expose the magnitude of the falsehood he believes Roosevelt is trying to put over on the American people.

Pushing his attack deeper, Dooley argues that Roosevelt's conceptualization of the American race underwrites and perpetuates the exclusion of

Irish Americans from positions of national power, undermining Roosevelt's claims to equal opportunity for all "true Americans" regardless of "creed or birthplace." "I wondher how he'll threat th' Anglo-Saxon fr'm now on," Dooley conjectures. "I'm proud iv bein' a mimber iv that gr-reat race, now that me attintion has been called to it. Gawd bless Anglo-Saxony, says I, with all me heart. It has made us a free counthry. But in handin' around th' medals afther th' victhry, I fain wud see a few pinned to manly coats that were not made in Bond Sthreet. Give all th' branches iv that noble herd a chance."[123] Dunne again exposes the contradictions in Anglo-Saxonism. Erasing the diversity of America's citizenry by claiming a homogeneous racial identity for the nation, those who draw on the claims of Anglo-Saxonism simultaneously assert their supremacy over the supposedly nonexistent other. If the Irish and the Germans are "Anglo-Saxons" or branches of the "English-speaking race," let them reap the rewards of political support, Dooley argues, but he does not expect much of the newly elected president.

Dooley suggests Roosevelt's prior and expected exclusion of Irish Americans from positions of power through an analogy to "a man be th' name iv Sheehan or Sullivan or Casey" whose work and connections to the Irish American community get a president elected. This Irish American kingmaker handpicks a presidential candidate, feeds him "canned principles," pulls him out of obscurity, creates a whirlwind campaign for him ("He supplies th' wind an' Casey supplies th' whirl"), writes his speeches, takes all the punches from the press, and uses his Irish connections nationwide to ensure that his candidate is elected. The next morning, Casey reads in the papers that the results are seen as a triumph for Anglo-Saxon policy. He does not "shout himsilf hoarse over that because his on'y acquaintance with an Anglo-Saxon policy was whin his fam'y was dhriven out iv th' County Kerry be a bailiff with an Anglo-Saxon bludgeon."[124] Instead, he quietly goes to see the president-elect with a list of several Irish Americans who worked hard on the campaign to be considered for cabinet posts. "'Ye can sind th' applications iv ye'er frinds to th' clerk iv th' civil service commission, who has charge iv th' day laborers,'" the new president responds, forgetting his obligations and putting the Irishmen down where he believes they belong. He has already decided to appoint the Honorable Peabody Perkins secretary of state; "'he is partic'larly fitted f'r th' place, havin' spint all but th' last six weeks iv his life in England. His appintmint is endorsed be th' London *Times*.'" The president has similarly offered the job of secretary of the interior to the Honorable Ponsonby Sanderson; "'he is th' high chief guy in th' Lile Orange Lodge, an' will know jus' how to handle th' public-school question.'"[125] For all of their patriotism, loyalty, and labor, the Irish Americans are shunted aside by the president in favor of native-born Americans of the most offensive, un-American type. The president plays ethnic politics when it works to his advantage, but when it is no longer needed, he turns his back on ethnic America.

In case there is any question as to whom Dooley's analogies refer, Hennessy makes clear his pained sense of betrayal by President Roosevelt. "'Well,'" says the loyal Democrat Mr. Hennessy at the end of this tirade, "'if I thought this was an Anglo-Saxon victhry I wud niver have voted th' way I did.'"[126] Choosing loyalty to Roosevelt over loyalty to the party, the Irish American finds himself bereft of the promise of equality, opportunity, and "true Americanism."

Roosevelt was outraged by this column. He insisted that Dunne, or at least Dooley, misrepresented him, and, writing to Dunne immediately after its appearance, he rebutted the column's claims one by one. Roosevelt began by reasserting his repudiation of Anglo-Saxonism. "If you have ever happened to see what I have written on the matter of the Anglo-Saxon business," he bristled, "you may have noticed that I have always insisted that we are not Anglo-Saxons at all—even admitting for the sake of argument, which I do not, that there are any Anglo-Saxons—but a new and mixed race—a race drawing its blood from many different sources." He then denied the claim that he owes his victory to the Irish. "No Casey hunted me up," Roosevelt insisted; rather, he hunted up George Cortelyou, a "Dutchman" like himself, to serve as campaign manager, "so there is nothing particularly Anglo-Saxon about our triumph." Had his campaign manager been an Irishman, he would most certainly have thanked him appropriately, Roosevelt implied, insisting that "if a man is good enough for me to profit by his services before election, he is good enough for me to do what I can for him after election; and I do not give a damn whether his name happens to be Casey, or Schwartzmeister, or Van Rensselaer, or Peabody." In fact, he contended, "my whole public life has been an emphatic protest against the Peabodys and Van Rensselaers arrogating to themselves any superiority over the Caseys and Schwartzmeisters. But in return, I will not . . . tolerate for one moment any assumption of superiority by the Caseys and Schwartzmeisters over the Peabodys and Van Rensselaers." And in a postscript longer than the letter, Roosevelt argued that it is more politically expedient to draw on Anglophobia than Anglomania, particularly if one wishes to win the Irish vote. But he could take pride in the fact that

> while I got, I think, a greater proportion of the Americans of Irish birth or parentage and of the Catholic religion than any previous republican candidate, I got this proportion purely because they knew I felt in sympathy with them and in touch with them, and that they and I had the same ideals and principles, and not by any demagogic appeals about creed or race, or by any demagogic attack upon England. I feel a sincere friendliness for England; but you may notice that I do not slop over about it, and that I do not in the least misunderstand England's attitude, or, for the matter of that, the attitude of any European nation as regards us.[127]

Roosevelt took pride in the fact that he could simultaneously be friendly toward England and win the Irish American vote, a sign that he does not play ethnic politics. He understood Irish support as a vote in favor of his Americanist principles over any partisan or nationalist loyalty, and he utterly rejected Dooley's suggestion that he was guilty of discriminatory Anglo-Saxonism. "There!" Roosevelt exclaimed. "You may think I have taken your article rather seriously, and so I have, because I think you are a force that counts and I do not want to see you count on the side of certain ugly and unpleasant tendencies in American life."[128] The vehemence of Roosevelt's reaction stemmed not only from his perception of Dunne's influence on the public but also from his understanding of the depth of the satirist's censure.

Roosevelt recognized Dunne's column as an attack on the president's personal claim to "true Americanism." As he said in his own defense, Roosevelt had built much of his public life and political rhetoric on the principle that "Americanism is a question of spirit, conviction, and purpose, not of creed or birthplace. . . . A Scandinavian, a German, or an Irishman who has really become an American has the right to stand on exactly the same footing as any native-born citizen in the land."[129] This was the principle on which Dooley and Dunne staked their identities as Americans. But the president's continued exclusion of Irish Americans from his cabinet, his appointment instead of native-born men no better than William Waldorf Astor, and his support for an alliance with Britain made him suspect in their eyes. Questioning Roosevelt's credentials as a populist progressive, Dooley suggests that Roosevelt represents the entrenched elite, not the people. He cuts through Roosevelt's rhetoric, uncovering the contradictions and ambivalences at the heart of his Americanism.

Unlike other ethnic writers who had won the president's support, Dunne stood his ground against Roosevelt's criticisms. He responded immediately, for "I cannot wait until I see you to make some sort of reply to the kind but firm whaling you administered to Mr. Dooley." And he critiqued Roosevelt directly from a brazenly ethnic American, progressive, and transnationalist perspective. "You say, my dear Mr. Roosevelt, that you feel a sincere friendliness for England. That must mean, the English government, and I hope you will forgive me for saying that I do not see how you can hold such a sentiment," Dunne writes respectfully, though neglecting to call Roosevelt "Mr. President."[130]

> If in the individual, . . . you hate and despise crookedness and cowardliness and injustice and insincerity and inefficiency, how can you like a government that has shown all these things in its dealings with other governments and especially in its dealings with us? I dislike and distrust the English government and the classes that control it because I am of Irish blood, because I have suffered in my own family from their cruelty, and especially because I believe they are as much the enemies of this country to-day as they were one hundred years ago, forty years ago or ten years ago.[131]

Roosevelt's failure to recognize the moral corruption of the imperialist English government is a failure of his progressivism, Dunne argues. He speaks to Roosevelt in this letter as the son of Irish immigrants and as a man of "Irish blood." His position emerges from the very sort of "Old World quarrel" and "national antipathy" that Roosevelt had declared "we have a right and duty to demand" immigrants leave behind when they enter the United States.[132] But Dunne suggests that his Irish hatred of England makes him a better progressive, indeed a better American, than even Roosevelt, for it gives him insight into the British government's attitude toward the United States and frees him of any lingering political or cultural sense of dependence on England. "I am not an Anglophobiac. I hope I am not a 'phobiac' on any subject," he says, defending himself against the implications of Roosevelt's criticism, "but I resent the present tendency" toward an alliance, "first, because I think it is very dangerous for this country; and secondly, because I believe it has created a general impression in England and Ireland that the century-old sympathy of this country for Ireland has disappeared."

Dunne's concerns both in this letter and in his column are for the welfare of the United States as well as of Ireland. "I would like to teach the young Irishmen of this country that they owe much to Ireland and that it is no part of their duty to accept without protest the social and political campaign in the Eastern states among university professors and associations of wholesale pawn-brokers to create an 'Anglo-Saxon alliance,'" he explains. In ways that would have been surprising to Philip Dunne, even in his nationally syndicated columns, Finley Peter Dunne perceives his audience and his mission as double. Dooley's vernacular wit speaks to young Irish Americans, politicizing and galvanizing the diasporic community to support the nationalist cause and to protest policies harmful to Ireland and to Irish Americans. At the same time, Dunne uses Dooley to exert direct pressure on the larger nation and particularly on its leaders whose ear the columnist had won through that same dialect humor. The "Anglo-Saxon Triumph" reminds the president and his party who put them back in office. In return for their vote, Dunne asserts, Irish Americans do not expect appointive office, though "in this respect every administration," including Roosevelt's, "has managed to dissemble its love even if it has not actually kicked us down the stairs." But, Dunne argues, speaking as the self-appointed representative for the Irish American community to the president of the United States, they desire "an understanding and a toleration of their hopes and ambitions," both in the United States and in Ireland. Dunne calls on Roosevelt both privately in his letter and publicly in his column to remember the source of his victory and to respond with meaningful political action. For his part, "what ever I can do to prevent the progress of this foolish [Anglo-Saxon] partnership," Dunne says, "I will do with all my heart. Probably it will not be much, but I take consolation in the fact that some pretty big follies have been laughed away in their time."[133] Through laughter of a distinctly ethnic sort, Dunne hoped to change the ideologies and policies of the nation.

The day Dooley lodged his attack on the notion of Roosevelt's Anglo-Saxon triumph, the president spoke before European ambassadors: "A young people of composite stock, we have kinship with many different nations, but we are identical with none of them and are developing a separate national stock, as we have already developed a separate national life," Roosevelt said on that day.

> We have in our veins the blood of the Englishman, the Irishman, the Welshman, the German and the Frenchman, the Dutchman, the Scandinavian, the Italian, the Magyar, the Finn, the Slav, so that to each of the great Powers of the Old World we can claim a more or less distant kinship by blood, and to each strain of blood we owe some peculiar quality in our national life or national character. As such is the case it is natural that we should have a peculiar feeling of nearness to each of many peoples across the water.[134]

Without denying a special connection to the English-speaking race, Roosevelt publicly reasserted his theory of the mixed American race, using it this time to claim relatedness and friendship to all European peoples. Roosevelt gave this speech at the signing of an arbitration treaty with Germany as a way of disclaiming the possibility of an American alliance with Britain against the kaiser. But his words resonate in response to the Irishman's criticisms. In the face of the suggestion that the president was pandering to the British and to Anglo elements in American culture, Roosevelt reemphasized his belief in the hybridity of the American race and its broad political implications.

But a shift in emphasis could not adequately answer the columnist's attack, as Roosevelt's uncomfortable letter seems to acknowledge. Dunne had lodged a very serious public assault on the president that cut through his rhetoric and unveiled his hypocrisy. Dunne claimed in newspapers throughout the country that despite all of Roosevelt's heartfelt calls to judge the individual by his "worth as a man only," the president failed to give Irish Americans a "square deal." And he located the source of this discrepancy in Roosevelt's notion of the American race, which, he claimed, remained Anglo-Saxonist at its crux.

Through Dooley, Dunne exposed the contradictions at the heart of Roosevelt's Americanism. And Roosevelt could not effectively defend himself, for to a degree unlike that of any other writer examined in this study, the satirist held great power in this relationship. More important, the blunt, funny, self-made Irish American Dunne had created was holding the president to his own standards. In his accented voice and with his transnational allegiances and ethnic concerns, the Irish immigrant saloonkeeper out-Rooseveleted Roosevelt, demanding an America true to its highest ideals. Dunne's Irish American critique of the nation, and of Roosevelt in particular, artfully revealed alternative sites and modes of "true Americanism" already implied in the works of Zangwill, Riis, and Stern, setting the stage for a new ethnic politics and new constructions of the national narrative that would emerge in full force only later in the twentieth century.

Epilogue

On December 24, 1999, the Taubenfeld family celebrated its fiftieth year in the United States. A party complete with American flags, Uncle Sam hats, pop-culture trivia games, and kosher Chinese food marked the occasion. The highlight of the day was to be a video made by the children and grandchildren of the immigrants, with photos and reminiscences about the early years and emotional testimonials to the first generation for their sacrifices on our behalf. As the family gathered around a large-screen TV, we were amazed to see in the opening frames of the video none other than former New York City mayor Ed Koch addressing us directly.

"Nat, Ike, and Rose Taubenfeld typify the immigrant experience," he told us of our parents and grandparents. "America is the great place that it is because it allows people to rise and to get the benefit of its bounty using their hands and their brains. And the Taubenfelds have done that. It's extraordinary. They're extraordinary." A thrill went through the room. Here was the nationally renowned former mayor celebrating our family's achievements for all posterity. Surely we had made it in America.

And yet there was something unsettling about the mayor's remarks. While he told us how extraordinary the Taubenfelds are, he also insisted that they are typical. They represent the immigrant experience; their success tells not of themselves but of the bounty and greatness of the nation. What could this mean for the immigrants who labored at immense personal cost to fashion a life here? What could it mean for the second and third generations who find ourselves beginning our own stories with those of our parents? How can we construct an individual sense of self within the stories the nation narrates about itself out of our experiences? The same questions that Rough Writing has posed about the national and personal meanings of ethnic experience and narrative more than one hundred years ago persist today as the United States continues to grapple with the place of newcomers in the nation and its narratives and as individuals struggle both to distinguish themselves and to belong.

Roosevelt recognized early on the need to build the nation's story out of the stories of individuals. As we have seen, from the last decade of the nineteenth century until his death in 1919, Theodore Roosevelt actively supported European immigrant and ethnic writing. He wrote prefaces and blurbs, reviews and commentaries, promoting the work of writers of diverse European backgrounds, including Israel Zangwill, Jacob Riis, Elizabeth Stern, and Finley Peter Dunne, who wrote about ethnic America. The stories he backed were tales of "true Americanism," of immigrants who seemed to "throw themselves heartily into our national life, cease to be Europeans, and become Americans like the rest of us."[1] As he wrote in the introduction to Elizabeth Stern's work, "When we tend to grow disheartened over some of the developments of our American civilization," such narratives remind us "what this same civilization holds for starved and noble souls who have elsewhere been denied what here we hold to be, as a matter of course, rights free to all."[2]

For Roosevelt and native-born readers, such texts upheld their idea of America and American uniqueness and identity. But these texts told other stories as well, tales of ambivalence and loss, tales of reconnection with homeland and home, tales of America's failures and faults, and alternative visions for its future. And yet they were engaged and incorporated into the "official narrative" of the United States, by its chief overseer, Theodore Roosevelt.

Though he excluded all Asians and Africans and called for all new European arrivals to "become Americans like the rest of us," though he had distinct ideas of who "the rest of us" were and pressured newcomers to conform, Roosevelt saw the need for immigrant and ethnic voices within his American narrative. And though he tried to subsume these voices into a particular tale of American race, gender, nationalism, class, and civic values, their own divergent stories lingered within. Their presence created and exposed dynamic tensions between the individual and the nation and between the stories each must tell. Each simultaneously served and pressured the other, altering its meaning and reshaping its future. In the nativist atmosphere of the 1920s and the claims to national unity and consensus of the mid-1930s to early 1960s, these stories would largely be forgotten. But they remained for the next generations to recover and revise in the construction of new individual and national American narratives.

NOTES

INTRODUCTION

1. Henry James, *The American Scene* (1907; New York: Penguin, 1994) 92–93.

2. John Bodnar, *The Transplanted: A History of Immigrants in Urban America* (Bloomington: Indiana UP, 1985), 217; Roger Daniels, *Guarding the Golden Door* (New York: Farrar, Straus and Giroux, 2005) 5–6.

3. James 92.

4. Horace Kallen quotes these words from his Harvard professor Barrett Wendell anonymously in "Democracy versus the Melting Pot," pt. 1 *Nation* 18 February 1915: 194. Priscilla Wald identifies Wendell as the source in her essay "Of Crucibles and Grandfathers: The East European Immigrants," *The Cambridge Companion to Jewish American Literature*, ed. Michael P. Kramer and Hana Wirth-Nesher (New York: Cambridge UP, 2003) 54.

5. The claim to be speaking for the people against special interest is James J. Connolly's definition of Progressivism, which he understands as a style of political rhetoric and behavior rather than an ideology that is the sole possession of any one class or group. See Connolly's *The Triumph of Ethnic Progressivism: Urban Political Culture in Boston, 1900–1925* (Cambridge: Harvard UP, 1998). I am grateful to the anonymous reviewer for NYU Press who led me to Connolly's work.

6. Theodore Roosevelt, "True Americanism," *The Forum*, April 1894, *The Works of Theodore Roosevelt*, national edition, ed. Hermann Hagedorn, vol. 13 (New York: Scribner's, 1926) 25 (hereafter cited as *Works*; unless otherwise noted, all citations refer to this edition).

7. Twelve years before Roosevelt's statement, the influential French philosopher Ernest Renan argued similarly that "a nation is a soul, a spiritual principle. Two things, which in truth are but one, constitute this soul or spiritual principle. One lies in the past, one in the present. One is the possession in common of a rich legacy of memories; the other is present-day consent, the desire to live together, the will to perpetuate the value of the heritage that one has received in an undivided form" (Renan, "What Is a Nation?" Lecture delivered at the Sorbonne, 11 March 1882, trans. Martin Thom, ed. Homi K. Bhabha, *Nation and Narration* [New York: Routledge, 1990] 19). For Renan as for Roosevelt, a nation is dependent on a shared sense of history and ideals and a shared desire to continue these into the future.

Contemporary theorists of the nation have argued that nation formation depends on the ways in which the state creates for its citizens a feeling of belonging. The role of narrative in creating identification and identity within the nation has been theorized most significantly by Benedict Anderson, *Imagined Communities: Reflections of the Origin and Spread of Nationalism*, rev. ed. (London: Verso, 1991); Etienne Balibar and Immanuel Wallerstein, *Race, Nation, Class: Ambiguous Identities*, trans. Chris Turner (London: Verso, 1991); and Homi K. Bhabha, ed., *Nation and Narration* (New York: Routledge, 1990). Pricilla Wald applies these principles to the narration of

Americanness in *Constituting Americans: Cultural Anxiety and Narrative Form* (Durham: Duke UP, 1996).

8. Roosevelt, "True Americanism" 19–20.

9. Theodore Roosevelt, "The Shaping of Public Opinion," *Works* 13:667.

10. Theodore Roosevelt, *The Winning of the West*, vol. 1 (1889; Lincoln: Bison Books, 1995) 1. Roosevelt's idea of the impact of the West on the American race was heavily influenced by Frederick Jackson Turner's "The Significance of the Frontier in American History," 1893, *The Frontier in American History* (New York: Henry Holt, 1920) 1–38.

11. Theodore Roosevelt, *New York*, 1891, *Works* 10:361–62.

12. Theodore Roosevelt, *Gouverneur Morris*, 1888, *Works* 7:237.

13. Theodore Roosevelt, *Autobiography*, 1913, *Works* 20:ix.

14. Theodore Roosevelt, "Nationalism in Literature and Art," 16 November 1916, *Literary Essays* (Philadelphia: Pavilion Press, 2004) 303.

15. Roosevelt, "Nationalism in Literature" 305.

16. Roosevelt's active engagement in the effort to theorize and establish a national literature has been well traced by Laurence J. Oliver through Roosevelt's extensive correspondence with Columbia University professor of English Brander Matthews. See Oliver, ed., *The Letters of Theodore Roosevelt and Brander Matthews* (Knoxville: U of Tennessee P, 1995); and Oliver's *Brander Matthews, Theodore Roosevelt and the Politics of American Literature 1880–1920* (Knoxville: U of Tennessee P, 1992).

17. Roosevelt, "Nationalism in Literature" 308.

18. Roosevelt, "True Americanism" 22.

19. Roosevelt, "True Americanism" 23–24.

20. Roosevelt, "True Americanism" 23.

21. The term "civil religion" was coined by Robert Bellah in his article "Civil Religion in America," *Daedalus* 96 (Winter 1967): 1–21.

22. For a provocative discussion of the nexus of race, civilization, and masculinity, as it pertains to Roosevelt, see Gail Bederman's *Manliness and Civilization: A Cultural History of Gender and Race in the United States, 1880–1917* (Chicago: U of Chicago P, 1995).

23. Roosevelt, "True Americanism" 23.

24. Roosevelt, "True Americanism" 24. As Theodore Roosevelt exemplified, throughout U.S. history, racial definitions of the nation have always coexisted with civic ones. America has simultaneously and contradictorily understood itself as a people united by shared democratic ideals, to which anyone can subscribe, and as a people united by race, to which only some by nature belong. Racial conceptions of the nation limit who is entitled to join the civic community of equal citizens. Ideological definitions of the nation in turn restrict the systems of political belief and personal identification to which racially acceptable citizens may subscribe. All must rally around common institutions, or else the nation, it was feared, would dissolve. For further discussion of the tension between these poles, see Michael Ignatieff's *Blood and Belonging: Journeys into New Nationalism* (1993; New York: Noonday Press, 1995), which establishes the distinction between civic and ethnic nationalism as a way of talking about competing criteria for national belonging (6–9); Rogers Smith's *Civic Ideals: Conflicting Visions of Citizenship in U.S. History* (New Haven: Yale UP, 1997), which relates these ideas to the American context, expanding the notion of ethnic nationalism to apply to all forms of what he calls "ascriptive Americanism," including race, ethnicity, and gender; Gary Gerstle's

American Crucible: Race and Nation in the Twentieth Century (Princeton: Princeton UP, 2001), which applies the distinction between civic and racial nationalism particularly to Roosevelt and the progressive state he helped create; and Desmond King's *Making Americans: Immigration, Race, and the Origins of the Diverse Democracy* (Cambridge: Harvard UP, 2000) 11–49.

25. Roosevelt, "True Americanism" 26.

26. Alfred P. Schultz, *Race or Mongrel: A Brief History of the Rise and Fall of the Ancient Races of Earth: A Theory That the Fall of Nations Is Due to Intermarriage with Alien Stocks: A Demonstration a Nation's Strength Is Due to Racial Purity: A Prophecy That America Will Sink to Early Decay Unless Immigration Is Rigorously Restricted* (Boston: L. C. Page, 1908) 266.

27. Much has been written in recent years of the nonwhite status ascribed to many European ethnic groups, particularly upon their entry into the United States. See, for instance, Matthew Frye Jacobson's *Whiteness of a Different Color: European Immigrants and the Alchemy of Race* (Cambridge: Harvard UP, 1998); Eric Goldstein's *The Price of Whiteness: Jews, Race, and American Identity* (Princeton: Princeton UP, 2006); Noel Ignatiev's *How the Irish Became White* (New York: Routledge, 1995); Karen Brodkin's *How the Jews Became White Folks and What That Says about Race in America* (New Brunswick: Rutgers UP, 1998); and Thomas Guglielmo's *White on Arrival: Italians, Race, Color, and Power in Chicago, 1890–1945* (New York: Oxford UP, 1998), among others.

28. Madison Grant, *The Passing of the Great Race* (1916; New York: Scribner's, 1921) 90.

29. Kallen, "Democracy versus the Melting Pot" 191.

30. Horace Kallen, "Democracy versus the Melting Pot," pt. 2, *Nation* 25 February 1915: 220. For Kallen, as for the vast majority in this period, "culture" was considered part of one's racial/biological inheritance. It was not until the popularization of the work of Franz Boas that culture became understood as a distinct concept. For an excellent discussion of the beginnings of the distinction between race and culture, see George W. Stocking Jr., *Race, Culture, and Evolution: Essays in the History of Anthropology* (1968; Chicago: U of Chicago P, 1982) 260–69. See also Michael A. Elliott, *The Culture Concept: Writing and Difference in the Age of Realism* (Minneapolis: U of Minnesota P, 2002).

31. Randolph S. Bourne, "Trans-national America," 1916, *Theories of Ethnicity: A Classical Reader*, ed. Werner Sollors (New York: New York UP, 1996) 98, 106.

32. Theodore Roosevelt, "Americanism," October 1915, *Works* 18:392.

33. My notion of an "official narrative" derives from Priscilla Wald's definition of "official stories" as those "that surface in the rhetoric of national movements and initiatives—legal, political, and literary." They are "official" because of "the authority they command, articulated as they are, in relation to the rights and privileges of individuals" (*Constituting Americans* 2).

34. Roosevelt, "True Americanism" 16.

35. Roosevelt, "True Americanism" 16.

36. For discussion of the meanings of literary regionalism in the United States and its relation to nationalism and national literature, see Carrie Tirado Bramen, *The Uses of Variety: Modern Americanism and the Quest for National Distinctiveness* (Cambridge: Harvard UP, 2000); Judith Fetterley and Marjorie Pryse, *Writing Out of Place: Regionalism, Women, and American Literary Culture* (Urbana: U of Illinois P, 2003); and Fetterley's "'Not in the Least American': Nineteenth-Century Literary Regionalism,"

College English 56 (December 1994): 877–95; Elizabeth Ammons and Valerie Rohy, introduction, *American Local Color Writing, 1880–1920*, ed. Elizabeth Ammons and Valerie Rohy (New York: Penguin, 1998) xxvi–xxviii; Roberto Maria Dainotto, "'All the Regions Do Smilingly Revolt': The Literature of Place and Region," *Critical Inquiry* 22 (Spring 1996): 486–505; June Howard, "Unraveling Regions, Unsettling Periods: Sarah Orne Jewett and American Literary History," *American Literature* 68(June 1996): 365–84; Amy Kaplan, "Nation, Region, Empire," *Columbia Literary History of the American Novel*, ed. Emory Elliott (New York: Columbia UP, 1991) 250–57; Eric Sundquist, "Realism and Regionalism," *Columbia Literary History of the United States*, ed. Emory Elliott (New York: Columbia UP 1988) 501–24.

37. Roosevelt, "Nationalism in Literature and Art" 459, emphasis mine. Like Hamlin Garland, Frank Norris, Edward Eggleston, and other "regionalists," Roosevelt called for the creation and depiction of America through literary representations of regional character and difference. In letters to Columbia University literary critic Brander Matthews in the same year in which he wrote "True Americanism," Roosevelt specifically praised the "Americanism" of Garland's critical work *Crumbling Idols*, in which Garland called for a distinctly national fiction achieved through an emphasis on the local (Oliver, *Letters*, 81–82). "Local color means national character," Garland argued, placing the regional in the service of the national (*Crumbling Idols* [1894; Gainesville: Scholars Facsimiles, 1952] 63. William Dean Howells similarly considered "our decentralized literature" to be our national literature ("American Literary Centres," *Literature and Life* [New York: Harper, 1902] 177.

38. Roosevelt, "True Americanism" 18.

39. Roosevelt, "True Americanism" 20. Roosevelt seems to refer to Henry James in particular here.

40. Roosevelt, "True Americanism" 17.

41. Benedict Anderson analyzes the role of "print capitalism" in creating national feeling in *Imagined Communities* 6.

42. Theodore Roosevelt, "Race Decadence," *Outlook*, 8 April 1911, *The Works of Theodore Roosevelt*, memorial edition, ed. Hermann Hagedorn, vol. 14 (New York: Scribner's, 1924) 155 (hereafter cited as *Works*, memorial edition).

43. Israel Zangwill was a British Jew. However, with *The Melting Pot*, Zangwill sought to create a place for all immigrants, eastern European Jews in particular, in the United States. For this reason, as well as for the popularity and impact of his play, he is central to this study.

44. As Werner Sollors has demonstrated in *Beyond Ethnicity: Consent and Descent in American Culture* (New York: Oxford UP, 1986), immigrant autobiographies of this period are generally constructed as "ethnic transformation" tales. As Mary Antin does in *The Promised Land* (1912; New York: Penguin, 1997), which helped shape the genre, immigrant autobiographers frequently testify that their ethnic selves have been killed off and replaced by new and improved American selves (32). Pricilla Wald labels such tales "conversion narratives" (*Constituting Americans* 246–52). William Boelhower analyzes these structures further in "The Brave New World of Immigrant Autobiography," *MELUS* 9 (Summer 1982): 5–23.

CHAPTER 1

1. Israel Zangwill, *The Melting Pot* (1909; New York: Arno Press, 1975) 33–34. The play

premiered on 5 October 1908 and was first published in 1909. All references to Zangwill's play (hereafter *MP*) are to this published edition unless otherwise indicated.

2. Theodore Roosevelt, "The Children of the Crucible," *The Foes of Our Own Household*, *Works* 19:30.

3. Israel Zangwill (IZ) to TR, 25 August 1908, Israel Zangwill Papers, Central Zionist Archives, Jerusalem, Israel, A120/559.

4. *New York Times* 10 October 1908. For more on the reception history of *The Melting Pot*, see Guy Szuberla's "Zangwill's *The Melting Pot* Plays Chicago," *MELUS* 20 (Autumn 1995): 3–20; and Joe Kraus's "How *The Melting Pot* Stirred America: The Reception of Zangwill's Play and Theater's Role in the American Assimilation Experience," *MELUS* 24 (Autumn 1999): 3–19.

5. Roosevelt originally wrote these words in a letter to Zangwill, 15 October 1908, Theodore Roosevelt Papers, Library of Congress, Washington, DC. For a collection of advertisements for *The Melting Pot*, see Zangwill Papers, A120/165.

6. As the *American Hebrew* remarked, "President Roosevelt has put his finger in the 'Melting Pot.' It was only to change a line or so, but nevertheless it has resulted in sufficient advertisement of the play" (3 October 1908).

7. TR to IZ, 15 October 1908, Roosevelt Papers.

8. "'Melting Pot' at Grand," review clipping, Zangwill Papers, A120/165. Others have agreed with this assessment more recently, including Andrew Heinze in *Jews and the American Soul: Human Nature in the 20th Century* (Princeton: Princeton UP, 2004) 27.

9. Roosevelt, "True Americanism" 25, 22, 24.

10. Roosevelt, "True Americanism" 17.

11. *MP* 28.

12. I have adopted Zangwill's spelling of Kishineff throughout.

13. Zangwill had approached Roosevelt to support his Zionist endeavors as well. In the aftermath of the 1904 Kishineff pogrom, which Roosevelt had strongly denounced, the British playwright lunched with the president and petitioned him to suspend his general policy of opposing diasporic nationalism in the United States. Describing the desperate need of eastern European Jewry for an independent colony to make home, he urged Roosevelt to sanction Jewish nationalist activism in the United States by declaring publicly that "it was open to all American Jews, without the faintest imputation on their patriotism, to take part in the foundation of such a colony." The president refused to make such a statement directly, but, according to Zangwill, he authorized his secretary of state, John Hay, to do so (for Zangwill's accounts of these events, see his *Watchman, What of the Night* [New York: American Jewish Congress, 1923] 21). Now, in 1908, faced with the possibility of the closing of the borders of the United States to eastern European and other immigrants, Zangwill wrote *The Melting Pot* as another deliberate political intervention on behalf of European Jewry, this time seeking to keep the United States open as an alternative haven for them.

14. When asked for his opinion of the play, Oscar Straus wrote to the *American Hebrew*, "It is a great play and remarkable for presenting an historical picture of a great three-fold present-day movement with graphic human colors, namely, it paints the Russian Pogrom, the immigration problem, and the American amalgamation process" (23 October 1908: 610). He avoided commenting on his view of these

three pressing issues. For more on Oscar Straus, see Naomi Cohen's *A Dual Heritage: The Public Career of Oscar S. Straus* (Philadelphia: Jewish Publication Society, 1969).

15. No reviewer, for either Jewish or general papers, mentions the coincidence of the play's premiere with the close of Yom Kippur.

16. See, for instance, Nathan Glazer and Daniel Patrick Moynihan's classic *Beyond the Melting Pot: The Negroes, Puerto Ricans, Jews, Italians and Irish of New York City* (Cambridge: MIT and Harvard UP, 1963), where, in arguing that the perpetuation of ethnicity in New York indicates that America is not a melting pot, they define the melting pot in terms of "a single American nationality" with a homogeneous culture and single mode of self identification, rather than as a single American race connected by blood and shared inheritable traits (290, 1–23). See also Milton Gordon's *Assimilation in American Life: The Role of Race, Religion, and National Origins* (New York: Oxford UP, 1964).

17. *MP* 33–34.

18. Roosevelt, "True Americanism" 24.

19. For a discussion of the Nietzschean element in Zangwill's thought, see Maurice Wohlgelernter's *Israel Zangwill: A Study* (New York: Columbia UP, 1964). Sander Gilman argues in *Multiculturalism and the Jews* (New York: Routledge, 2006) that Zangwill presents "the Jew as Zarathustra" (76–77).

20. *MP* 95, 97.

21. *MP* 158, 157.

22. *MP* 184–85.

23. Sacvan Bercovitch, *The American Jeremiad* (Madison: U of Wisconsin P, 1978) 9ff.

24. *MP* 87.

25. The reversal of the Puritan typology was a common device by which Jewish writers and activists sought to claim a hallowed place for themselves within America (see Michael P. Kramer's "New English Typology and the Jewish Question," *Studies in Puritan American Spirituality* 3 [December 1992]: 97–124). Orm Øverland analyzes such "homemaking myths" cross-culturally in *Immigrant Minds, American Identities: Making the United States Home, 1870–1930* (Champaign: U of Illinois P, 2000). For further discussion of the Jewish vision in Zangwill's drama, see Edna Nahshon's *From the Ghetto to the Melting Pot: Israel Zangwill's Jewish Plays* (Detroit: Wayne State UP, 2006) 1–3, 219–21.

26. Bederman 25–27.

27. Gail Bederman, Gary Gerstle, and Richard Slotkin emphasize the place of race conflict and battle in Roosevelt's understanding of evolution (see Bederman 178–215; Gerstle 17–32; and Slotkin, *Gunfighter Nation: The Myth of the Frontier in Twentieth-Century America* [Norman: U of Oklahoma P, 1998] 29–62). Roosevelt did indeed frequently articulate the notion of forging a superior American race through masculine race conflict. See, for instance, Roosevelt's *The Winning of the West*; "The Strenuous Life," *Works* 13:319–31; and "Expansion and Peace," *Works* 13:332–40. However, for Roosevelt, race conflict was not the only or even the preferred explanation of evolutionary progress. As he wrote in his essay "Social Evolution" (1895), "While for any progress at all there must be some rivalry in selection, . . . the rivalry of natural selection is but one of the features in progress" (*Works* 13:225. For further discussion of Roosevelt's selective use of Darwinism, see Thomas G. Dyer's superb *Theodore Roosevelt and the Idea of Race* (Baton Rouge: Louisiana State UP, 1980) 32–37.

28. For more on the violence of the melting-pot image, see Wald, *Constituting Americans* 280–81.

29. *MP* 96.

30. *MP* 96. The image of America as a mother in whose womb the immigrant is reborn dates back to J. Hector St. John de Crèvecoeur, who wrote in his *Letters from an American Farmer*: "He [an immigrant] becomes an American by being received in the broad lap of our great *Alma Mater*. Here individuals of all nations are melted into a new race of men" (39). Like Zangwill's imagery, Crèvecoeur's metaphor of men melting in the female lap can also be seen as either maternal or sexual. Werner Sollors suggests that it is both. In the lap of Alma Mater, the male immigrant must "symbolically penetrate an adopted mother-goddess in order to become a self-made man." The mother must be incestuously violated in order for the immigrant to be reborn as an American (Sollors, "The Rebirth of All Americans in the Great American Melting Pot: Notes toward the Vindication of a Rejected Popular Symbol; or: An Ethnic Variety of Religious Experience," *Prospects: The Annual of American Cultural Studies* 5 [1980]: 79–110).

31. The "logical consequence" of intermixture is intermarriage, writes Zangwill, who was himself married to a Christian Englishwoman. Israel Zangwill, *Speeches, Articles and Letters of Israel Zangwill* (London: Soncino Press, 1937) 107.

32. *MP* 184.

33. As Robert J. C. Young puts it in his study of hybridity, "Theories of race were thus also covert theories of desire" (*Colonial Desire: Hybridity in Theory, Culture and Race* [New York: Routledge, 1995] 9).

34. *MP* 170, 46.

35. Claudia Stokes, "The American Messiah: Assimilation and Cultural Exchange in Israel Zangwill's *The Melting Pot*," MA essay, Columbia U, 1994, 29–33.

36. *MP* afterword 207.

37. Not surprisingly, many in the Jewish community were outraged by what they saw as the play's advocacy of intermarriage (Nahshon 247–49).

38. *MP* 3.

39. *MP* 4.

40. *MP* 48.

41. *MP* 49.

42. Neil Larry Shumsky, "Zangwill's *The Melting Pot*: Ethnic Tensions on Stage," *American Quarterly* 27 (March 1975): 35–41; Yasmeen Abu-Laban and Victoria Lamont, "Crossing Borders: Interdisciplinarity, Immigration and the Melting Pot in the American Cultural Imaginary," *Canadian Review of American Studies* 27.2 (1997): 33–35.

43. IZ to Joseph Jacobs, 22 September 1909, Zangwill Papers, A120/407, in response to Jacobs's review, "The Tragedy of Kishineff: Israel Zangwill's 'Melting Pot,'" *American Hebrew* (10 September 1909): 407–8.

44. *MP* 97.

45. *MP* 154.

46. *MP* 155.

47. *MP* 180.

48. *MP* 180.

49. *MP* 159.

50. Ernest Renan, "What Is a Nation?" lecture delivered at the Sorbonne, 11 March 1882, trans. Martin Thom, ed. Homi K. Bhabha, *Nation and Narration* (New York: Routledge, 1990) 11.

51. Renan 15.

52. Sollors, *Beyond Ethnicity* 3–19, 74.

53. Sollors, *Beyond Ethnicity* 70, 72.

54. Roosevelt, "True Americanism" 17.

55. Theodore Roosevelt, "The Monroe Doctrine," *The Bachelor of Arts*, March 1896, *Works* 13:172.

56. The original version is reported in the *London Times* 12 October 1908: 6.

57. Reported in the *London Times* 12 October 1908: 6.

58. Clearly uncomfortable with the fact that Roosevelt held final power over his work, Zangwill feebly attempted to claim independence from his patron, insisting in interviews that it was his own reconsideration of his words, rather than pressure from the president, that led him to alter his text (see *London Times* 2 October 1908: 6). He continued to denounce American's lax attitudes toward marriage (see, for instance, "Divorce in America," *Daily Telegraph* November 1908, Zangwill Papers, A120/165). But when it came to his play, the desire to maintain Roosevelt's support clearly won out.

59. The eastern European Jewish immigrant community and many scholars writing about its experiences have often argued that Jews at this time, without a homeland of their own to divide their loyalties, could become exceptional Americans. This argument is implicit in Zangwill's decision to make David a pogrom orphan and strengthens his case for the continued admission of eastern European Jewish immigrants into the United States. As Rebecca Kobrin has recently argued, however, Jewish immigrants often longed for the lands of their birth in eastern Europe and created new strategies to remain connected with their former homes (see Kobrin's *Between Exile and Empire: Jewish Bialystock and Its Diaspora* (Bloomington: Indiana UP, forthcoming).

60. *MP* 86.

61. *MP* 67.

62. *MP* 112.

63. Jacobson, *Whiteness* 78.

64. *MP* 88.

65. Rogers Smith and Gary Gerstle, among others, have demonstrated the inherent tension between conceptions of America as a people bonded by shared race and as a people united by shared democratic ideals. Both notions, present in Roosevelt's thought and in Zangwill's play, have been shown to exist simultaneously throughout the nation's history. Civic nationalism suggests that an act of will, of embracing American values, can make one an American. Racial nationalism insists that one must be of the American race to be an American. The idea of the melting pot has often been used as a symbol for civic nationalism (Gerstle 6), of the nation's essential openness to newcomers who can join by sloughing off previous affiliations and pledging themselves wholeheartedly to America and its ideals. The fact that only certain peoples have been considered fit to melt into the nation has been seen to embody the encroachment of racial nationalism on civic ideals. What has been missed in this analysis is that the notion of the melting pot is itself a form of racial nationalism. It is more democratic than we generally think because it admits newcomers of diverse origins. But the melting pot imagines they are joining a nation defined by race. For those immigrants allowed full participation in America, it imagines and demands racial transmogrification, the alteration of their very physical composition, as a prerequisite and a means for the ultimate fulfillment of the civic ideals of "true Americanism."

66. Schultz 324–25.

67. William Z. Ripley, *The Races of Europe: A Sociological Study* (1896; London: K. Paul Trench, 1913).

68. Proponents of the idea that races cannot acclimate to new geographic regions include Ripley 586–90; Paul Topinard, *Anthropology* (1880; London: Chapman and Hall, 1890) 397; A. H. Keane, *Man Past and Present* (1899; Cambridge: Cambridge UP, 1920) 13; and Josiah Clark Nott and George

R. Gliddon, "Acclimation," *Indigenous Races of the Earth* (Philadelphia: Lippincott, 1897). For further discussion of acclimatization, see Stocking, *Race* 53–55; and Nancy Stepan, *The Idea of Race in Science: Great Britain 1800–1960* (London: Macmillan, 1982) 106.

69. One of the primary popularizers of the belief in the absolute sterility of human racial intermixtures was Josiah Clark Nott. See, for instance, his "Hybridity of Animals, Viewed in Connection with the Natural History of Mankind," in Nott and Gliddon, *Types of Mankind* (Philadelphia: Lippincott, 1854) 372–410. Werner Sollors provides a useful history of this idea in *Neither Black Nor White Yet Both: Thematic Explorations of Interracial Literature* (New York: Oxford UP, 1997) 129–35, as does Stocking, *Race* 48–50.

70. The argument that the fertility of a union depends on the degree of racial proximity between the individuals involved was articulated most influentially by Paul Broca in *On the Phenomena of Hybridity in the Genus Homo* (London: Longman, Green, 1864). According to Robert J. C. Young, who provides an excellent summary of the development of notions of hybridity, this idea dominated race theory until the 1930s (6–19).

71. Zangwill was not the first to argue for hybrid superiority. This idea had already been articulated by James Cowles Prichard in *The Natural History of Man* (1843) and others who argued that intermixing leads to increased "vigor" (Sollors, *Neither* 133–34). For discussions of Prichard and how and why his liberal view fell largely into disrepute, see George W. Stocking, *Victorian Anthropology* (New York: Free Press, 1987) 46–77; Stepan 31–46, 109–10; and Young 10–11.

72. The First Universal Races Congress, held at the University of London, 26–29 July 1911, was a self-proclaimed "assemblage of all the races of the world. Accordingly there will be papers presented on China, Japan Turkey, Persia, the Jewish race, India, Egypt, Haitie, the American Negro and Indian, and the Negro of the West and South Africa." Papers were written by "a member of the particular people or race concerned." The stated goal of the congress was "to discuss, in light of modern knowledge and modern conscience, the general relations subsisting between these various races, with a view to encouraging between them a fuller understanding, the most friendly feelings, and a heartier cooperation" ("The First Universal Races Congress. An Appeal," Zangwill Papers, A120/484). Asked to represent the Jewish race, Zangwill agreed, but he protested the lumping together of Jews with "a list of races mainly coloured." Critiquing the very premise of the Congress, he added: "This list lends to the Races Congress an air of condescension on the part of the dominant white. Surely this is a mistake, and a paper or two should be added on such curious races as say the English and the Germans" (IZ to George Spiller, 23 January 1911, Zangwill Papers, A120/484). Zangwill resented the ways in which Jews were de-Westernized and nonwhite races were exoticized by the European coordinators of the meeting, who took for granted that their own races were the norm and therefore not objects of curiosity. In his speech he would attack assumptions that the races featured in the Congress were significantly different or less human than others.

73. Claims that racial intermixture was impossible or degenerative generally stemmed from what George Stocking Jr. has identified as a resurgence of polygenic thinking in the late nineteenth and early twentieth centuries (*Race* 42–68).

Polygenism—the belief that the races of humanity stem from different ancestors, or, more moderately, the belief that the races diverged so early in the evolution of humanity as to make them entirely different species or types—made the crossing of distinct race lines seem a biological danger or impossibility. Employed in the American context, polygenism and the distinction it made between closely (eugenesic) and distantly (dysgenesic) related races was used by many immigration restrictionists to argue for the need to keep out peoples who would weaken the American stock, including the "new immigrants" from eastern and southern Europe (*Race* 50).

74. Israel Zangwill, *The Problem of the Jewish Race* (New York: Judean Publishing Company, 191[2]) 15–16.

75. For an excellent discussion of representations of the Jew as actor or dissembler in English culture, see James Shapiro, *Shakespeare and the Jews* (New York: Columbia UP, 1996) 156–65.

76. Zangwill, *Problem* 12.

77. Zangwill, *Problem* 12. In this, Zangwill predates Woody Allen's *Zelig*, which suggests the same.

78. Zangwill, *Problem* 16.

79. Zangwill, *Problem* 16–17.

80. Zangwill, *Problem* 17.

81. Israel Zangwill, afterword, *The Melting Pot: Drama in Four Acts* (1914; New York: Macmillan, 1917) 207, 214.

82. Seeming to go back on the liberal vision of his drama, Zangwill writes in the afterword: "This is not to deny that the prognathous face is an ugly and undesirable type of countenance or that it connotes a lower average of intellect and ethics, or that white and black are as yet too far apart for profitable fusion. Melanophobia, or fear of the black, may be pragmatically as valuable a racial defense for the white as the counter-instinct of philoleucosis, or love of the white, is a force of racial uplifting for the black" (206). Never questioning the construction of the black face as ugly and as an outward sign of internal deficiencies (though he himself had been described as possessing "Negroid" features by none other than Theodore Herzl), Zangwill understands repulsion as a positive inborn instinct that safeguards the white race (*The Complete Diaries of Theodore Herzl*, ed. Raphael Pati, trans. Harry Zohn [New York: Herzl Press and Thomas Yoseloff, 1960] 276). As the opposite of the desire that fuels the melting pot, white repulsion will keep blacks out. But though he speaks about disgust in biological terms, Zangwill does recognize that it is largely an emotion born of social prejudice. "Indeed it is as much social prejudice as racial antipathy that to-day divides black and white in the New World," he writes, and "the accusations against the black are largely panic-born myths.... The devil is not so black nor the black so devilish as he is painted" (205). Citing the "large minority" of blacks and whites who have interbred throughout the world, Zangwill claims that prejudice, not preservational instinct, plays the primary role in keeping blacks and whites apart in the United States, and he insists that "it is equally certain that there are at work forces of attraction as well as of repulsion, and that even upon the Negro the 'Melting Pot' of America will not fail to act" (205).

83. Zangwill, afterword, 205.

84. IZ to Joseph Jacobs, 22 September 1909, Zangwill Papers, A120/407.

85. *MP* 72.

86. Amy Leslie, writing for the *Chicago Daily News*, criticized Zangwill for including "grotesque little religious ceremonies," "puerile and frivolous" with "callous respect for all

sorts of religious eccentricities even unto the putting on of long hooked false noses by men and women in the Jewish feast of all souls," which she believes is offensive to both Jewish and Christian audience members ("Gave Play at Grand," Review of *The Melting Pot*, *Chicago Daily News* 21 October 1908). The reviewer for the *Inter Ocean* considered the noses "undignified," making one think of "Punch and Judy" (21 October 1908, Zangwill Papers, A120/165). The *New York Times* felt that Zangwill was insincere in his depiction of the Jewish people and their customs, using them for comic relief with "cheap humor ... emphasized by the employment of abnormally large false noses, designed to make the Christians howl with merriment" (Adolph Klauber, "A Spread Eagle Play by Israel Zangwill," *New York Times* 2 September 1909: 10). Another reviewer for the same paper expressed doubt whether even Zangwill, "with exceptional opportunity for studying the race, has ever seen a typical orthodox mother in Israel making merry on Purim with an Irish housemaid as companion in the dance and a false nose to emphasize a racial trait" ("New Zangwill Play Cheap and Tawdry," *New York Times* 7 September 1909: 9).

87. James 92.

88. The *Baltimore Jewish Comment* wrote: "There is [sic] also a lot of Jewish customs dragged in by the heels, mystifying the non-Jew and repelling the Jew, whether orthodox or assimilationist" (9 October 1908: 1). This reviewer was upset not only by the grotesque noses but by the representation of Jewish customs within the play altogether. "Jews will ask themselves, what does Mr. Zangwill mean by compelling a character to mumble upon the English stage blessings in Hebrew? To the non-Jew they are so much gibberish, signifying nothing. To the Jew they are disgusting—caricatures painful in the extreme," he or she writes. "No Jewish practices, perhaps, are too sacred to be seriously treated on the stage; the fault here is that serious treatment was intended and there is only bewilderment or repulsion" (1).

89. Abu-Laban and Lamont 34.

90. Israel Zangwill, "A Land of Refuge," 8 December 1907, Manchester Hippodrome, *Speeches* 241.

91. In his article "Zangwill's *The Melting Pot*: Ethnic Tensions on Stage," Neil Shumsky analyzes Zangwill's idea of America as the site of a universalized Judaism, but he sees this as separate from race (40).

92. Israel Zangwill, *Chosen Peoples: The Hebraic Ideal versus the Teutonic* (New York: Macmillan, 1919) 37.

93. Israel Zangwill, *Voice of Jerusalem* (New York: Macmillan, 1921) 9.

94. Israel Zangwill, "The Ghetto," c. 1890, *Speeches* 27.

95. The idea of a universal Judaism centered in America and transmitted by a new people seems completely at odds with Zangwill's simultaneous support of the Zionist cause. One calls for the complete "denationalization" of Jewishness and the other for "renationalization" of the Jewish people in an autonomous land (Zangwill, "Zion, Whence Cometh My Help," July 1903, *Speeches*, 81). Many critics have been puzzled by the fact that Zangwill worked simultaneously promoting both amalgamation and racial self-preservation within a homeland. Most reconcile the apparent contradiction by claiming that Zangwill envisioned one solution for cosmopolitan Jews like himself, and the other for the ghetto Jews of eastern Europe desperate to escape from persecution and seeking to preserve their traditional ways (see, for instance, Joseph H. Udelson, *Dreamer of the Ghetto: The Life and Works of Israel Zangwill* [Tuscaloosa: U of Alabama P,

1990] 151–89). Many scholars argue further that Zangwill's bifurcated solution to the problem of Jewish oppression reveals his own conflict between the desire to lose his Jewishness, epitomized by his marriage with the Christian British author Edith Ayrton, and the desire to recapture and retain the spirit of Judaism that nourished him as a child (Udelson 1–10; Wohlgelernter 20–30; Arthur Mann, "The Melting Pot," *Uprooted Americans: Essays to Honor Oscar Handlin*, ed. Richard L. Bushman, Neil Harris, David Rothman, et al. [Boston: Little, Brown, 1979] 295).

Though clearly in tension, these two aspects of Zangwill's life and social commitments were not completely at odds. Though he married a Christian woman and raised his children without any religion, he and his wife were personally dedicated to building a Jewish state. "I am not a Jewess. I am an English woman," Edith Ayrton Zangwill told the *New York Sun* in 1904, tellingly defining Englishness as excluding the Jew. "But," she continued, "if—or when—the [Zionist] scheme becomes an established fact we intend to make our home wherever the colony for the Jews shall have been established" ("Mr. Zangwill Discusses His Plays and Tells Why He Is Against Happy Endings," *New York Sun* November 1904: 9). The Zangwill family sought to combine both alternatives within their own lives and within the life of the Jewish people.

For Zangwill, the alternatives of amalgamation and Jewish territorialism stemmed from the same notion of race and mission. Believing in the morality and essential justice of the Jewish race soul, he wished to disseminate its message through all possible means. He felt that Jews must merge their blood and racial culture with those of the rest of the world as a way of promulgating and universalizing Jewish ideals. In this scheme, America, a land built on a Hebraic ethics and a place where all blood types are coming together into one new race, would be the center of Hebraism, serving as a beacon to the world. At the same time, he believed that the Jewish race must persist and be allowed to develop in its own direction on its own land. "In short it was the Jewish spirit that founded America. But where was the Jewish spirit in the Jews?" he asks (*The East African Question: Zionism and England's Offer* rpt. from *The Maccabaean* [New York: Maccabaean, December 1904], 55). "The comedy and tragedy of Jewish existence to-day derive primarily from the absence of a territory in which the race could live its own life" (*Problem* 8). The purpose of a Jewish state for Zangwill is not only to provide a haven for oppressed Jews throughout the world but to preserve and develop the unique features of the Jewish race, to "save the Jew's body and the Jew's soul" (*East African Question* 18–19).

The result of Zangwill's twin visions, then, would be the creation of two cities upon a hill: one in the soon to be founded Jewish land, in which the Jewish race itself would actualize its moral mission, establishing "not only a colony, but an object lesson in civilization" ("A Land of Refuge" 245), and the other in the United States, where Hebraic ideals would be universalized and promulgated by a mixed race combining the dominant features of all its elements. Zangwill's hopes for the future of the Jew, America, and indeed the world rely on his faith that what is most evolved and/or genetically dominant will be perpetuated within both distinct nations and hybrid nations.

96. Theodore Roosevelt, "General Sheridan," *Works* 11:222.

97. Roosevelt, "Children of the Crucible" 30.

98. Dyer 37–44.

99. Peter Bowler, *The Eclipse of Darwinism: Anti-Darwinian Evolution Theories in the Decades around 1900* (Baltimore: Johns Hopkins UP, 1983) 62–63.

100. Stocking, *Race* 47; Dyer 43.

101. As Roosevelt put it, "Society progresses . . . due mainly to the transmission of acquired characters, a process which in every civilized state operates so strongly as to counterbalance the operation of that baleful law of natural selection" ("National Life and Character," *Works*, memorial edition, 14:249). Many historians and critics have identified Roosevelt with eugenics. (See, for instance, John Nickel, "Eugenics and the Fiction of Pauline Hopkins," *Evolution and Eugenics in American Literature and Culture, 1880–1940: Essays on Ideological Conflict and Complicity*, ed. Lois A. Cuddy and Claire M. Roche [Lewisburg: Bucknell UP, 2003] 137; Michael E. McGerr, *A Fierce Discontent: The Rise and Fall of the Progressive Movement in America, 1870–1920* [New York: Simon and Schuster, 2003] 214; Edward John Larson, *Sex, Race, and Science: Eugenics in the Deep South* [Baltimore: Johns Hopkins UP, 1995] 30; among others). But though he did understand Americanness, at least in part, racially, and he did worry about insufficient childbearing, Roosevelt's notion of race was not based in genetics, as was theirs, complicating his affinities with some of their practices.

102. Dyer 33.

103. Roosevelt, "Biological Analogies in History," 1910, *Literary Essays* (New York: Pavilion Press, 2004) 51.

104. Thomas Kuhn, *The Structure of Scientific Revolutions* (1962; Chicago: U of Chicago P, 1996) 66–91; Bowler 11.

105. Roosevelt, "Biological Analogies" 37.

106. Roosevelt, "Biological Analogies" 50.

107. Dyer 42–44; Bederman 29.

108. It is interesting to note that Roosevelt wrote the preface to Emmett J. Scott and Lyman B. Stowe's biography of Washington, *Booker T. Washington, Builder of a Civilization* (Garden City: Doubleday, Page, 1916) ix–xv. He refused, however, to provide similar support for *The Autobiography of an Ex-Colored Man* (1912, rpt. in *Three Negro Classics* [New York: Avon, 1965]), published anonymously by James Weldon Johnson. Johnson had written the 1904 campaign song "You're All Right, Teddy" for Roosevelt, and Roosevelt's close friend Professor Brander Matthews had appealed to Roosevelt on Johnson's behalf, but he would not publicly back the work. As he wrote to Matthews, after much urging by the professor, "I read the autobiography you sent me and was much impressed by it. Ugh! There is not any more puzzling a problem in this country than the problem of color. It is not as urgent, or as menacing, as other problems, but it seems more utterly insoluble. The trouble is that the conflict in many of its phases is not between right and wrong, but between two rights" (TR to Matthews, 7 January 1913, in Oliver, *Letters* 200). Roosevelt was willing to support Washington's moderate approach to "the problem of color" but not Johnson's fictional account of passing that questioned the very assumptions on which racial qualifications for Americanism were based.

109. The place of the African American in Roosevelt's vision of the United States deserves further attention. More complete discussions can be found in Amy Kaplan's "Black and Blue on San Juan Hill," *Cultures of US Imperialism*, ed. Amy Kaplan and Donald E. Pease (Durham: Duke UP, 1993) 219–36; Willard B. Gatewood Jr., *"Smoked Yankees" and the Struggle for Empire: Letters from Negro Soldiers 1898–1902* (Fayetteville,

U of Arkansas Press, 1987); and Gatewood's *Theodore Roosevelt and the Art of Controversy: Episodes of the White House Years* (Baton Rouge: Louisiana State UP, 1970), as well as in Gerstle 14–43, Smith 410–60, and Dyer 89–122.

110. Roosevelt, "True Americanism" 23.

111. Roosevelt, *Autobiography* 372.

112. [Roosevelt,] "Men," *Ladies' Home Journal* March 1917: 24.

113. TR to IZ, 27 November 1912, Roosevelt Papers.

114. For an analysis of the shifting and variable meanings of the term the "melting pot," see Philip Gleason's "Melting-Pot: Symbol of Fusion or Confusion," *American Quarterly* 16 (1964): 20–46; and his later "Confusion Compounded: The Melting Pot in the 1960s and 1970s," *Ethnicity* 6 (1979): 10–20.

CHAPTER 2

1. Jacob A. Riis, *The Making of an American* (1901; New York: Macmillan, 1928) 256. All citations to *Making* refer to this edition unless otherwise indicated.

2. Theodore Roosevelt, introduction, *The Making of an American*.

3. Roosevelt, "True Americanism" 23–24.

4. Theodore Roosevelt, "Americanism," October 1915, *Works* 18:392–93.

5. Roosevelt, "International Duty and Hyphenated Americanism," *Works* 18:278.

6. Kobrin. A multitude of studies exists examining the experience of immigrants at the turn of the twentieth century and beyond from the perspective of uprootedness and adjustment. Two examples from different eras are Oscar Handlin's classic *The Uprooted: The Epic Story of the Great Migrations That Made the American People* (1951; Boston: Little, Brown, 1996) and Ronald Takaki's *A Different Mirror: A History of Multicultural America* (Boston: Little, Brown, 1994). Recent studies that begin to examine the question of transnationalism during this period include Matthew Frye Jacobson, *Special Sorrows: The Diasporic Imagination of Irish, Polish and Jewish Immigrants in the United States* (Cambridge: Harvard UP, 1995); Kerby Miller, *Emigrants and Exiles: Ireland and the Irish Exodus to North America* (New York: Oxford UP, 1985); Nancy Foner, *From Ellis Island to JFK: New York's Two Great Waves of Immigration* (New Haven: Yale UP, 2000).

7. For discussions of contemporary transnationalism, see, for instance, Robin Cohen's *Global Diasporas: An Introduction* (Seattle: U of Washington P, 1997); Jana Evans Braziel and Anita Mannur's *Theorizing Diaspora* (New York: Blackwell, 2003); and the works of Nina Glick Schiller, Linda Basch, and Cristina Szanton Blanc, including *Towards a Transnational Perspective on Migration: Race, Class, Ethnicity and Nationalism Reconsidered* (New York: New York Academy of Sciences, 1992); *Nations Unbound: Transnational Projects, Postcolonial Predicaments, and Deterritorialized Nation States* (New York: Gordon and Breach, 1994); and "From Immigrant to Transmigrant: Theorizing Transnational Migration," *Anthropological Quarterly* 68.1 (1995): 48–63. For the impact of transnationalism on U.S. literature, see Inderpal Grewal, *Transnational America: Feminisms, Diasporas, Neoliberalism* (Durham: Duke UP, 2005); Coleen Glenney Boggs, *Transnationalism and American Literature* (New York: Routledge, 2007), among others.

8. Riis, *Making* 255–56. Riis frequently describes his fervent patriotism to both countries in terms of love of both flags. See, for instance, *Making* 29: "All the hot blood of youth was surging through me. I

remembered the defeat, the humiliation of the flag I loved—aye! and love yet, for there is no flag like the flag of my fathers, save only that of my children and of my manhood." As Priscilla Wald notes in *Constituting Americans*, Riis draws on the preponderance of rituals surrounding the American flag in this era (251). But he also uses these nationalist images, familiar to his American readers, to express his simultaneous loyalty to Denmark. It is striking that Riis does not limit his claims of the value of dual loyalty, symbolized by double flags, to himself or even to Danes. He writes in *The Battle with the Slum* (1902; New York: Dover, 1998): "You cannot have too much of the flag in the right way.... Just go into one of the Children's Aid Society's ragged schools, where the children are practically all from abroad and see how they take to it. Watch an Italian parade, in which it is always borne side by side with the standard of United Italy, and if you had any doubts about what it stands for you will change your mind quickly.... And it looks fine in the landscape always. It always makes me think there that I added to the red and white of my fathers' flag only the blue of heaven, where wrongs are righted, and I feel better for it. Why should it not have the same effect on others? I know it has" (210–11). Although he emphasizes the symbolic importance of the U.S. flag to immigrants in this passage, Riis recognizes that love of the United States does not replace love of native land in the immigrant's heart but is added to it, and, as we shall see, he embraces and encourages this cumulative approach to patriotism.

9. Jacob Riis, *Hero Tales of the Far North* (1910; New York: Macmillan, 1919) viii. All subsequent citations to this text refer to this edition.

10. The title *Hero Tales of the Far North* links this text to Roosevelt's own *Hero Tales from American History*, which he wrote with Henry Cabot Lodge in 1895. In their introduction to this work, Lodge and Roosevelt spell out the virtues they wish to teach by example with this book. "Its purpose ... is to tell in simple fashion the story of some Americans who showed that they knew how to live and how to die; ... and who joined to the stern and manly qualities which are essential to the well-being of a masterful race the virtues of gentleness, of patriotism, and of lofty adherence to an ideal.... No citizen of a free State should wrong any man; but it is not enough merely to refrain from infringing on the rights of others; he must also be able and willing to stand up for his own rights and those of his country" (*Works* 10:xxiii–xxiv). These ideals of manliness, patriotism, and defense of individual and national rights exemplified in a "master race" are, as we shall later see, what Riis also attempts to display as inherent in the heroes of his northern tales and the citizens of his homeland.

11. Theodore Roosevelt, introduction, *The Making of an American* (New York: Macmillan, 1928) 256. This introduction is a reprint of Roosevelt's obituary "Jacob Riis," *Outlook* 6 June 1914: 284.

12. Immediately after Roosevelt's inauguration as vice president, Riis wrote to him, "My dear Colonel, Or what shall I call you now? Vice President is so long. Colonel is good, and I like it" (27 March 1901). After Roosevelt's terms as president (at which time Riis addressed him as Mr. President), Riis, like many other Americans, went back to calling him "Colonel," seeming to find this title most evocative of the masculine, fighting image Roosevelt cultivated and Riis valued and helped promote. As for Roosevelt's calling him "Jake," Riis wrote in *Theodore Roosevelt the Citizen* (New York:

Outlook, 1904): "He may call me Jake and I like nothing better. But though I am ten years older than he, he was always Mr. Roosevelt to me" (9). This claim reveals an imbalance in the dynamics of power between the immigrant writer and the president that all their declarations of friendship and mutual admiration never erased.

13. Riis, *Theodore Roosevelt* 131. See also Riis, *Making* 212.

14. TR to Jacob Riis (JR), 11 June 1903, Roosevelt Papers. Unless otherwise noted, all quotations from the Roosevelt–Riis correspondence are taken from this collection.

15. See, for example, Roosevelt's letters and description of letters to Leonard Wood and Gifford Pinchot on Riis's behalf (TR to JR regarding letter to Wood, 17 February 1900; TR to Pinchot, 16 April 1901).

16. "There was never a better American than Jacob Riis, who was born in Denmark and whom I always thought about the best American I ever knew." Theodore Roosevelt, "International Duty and Hyphenated Americanism," *Works* 18:280–81.

17. Jacob Riis, *How the Other Half Lives* (1890; New York: Dover, 1971) 1.

18. Riis, *How the Other Half Lives* 2.

19. Riis, *How the Other Half Lives* 229.

20. Riis, *How the Other Half Lives* 143.

21. Riis, *How the Other Half Lives* 137.

22. Riis, *How the Other Half Lives* 2.

23. TR to JR, 25 October 1897.

24. The Lexow Committee was appointed by the New York legislature in March 1894 to investigate Rev. Charles Parkhurst's allegations of extreme corruption in the New York Police Department. Its shocking findings led to the temporary ouster of Tammany government from New York City and the election of Republican mayor William Strong in November 1894. Strong selected Roosevelt to spearhead police reform. (Actually, Strong originally tapped Roosevelt for the position of sanitation commissioner, but Roosevelt refused.) For more on Parkhurst, police corruption, the Lexow Committee, and Roosevelt's term as police commissioner, see, for instance, Jacob Riis and Lincoln Steffens's autobiographies; H. Paul Jeffers's *Commissioner Roosevelt: The Story of Theodore Roosevelt and the New York City Police, 1895–1897* (New York: Wiley, 1994); Edmund Morris's *The Rise of Theodore Roosevelt* (New York: Coward, McCann, and Geoghegan, 1979); David McCullough's *Mornings on Horseback: The Story of an Extraordinary Family, a Vanished Way of Life, and the Unique Child Who Became Theodore Roosevelt* (1981; New York: Simon and Schuster, 2001); and Paul Grondahl's *"I Rose Like a Rocket": The Political Education of Theodore Roosevelt* (New York: Free Press, 2004).

25. Roosevelt, *Autobiography* 83.

26. Lincoln Steffens, *The Autobiography of Lincoln Steffens* (1931; New York: Harcourt, Brace, and World, 1958) 257–58.

27. Roosevelt, *Autobiography* 176–77.

28. For a discussion of Roosevelt's uses of the press, see Harry H. Stein, "Theodore Roosevelt and the Press: Lincoln Steffens," *Mid-America* 54 (April 1972): 94–197. See also, Morris, *Rise of Theodore Roosevelt* 501–11; H. W. Brands, *TR: The Last Romantic* (New York: Basic Books, 1997) 280–81; Nathan Miller, *Theodore Roosevelt: A Life* (New York: William Morrow, 1992) 232–33; John Milton Cooper, *The Warrior and the Priest: Woodrow Wilson and Theodore Roosevelt* (Cambridge: Harvard UP, 1983); Jeffers 155–58; and Jeffrey Tulis, *The Rhetorical Presidency* (Princeton: Princeton UP, 1987).

29. *World*, 22 May 1895, as quoted in Morris, *Rise of Theodore Roosevelt* 488. James J. Connolly argues that publicity was

one of the hallmarks of progressive politics, which rather than drawing on partisan loyalties, used mass media to appeal to individual voters. In particular, candidates sought to create an image of themselves as spokespeople for the "community at large" or "the people" against corruption and special interest. See Connolly's *Triumph of Ethnic Progressivism* 3–5, 105, 133–38.

30. Virtually every biography of Roosevelt recounts this incident, including Riis's *Theodore Roosevelt* 144ff.

31. Morris, *Rise of Theodore Roosevelt* 494.

32. Kathleen Dalton, among others, argues that Roosevelt's police work and his work with Riis shaped his view of immigrants (*Theodore Roosevelt: A Strenuous Life* [New York: Vintage, 2003]) 158. Roosevelt suggests the same in his article "How I Became a Progressive" (1921), where he writes, "Looking back, it seems to me that I made my greatest strides forward while I was police commissioner, and this largely through my intimacy with Jacob Riis, for he opened all kinds of windows into the matter for me" (*Works* 17:317).

33. Roosevelt, *Autobiography* 174.

34. The closings of the police lodging houses and the Hearst soup kitchens, for instance, were condemned by many who saw these measures as hurting the poor by taking away much-needed free lodging and food.

35. TR to JR, 12 June 1899.

36. Though suffering from ultimately fatal heart disease, Riis traveled to Michigan in May 1913 to testify to Roosevelt's sobriety in a libel suit brought by the former president against a newspaper accusing him of perpetual drunkenness.

37. In *Theodore Roosevelt the Citizen*, Riis works assiduously to correct Roosevelt's public image. He attempts to prove that Roosevelt is not rash and pugilistic (33–34, 158–60) and not a posturing politician, but that he is consistent in his private and political life and actually does not know how to dissimulate (55, 65, 68 89, 292, 345–47, 352, 413). Riis also argues that contrary to the claims that the president is not religious, Roosevelt believes in basic Christian principles (305–7), and despite claims that he is not impartial, he is fair to both labor and capital and does not favor either (371–82). Riis also defends many of Roosevelt's actions, including his part in the anthracite coal strike of 1902 (373–80), his efforts to build a canal in Panama (384), and his decision to invite Booker T. Washington to dinner in the White House (369–70). His book is clearly a defense of Roosevelt, and one which Roosevelt embraced.

38. The two men constantly apologize for imposing, but they continue to ask favors of each other all the time. See, for instance, Roosevelt's apology to Riis (27 December 1899): "Mrs. Roosevelt and I feel that we impose upon your friendship often in asking you about these charitable cases. The trouble is, old man, that when one is really good, he is sure to be imposed upon by his friends." Riis writes in a similar tone on 15 January 1900: "I am sorry to add as much as one feather's weight to your cares at this time, with a fight carving up the state, but I should not serve you faithfully if I reported otherwise."

39. TR to JR, 4 August 1900.

40. TR to JR, 12 November 1902.

41. JR to TR, 23 November 1900.

42. At the same time that Jacob Riis raised his class status in America, Elisabeth's status had fallen in Denmark. She had been engaged to a lieutenant in the Danish army, a match her family approved of until the man, many years her senior,

contracted tuberculosis. Against her parent's wishes, Elisabeth insisted on going to live with her fiancé's family near the sanitarium where he lay dying. After his death, her parents would not accept her back into their household and urged her to support herself as a governess. When Jacob heard of the death of Elisabeth's fiancé, he wrote to her mother of his intentions to marry Elisabeth, and her parents, who had once opposed his suit, now encouraged their daughter to accept it. This turn of events indicates that Riis became acceptable to the Gjortz family not so much because America had enhanced his status but because a failed engagement had lowered Elisabeth's. In fact, for many in Ribe, emigration to America was seen as a betrayal, not as an act of self-improvement.

43. See Edith Patterson Meyer's *"Not Charity, but Justice"; The Story of Jacob A. Riis* (New York: Vanguard, 1974) 120.

44. See Kate Riis Owre's letter to Riis's biographer Louise Ware, 6 December 1934. Unless otherwise indicated, citations to all of the Riis family and personal correspondence, with the exception of letters to and from Roosevelt, have been taken from the Jacob A. Riis Collection at the Library of Congress.

45. JR to Emma Riis, 1 April [1907]. In this letter, Riis writes to his sister back in Ribe, "Clara reads Danish easily. I wish I had given all our children a thorough knowledge of our language." Citations from the correspondence between Emma and Jacob Riis are from the English translations accompanying their Danish letters in this collection.

46. Roosevelt, "True Americanism" 24.

47. The king bestowed this medal upon Riis shortly after a meeting of the two at the palace, at which time "he asked me about the Danes in America and I told him they were good citizens, better for not forgetting their motherland and him. . . . He patted my hand with a glad little laugh, and bade me tell them how much he appreciated it, and how kindly his thoughts were of them all" (*Making* 276). Riis seeks to use his good American citizenship to win acceptance not only in the United States but in Denmark as well. He feels that the people of Ribe who knew him as a failed carpenter and failed lover during his adolescence view his emigration as abandonment of home and country, and he wishes to justify himself to them through his actions and fame in the United States. Writing in *The Old Town* of how at a royal banquet in Ribe, King Christian rose to drink to Jacob Riis, Riis admits:

> I was never so proud in all my days. For there sat my old townsmen, with whom I had been, shall we say, just a bit off-color in spite of all, because I did not do according to the rules, but broke over the traces every way, and went off to America to do mercy knows what outlandish stunts in the way of earning a living. There they sat now, in their own town, and saw the King himself toast me before their very faces! I did think my measure was full when I beheld the President of the United States take my wife in to dinner in the White House—I know I nearly burst with pride in her and in him— but now indeed, it was running over.

And years later he writes to his sister Emma how he is looking forward to Theodore Roosevelt's planned trip to Denmark "because I am sure he will not let an opportunity pass without saying a word about our friendship" (19 April 1910). Having the most powerful men of both his countries recognize and praise him for his good citizenship is Riis's greatest desire and strongest affirmation of his success.

48. Riis, *Making* 274. Riis describes this incident in his letter to Elisabeth of 8 April 1904 and in *Theodore Roosevelt the Citizen* (281–82), though he changes the story from a White House breakfast to a dinner. In the campaign biography Riis portrays the incident not as a bold declaration of Danish nationalism but as an embarrassing breech of etiquette: he had believed wearing the cross would "do [Roosevelt] the highest honor" but quickly discovered that not even the diplomats at the table wore any sort of decoration. Sensing his embarrassment, the president approached his old friend and whispered to him that he was honored by the cross and understood Riis's motives for wearing it. "So he knew, and it was all right. The others might stare. It is just an instance of the loyalty that is one of the traits in the man which bind you to him with hoops of steel once you are close to him," Riis explains. With these words, Riis transforms this story of his self-identification as a knight of the Danish crown into a paean to Roosevelt, illustrating the great sensitivity of the president, which makes him deserving of the people's highest loyalty.

49. In his pivotal work, *Special Sorrows*, Matthew Frye Jacobson makes this important distinction between symbolic ethnicity and diasporic nationalism, focusing on the political content of many immigrants' ethnic identities and complicating the notion of Americanization (220–22, 230–40).

50. The history of Slesvig, or Schleswig in German, is far more complex than Riis ever acknowledges in his English writings. This duchy, whose population consisted of both ethnic Danes, primarily in the north, and ethnic Germans, primarily in the south, had been a site of contest between the German states and Denmark from the eleventh century through World War I. The will of its people in the nineteenth century was divided among those who wished complete incorporation into Denmark and others who wished complete incorporation into the German Confederation, loose affiliation with either or both of these governments, or union with the neighboring duchy of Holstein and national independence from both Germany and Denmark. The fate of the region in this period was ultimately determined by Bismarck's 1864 defeat of the Danish army and his subsequent absorption of Slesvig-Holstein into the German Confederation. With this defeat, the Danish government turned inward, seeking to build up its own economy rather than fighting for lost territory—a choice that infuriated Danes like Riis, who praised the development of the Danish heath but demanded also the restoration of Danish land and pride through military conquest and expressed their nationalism by championing Slesvig as a cause. See, for instance, Jacob A. Riis, "Children of the Danish Heath," *Century* (July 1912): 449–54; and Riis, *Making* 254–55. For a complete history of the region, which is fascinating both in itself and for the biases it reveals in Riis's presentation of the issue to his American audience, see W. Glyn Jones's *Denmark: A Modern History* (London: Croom Helm, 1986) 3–73; Palle Lauring's *A History of the Kingdom of Denmark*, trans. David Hohnen (Copenhagen: Host and Son, 1968) 211–38; and Waldemar Westergaard's *Denmark and Slesvig, 1848–1864* (London: Oxford UP, 1946).

51. Riis, *Making* 29.

52. Roosevelt, "True Americanism" 24.

53. Riis, *Making* 255.

54. For other examples of Riis's requests on behalf of Danish immigrants, see JR to TR, 2 July 1901 and 11 February 1908; and Elisabeth Riis to TR on behalf of the American legation in Copenhagen, 16 January 1905. The fact that Danish immigrants solicited Riis's aid indicates that they viewed him as a prominent Danish American with connections in high places. (Riis also complained that they mistakenly believed he was wealthy and could help them financially.) Wherever he went in the United States, Riis was perceived as a Danish American, or, ironically—considering his nationalist antipathy—as a German-American. In Riverside, California, for instance, he was greeted with Danish and U.S. flags and a band playing "King Christian" celebrating Riis's hyphenated identity (JR to Elisabeth Riis, 4 January 1905).

55. LM Jacobsen to JR, 8 April 1901, enclosed by Riis in 11 April 1901 letter to Roosevelt, Roosevelt Presidential Papers. Most Danish emigration to America in the late nineteenth century came from Slesvig and southern Denmark, where, according to George R. Nielsen, in addition to economic factors, "the unwillingness to undergo Germanization combined with the disillusionment with Denmark and a loss of faith in the future caused many Danes to think of migration" (*The Danish Americans* [Boston: Twayne, 1984] 27).

56. JR to TR, 13 April 1901.

57. TR to JR, 16 April 1901.

58. Elisabeth Riis to TR, 19 February 1905.

59. Jacob Riis, *The Old Town* (New York: Macmillan, 1909) 265. According to Jacob, in this version of the story, the prince said of Dagmar, "You may believe that if my sister had the influence you think, many a burden would be eased for that unhappy people."

60. The letter from this inquiring woman was destroyed, but its content can be surmised from Riis's response. Much to the frustration of his family after his death, Riis, as a rule, destroyed almost all the correspondence he received (see Emma Riis to Kate Riis Owre, 27 May 1917). He saved only letters that he considered extremely meaningful—such as Elisabeth's letter accepting his hand—or from exceptionally prominent people, including Roosevelt.

61. JR to anonymous, 23 September 1903.

62. Sollors, *Beyond Ethnicity* 149.

63. Sollors, *Beyond Ethnicity* 149–73.

64. Riis, *Making* 5.

65. Roosevelt, "Monroe Doctrine" 172.

66. Riis, *Making* 152. Sollors provides multiple examples of the image of the ethnic wife as a reminder of the male immigrant's past. As in Abraham Cahan's *Yekl: A Tale of the New York Ghetto*, where marriage is an old-world arrangement, the ethnic wife often stands in for descent relationships (Sollors, *Beyond Ethnicity* 157). But Riis uses his ethnic wife, Elisabeth, to represent the male immigrant's fantasy of a successful synthesis of both his worlds.

67. The reality of Riis's home life was far from the way he made it appear in his writings. His son John frequently ran away from home and school and later could not or would not hold down a job. Three of his children had failed marriages, with at least two ending ultimately in divorce. Florence Riis, wife of the eldest child, Edward, refused to establish a home and insisted on living in boardinghouses—one of the very things Riis had strongly campaigned against in his writings, where he declared: "Ours, to fulfill its destiny, must be a nation of homes. Down with the boarding-house!" (*Making* 115). Florence also refused to have children and had at least four abortions

(JR to John, 19 September 1911), flouting what Roosevelt declared to the nation as the primary responsibility of the American woman. Riis himself attempted to break up the marriage of his eldest daughter, Clara, to Dr. William Fiske, who had trouble supporting his family and frequently turned to his father-in-law for money. In 1909, Riis forced the separation of Clara and her husband until Dr. Fiske worked his way out of debt, and he posted surveillance on his daughter in California to be sure that she had no contact with her husband (A. Bradford to JR, 22 August 1909, Jacob A. Riis Collection, New York Public Library [NYPL]). "Shame on you! And you posing as a high minded doer of good! What must your sainted Elisabeth think of you," scrawled the enraged Dr. Fiske to Riis, whom he saw as little more than a hypocrite (William C. Fiske to JR, 12 August 1909, Riis Collection, NYPL; all extant letters between Riis and Dr. Fiske are found in this collection).

There is no doubt that this was far from an ideal family, yet Riis creates a myth of blissful domesticity. Riis never refers to any of his family in his later public writings and actively seeks to perpetuate the earlier image of his idyllic family, focusing in later years on the farm he bought with his second wife, Mary, and on his youngest son, William, or Vivi, as Riis called him, who of all the boys had the best relationship with his father.

Why all the secrecy about his family? Riis saw his children as a threat to his claims of expertise on questions of family and the home. In a letter to John in February 1904, for instance, Riis says: "From letters just received from your mother, I learn that you are now in Denver.... When I was there I spoke to a mighty audience of young men, and laid down the life rules of a decent, orderly and useful life for them. It is up to you, John, to show them that in our family we practice as we preach, or try to" (JR to John Riis, 28 February 1904). Fearing for his own reputation and authority, Riis never mentions John's problems, or Clara's husband, or Ed and Florence's lack of home life to his readers. Not that the public was entitled to know of such personal details, but when writing of his home, Riis insists on portraying it as the opposite of what it really was. He needed the world to believe that his was an idyllic home from which "proceeds civic virtue." And his readers largely believed this portrayal. As Edith Kellogg Dunton wrote in her review of *The Making of an American* for *The Dial*, "How fatal it would be should his readers miss seeing that here is a man whose house of life has no back door and no alley windows. The whole of Mr. Riis is in his book, then, and the real Mr. Riis" (1 January 1902: 8).

68. Riis, *Making* 2.

69. For a discussion of Riis's use of romanticism and sentimentality combined with realism in *How the Other Half Lives*, see David Leviatin in "Framing the Poor: The Irresistibility of How the Other Half Lives," introduction to *How the Other Half Lives* (New York: Bedford, 1996) 8, 33, 40.

70. Riis's use of sentimentalism and melodrama can be seen most clearly in his tales about children and Christmas collected in *Out of Mulberry Street: Stories of Tenement Life in New York City* (New York: Century, 1898); *Children of the Tenements* (1903; Upper Saddle River, NJ: Gregg Press, 1970); *Christmas Stories* (New York: Macmillan, 1923); and *Nibsy's Christmas* (1893; Freeport: Books for Libraries Press, 1969).

71. Wald, *Constituting Americans* 279.

72. Readers were drawn to *The Making of an American* largely because of its love

story and Jake's portrayal of his wife. In one illustrative letter, Jacob wrote to Elisabeth while on a lecture tour in the Midwest: "I wish I could have you with me on a sample trip so that you might see how very large share of the welcome that greets me everywhere is for you. All the men are in love with you . . . and sometimes the women too. *I* am all right, but they *love* you. Do you say that it is as I have painted you? Yes, but I am a realist, and I paint right every time" (JR to ER from Evansville, Indiana, 21 March 1905).

When Elisabeth was sick and after her death in May 1905, Jacob received numerous letters of condolence from people who knew her and his love for her only through *Making*. Thomas Evens, secretary of the Christian Association of the University, wrote: "Your beautiful love-story told in 'The Making of an American' reached my heart as I read it some years ago—I do so like to think of you two together—so devoted—so ideal" (9 May 1905, Riis Collection, NYPL). He accepted Riis's portrayal of his marriage as reality. Interestingly, P. Kellogg of New York compared Elisabeth to a fictional character: "In 'The Making of an American,' you drew the picture of Mrs. Riis with such a kindling touch that to one who did not know her outside those pages, her death came with the sadness of some gentle heroine of fiction whom you have known and loved through many chapters" (18 May 1905,Riis Collection, NYPL). Riis's combination of romance and realism in his autobiography made his text accessible and enjoyable to audiences who chose to read through the prism of either or both genres.

73. Riis, *Making* 111.
74. Riis, *Making* 111, 113.
75. Riis, *Making* 152.

76. Riis, *Making* 257.
77. It is interesting to note that Jacob Riis's father expressed a similar conflict in the definition of home in his letters to his son. On 28 March 1873, in the same letter in which he informs his son of Elisabeth's engagement to a soldier, Niels Edward Riis writes: "God knows we wish your future may be bright wherever you are, whether the far America shall be your home, or your native country. I hope you will find your home very soon, where loving hearts and peace will be yours." In this part of the letter, Niels Riis defines home as a place of love, urging his son to seek comfort from his disappointment over Elisabeth by establishing a home, presumably through marriage, in either America or Denmark. But in the rest of the letter, the elder Riis consistently defines Denmark as Jacob's real home, to which he should ideally return. "If you were really so lucky as to acquire a capital, so you could come home to us to stay forever, I will really say you have been fortunate," he writes. The conflict between marital home and parental home, the United States and Denmark, seems to begin for Jacob with his father.

78. Riis, *Making* 98. Riis claims in *Making* that its seventh chapter, entitled "Elizabeth Tells Her Story," was written by Elisabeth herself. While some believe that he staged her voice, the manuscript of *The Making of an American* reveals that the chapter is written in Elisabeth's hand with minor corrections by her husband, most of which attempt either to play down her love for her dead fiancé, Raymond, and the tensions it caused in her family or to Americanize her diction.

79. Elisabeth Riis to Clara Riis Fiske, 4 August 1904, Jacob A. Riis Collection, Museum of the City of New York.

80. "The child is a creature of environment," he say most explicitly in *The Children of the Poor* (New York: Scribner's, 1892) 4.

81. Jacob Riis, *The Peril and Preservation of the Home* (Philadelphia: George W. Jacobs, 1903) 24.

82. Riis, *Making* 206–7.

83. Riis further emphasizes the value of land and real estate ownership in instilling patriotic values and active citizenship. In *The Peril and Preservation of the Home*, for instance, he writes that "the ideal [home], always in my mind, is that of a man with his feet upon the soil and his children growing up there. So, it seems to me, we should have responsible citizenship by the surest road. But that ideal is unattainable in our cities. We must find another there" (24). Though he recognizes the infeasibility of the agrarian ideal in the modern industrial and urban age, Riis is Jeffersonian in his belief that landownership creates stability and good citizenship in a republican government. Based on this ideology, he encouraged the resettlement efforts of men like Jacob Schiff, who sought to bring Jewish immigrants from the Lower East Side of New York to rural New Jersey to become workers and eventually owners of the land (see *Children of the Tenements* 365–87), and in 1912, Riis invested virtually all his savings into purchasing a farm of his own in Barre, Massachusetts, where he and his second wife, Mary, attempted to practice scientific farming and encourage cooperative farming. Justifying his purchase of Pine Brook Farm to his sister, Riis wrote: "The day is not far off when the freest and safest man will be the one who has a piece of land and knows how to till it" (JR to Emma Riis 28 June 1912). For further discussion of Riis's Jeffersonianism, see James B. Lane's *Jacob A. Riis and the American City* (Port Washington: Kennikat Press, 1974) 217.

84. Riis, *Making* 230.

85. Riis's love for his homeland keeps him from claiming the United States as his only country. At least one reader of *The Making of an American* picked up on this strain in Riis's narrative. Born in Slesvig, a region under Danish control until Prussian occupation in 1864, a Mr. Jacobsen wrote to Riis in a letter addressed "Dear Sir and Landsmand," saying: "I think however that I can make still a better American than yourself, because you came from a country that you could love and I came from a land and country that I hated. I cut the bridges behind me and am an American by adoption" (see 8 April 1901 letter from Jacobsen to Riis, enclosed by Riis in 11 April 1901 letter to Roosevelt, Roosevelt Presidential Papers).

86. Jacobson, *Special Sorrows* 141–57. Jacobson demonstrates further that these immigrants' reactions to the United States' becoming an imperial power itself in the aftermath of the war were dictated by the ways in which they viewed the indigenous populations colonized by the United States. Those who viewed the war in the Philippines through the prism of national rights decried U.S. imperialism, while those who viewed it through the prism of race supported U.S. "tutelage" of nonwhite, non-Christian peoples (179–99). Riis, whose missionizing tendency was always a matter of concern among the Jewish and Catholic immigrants with whom he worked in New York City (see, for instance, Jeffery Gurock's "Jacob A. Riis: Christian Friend or Missionary Foe: Two Jewish Views," *American Jewish History* 71 [September 1981]: 29–47), fits the latter racial paradigm, advocating self-determination for Cuba but not for the Philippines. Yet he continues to work for the "liberation of German-occupied" Slesvig,

whose Danishness and desire for Danish control he never questions.

87. Riis, *Making* 244–45. For years, Riis had written articles about American life for Danish newspapers in his homeland. He viewed this work as a means to bridge the distance between himself and Denmark and to retain his connection to its language and culture. As he wrote to his sister Emma back in Ribe, "The fact is that those blessed letters to Nordisk tidende cause me more trouble than anything else. In them, I try . . . to analyze conditions and sometimes I feel that it comes difficult for me now to write Danish. But then that is why I write, otherwise I would forget it entirely" (JR to Emma Riis, 10 July 1895). These articles embody the compound identity Riis sought to forge, for they both preserved Riis's Danishness and simultaneously asserted his Americanness by establishing him as an authority on American conditions. But when he reported on the Spanish-American War, the Danish papers rejected his articles. "The Cuban campaign wrecked a promising career which I had been building for some ten or fifteen years with toilsome effort," he claims. "It was for a Danish newspaper I wrote with much approval, but when the war came, they did not take the same view of things that I did, and fell to suppressing or mutilating my letters, whereupon our connections ceased abruptly. My letters were, explained the editor to me a year or two later when I saw him in Copenhagen, so—er-r—ultra-patriotic, so—er-r—youthful in their enthusiasm, that—huh! I interrupted him with the remark that I was glad we were young enough yet in my country to get up a shout for the flag in a fight, and left him to think it over" (*Making* 244–45). Riis's reaction to the paper's editor reveals that his goal in writing these articles was not only to report on American nationalism but to infuse this nationalist spirit into Danes in order to inspire them to fight their own liberationist battle. Riis deployed American nationalism to evoke Danish nationalism in his homeland, fashioning himself as an ardent, youthful, masculine, Roosevelt-like figure in ways that the Danish press could not stomach.

88. Riis, *Theodore Roosevelt* 385–86.

89. In this representation of heroes of the "Far North," Riis expresses a Pan-Scandinavianism, celebrating not only Danish heroes but Swedish ones as well, even when these Swedes prove their heroism in wars against Denmark.

90. See W. Glyn Jones (53) on this Danish literary movement.

91. For a discussion of these "galvanizing poetics," see Jacobson, *Special Sorrows* 94–137.

92. Riis, *Hero Tales* vii.

93. Riis, *Hero Tales* vii.

94. Riis, *Hero Tales* vii–viii.

95. Riis believes that most European immigrants have the making of good American citizens within them, but that "the one immigrant who does not keep step, who, having fallen out of the ranks, has been ordered to the rear, is the Chinaman, who brought neither wife nor children to push him ahead. He left them behind that he might not become an American, and by the standard he himself set up he has been judged" (*Children of the Poor* 8–9). Riis is not interested in Chinese immigrants' history, or heroes, or even in their version of the story of their immigration. He sees them as a world apart and their lives and values as unworthy of America or its literature. His vision of shared national narratives is entirely Eurocentric.

96. Riis, *Hero Tales* viii.

97. See, for instance, Bourne's essay "Trans-national America" 86–97.

98. One way to understand Riis's insistence on nationalist immigrants is as a reaction against anarchists. In *Murdering McKinley: The Making of Theodore Roosevelt's America* (New York: Hill and Wang, 2003), Eric Rauchway argues that what Roosevelt feared most of immigrants was anarchism (146, 194, 201).

99. Sollors, *Beyond Ethnicity* 153.

100. Most earlier social critics blamed the poor themselves for their poverty, claiming that they were slothful, sinful, or biologically inferior to the middle class. For examples of this approach, see E. H. Chapin's *Humanity in the City* (New York: DeWitt and Davenport, 1854); Charles Loring Brace's *The Dangerous Classes of New York and Twenty Years' Work among Them* (New York: Wynkoop and Hallenbeck, 1872); and Josiah Strong's *Our Country: Its Possible Future and Its Present Crisis* (1885; Cambridge, MA: Belknap, 1963). For a comparison between such interpretations of poverty and Riis's, see Lane's *Jacob A. Riis and the American City* 52–54, 66–67, 89; and Keith Gandal's outstanding study *The Virtues of the Vicious: Jacob Riis, Stephen Crane, and the Spectacle of the Slum* (New York: Oxford UP, 1997).

101. Riis, *How the Other Half Lives* 93, emphasis mine. In later works Riis acknowledges that some of these "instincts" might have environmental causes. In a chapter of *The Battle with the Slum*, entitled "Pietro and the Jew," he suggests that Jews in eastern Europe "had been trained to lie for their safety; had been forbidden to work at trades, to own land; had been taught that only gold could buy them freedom from torture" (192). But though he recognizes that society produced some of the traits he observes, Riis never entirely gives up the language or theory of inborn racial characteristics.

102. Riis, *How the Other Half Lives* 43, emphasis mine.

103. Riis, *How the Other Half Lives* 80, emphasis mine.

104. Riis, *Making* 266.

105. Roosevelt, *Winning of the West* 1:20–21.

106. Roosevelt, *Winning of the West* 1:1.

107. Theodore Roosevelt. "Americans of Irish Origin," 17 March 1905, *Works* 16:40.

108. Roosevelt, *Gouverneur Morris* 324.

109. Roosevelt, *Gouverneur Morris* 326.

110. For an example of the association Roosevelt makes between frontiersman and Viking, see his *Thomas Hart Benton*, 1887, *Works* 7:5, 115. For further discussion of the analogy, see Dyer 49–54.

111. Roosevelt, *Winning of the West* 1:3. Speaking of the Germanic conquest of southern Europe, Roosevelt writes that "the Latin nations . . . [were] strengthened by the infusion of northern blood, sprang anew into vigorous life."

112. Øverland 1–22, 120–44. Øverland provides a superb, cross-cultural analysis of the myths of belonging created by ethnic groups in this period to assert both their Americanness and the appropriateness of perpetuating their ethnicity within the nation. He discusses in particular the ways in which Norwegian immigrants used the image of the Viking and of Norway as the source of democracy to make a place for themselves in America (144–73). Riis uses the same imagery for Danes.

113. JR to Dr. William Fiske, 28 August 1904, Riis Collection, Museum of the City of New York.

114. Riis, *Hero Tales* 145.

115. Riis, *Old Town* 44.

116. Riis, *Making* 270.

117. Riis, *Making* 283–84.

118. Wald, *Constituting Americans* 250.

119. The fact Riis does not provide the name of the town where these events occurred, but identifies the location as just outside of Elsinore, home of Hamlet, supports the suggestion that Riis views this as a moment of psychological or philosophical crisis. Furthermore, in his notes for his lectures on *The Making of an American*, Riis adds to the paragraph describing his illness and recovery: "The world was dark and dreary, until all at once a ship sailed by with the stars and stripes flung to the breeze. That moment I knew what ailed me. I was just homesick" (manuscript page 15, Riis Collection, Library of Congress, Reel 5).

120. See Dorothy Burton Skardal's *The Divided Heart: Scandinavian Immigrant Experience through Literary Sources* (Lincoln: U of Nebraska P, 1974) 115.

121. The view of Riis as an immigrant author who at least attempted to present a completely Americanized self has been perpetuated by Emma Louise Ware in *Jacob A. Riis: Police Reporter, Reformer, Useful Citizen* (New York: Appleton-Century, 1939); Roy Lubove in *The Progressives and the Slums: Tenement House Reform in New York City, 1890–1917* (Westport: Greenwood Press, 1974) 61–62; Louis Fried in *Makers of the City* (Amherst: U of Massachusetts P, 1990); Leviatin; and Wald, *Constituting Americans* 250–51.

122. Kallen 193.

123. Wald, *Constituting Americans* 251. The manuscript of *The Making of an American* reveals that Riis chose to pull himself out of this sentence claiming the discovery of an American made, deliberately depersonalizing it. He edited it as follows: "There remains to tell how I found out that in me he was made" (manuscript page 498, Riis Collection, NYPL, Box 4).

124. Manuscript p. 498. Strikethroughs indicate words crossed out by Riis.

125. Roosevelt, "True Americanism" 22.

126. JR to TR, 13 April 1901.

127. Roosevelt's reaction to the actual chapter does not remain, but he does respond initially, saying: "Indeed I will let you know about that chapter, but in as much as I am utterly unable to conceive of your writing anything that is not alright, I guess my verdict can be anticipated" (TR to JR, 16 April 1901). Riis solicited Roosevelt's opinion about drafts of his articles and about published pieces on many other occasions as well. There are more extant letters containing Roosevelt's replies to such requests than Riis's actual requests, but the context is clear. See, for instance, TR to JR 25 February 1898, 11 April 1901; JR to TR 23 June 1901, 9 May 1902, 11 January 1904.

128. JR to TR, 15 July 1904.

129. TR to JR, 30 July 1904.

130. Examining immigrant autobiography of the early twentieth century, William Boelhower argues that they all share a single story, structure, and double consciousness (see Boelhower 5–23). For examples of transformation narratives in immigrant autobiographies of the period, see, for instance, Mary Antin's *The Promised Land*; Edward Bok's *The Americanization of Edward Bok: The Autobiography of a Dutch Boy Fifty Years After* (1920; New York: Scribner's, 1924); and Edward Steiner's *From Alien to Citizen* (1914; New York: Arno Press, 1975). Steiner's narrative is a bit different in that he depicts not only his transformation into an American but also his literal conversion from Jew to Christian.

131. Riis, *Old Town* 230.

132. Imagining heaven like Ribe, Riis writes: "And I saw the old town no more. But in my dreams, I walk its peaceful

streets, listen to the whisper of the reeds in the dry moats of the castle hill, and hear my mother call me once more her boy. And I know that I shall find them, with my lost childhood, when we all reach home at last" (*Making* 270). In this passage, home is celestial, and Riis envisions it as a final and permanent return to mother and Ribe, with any reference to the United States conspicuously absent.

133. JR to TR, 20 October 1902.

134. JR to TR, 7 August 7 1908.

135. *The Critic* (May 1904) 462.

136. TR to JR, 7 May 1897.

137. Even a quick comparison of Roosevelt's correspondence with "Jake" versus his correspondence with a friend like Cecil Spring Roth (whom TR calls "Springy") reveals the reserved, more formal nature of his friendship with Riis.

138. Hans P. Vought discusses Roosevelt's simultaneous use and denial of ethnic politics more generally in *The Bully Pulpit and the Melting Pot: American Presidents and the Immigrant, 1897–1933* (Macon: Mercer UP, 2004) 37, 45.

139. TR to JR, 10 November 1904.

140. TR to JR, 18 March 1902. For a complete history of the U.S. purchase of the Danish West Indies, see Charles Callan Tansill's *The Purchase of the Danish West Indies* (New York: Greenwood Press, 1968).

141. JR to TR, 17 March 1902. The end of Riis's letter is noteworthy in that it suggests that he harbored a utopian vision of nationhood, distinct from the present United States. He warns the president, "What I might do as the little pooh-bah of three islands there is absolutely no telling. Very likely tow them off into unknown seas and start a little kingdom of my own."

142. Theodore Roosevelt, "The Duties of American Citizenship," 1893, *Works* 13:296.

143. Roosevelt, *Autobiography* 66.

144. Roosevelt, "True Americanism" 25.

145. Roosevelt, "The Duties of American Citizenship" 283.

146. Riis, *Battle with the Slum* 7.

147. Riis, *Battle with the Slum* 362.

148. Riis, *Battle with the Slum* 414.

149. Riis, *Making* 151, 272.

150. Riis, *Making* 83–84.

151. Riis, *Making* 199.

152. Riis, *Making* 198.

153. See Richard Hofstadter, *The Age of Reform: From Bryan to FDR* (New York: Vintage, 1955) 9, 183–85. Riis is also keenly aware of and even sympathetic to the allegiance of the poor and immigrant to the boss, and he actively seeks to make reform more appealing to such individuals. In *The Battle with the Slum*, he writes:

> To the poor people of his district the boss is a friend in need. He is one of them. He does not want to reform them; far from it. No doubt it is very ungrateful of them, but the poor people have no desire of being reformed. They do not think that they need to be. They consider their moral standards quite as high as those of the rich, and resent being told that they are mistaken. The reformer comes to them from another world to tell them these things, and goes his way. The boss lives among them. He helped John to a job on the pipes in their hard winter, and got Mike on the force. They know him as a good neighbor, and trust him to their harm. He drags their standard ever father down. The question for those who are trying to help them is how to make them transfer their allegiance and trust their real friends instead. (428–29)

154. Eric Rauchway suggests that Riis was well aware that Roosevelt was a calculating politician who had determined the political value of friendship with Riis (142).

155. JR to TR, 7 November 1902.

156. TR to JR, 12 November 1902.

157. JR to TR, 14 November 1902. Riis also makes explicit the personal value of Roosevelt's friendship in a note to the then vice president, thanking him for his letter to Riis's newborn granddaughter, Virginia Fiske (daughter of Clara Riis and Dr. Fiske). "She may never come to know her grandfather's friend," Riis wrote, "but her country's history will tell her how noble he was, and she will think more of me because of him" (23 June 1901). Riis believes that his family (and undoubtedly the world at large) will hold him in greater esteem because of his friendship with Roosevelt.

158. When Riis originally used Roosevelt's photo as the frontispiece to *The Ten Year's War*, Roosevelt wrote similarly to the author: "I take the greatest pride in having my name in your handwriting at the front of your book and my photograph thought worthy to put in it. If I were foolish enough to need any reward for what I had done, I should feel that I had it ten times over in what you have said about me, old man, in this book. Most of it is undeserved.... But I won't pretend to say that I regret to have it in, for I do not, and it will ever be a source of keen pride to me to show to my children" (17 February 1900).

CHAPTER 3

1. Theodore Roosevelt, "The Woman and the Home," address before the National Congress of Mothers, Washington, DC, 13 March 1905, *Works* 16:164–65.

2. [Elizabeth Gertrude Stern], "My Mother and I: The Story of How I Became an American Woman," *Ladies' Home Journal* October 1916: 86; *My Mother and I* (New York: Macmillan, 1917) 168. In order to uncover Stern's text as Roosevelt and Bok read it, all quotations from "My Mother and I" and Roosevelt's introduction are taken from the *Ladies' Home Journal* (hereafter *LHJ*) edition unless otherwise indicated. Variants in the Macmillan edition will be noted and cited as *My Mother*.

3. "My Mother" 86; *My Mother* 168.

4. "My Mother" 21; *My Mother* 9.

5. "America's Possibilities for the Immigrant," review of *My Mother and I, Nation* 30 August 1917: 225.

6. This question has remained virtually unexplored by scholars. As Susanne Amy Shavelson comments in a footnote to her dissertation: "While it is remarkable that the former president provided the foreword for Stern's narrative, neither the reviews of Stern's book nor the criticism written on it to date seems to find it so. Future work on *My Mother and I* might consider how Roosevelt came to endorse this work" ("From Amerike to America: Language and Identity in the Yiddish and English Autobiographies of Jewish Immigrant Women," diss. U Michigan, 1996, 121).

7. In 1904, the *LHJ* became the first magazine to reach a circulation of more than one million (*A Short History of the* Ladies' Home Journal [Philadelphia: Curtis, 1953] 19 in the Curtis Publishing Company Papers, Special Collections, Van Pelt Library, University of Pennsylvania).

8. In her introduction to the 1986 reprint of Stern's work *I Am a Woman—and a Jew* (New York: Markus Wiener, 1986), Ellen Umansky states that Stern sent her manuscript to Roosevelt, who then sent it on to Bok. She writes, "The Journal claimed that

the manuscript had been sent to Roosevelt, who then brought it to The Journal's attention" (v). Actually, the *LHJ* never explicitly indicated the order of events, but printed before Stern's story: "With an appreciation by Theodore Roosevelt to whom the manuscript was sent" (21). According to the autobiographies of Bok and Stern's son, Thomas Noel Stern, however, Stern's contact was with Bok and never with Roosevelt. The absence of any correspondence between Elizabeth Stern and the former president corroborates this version of events.

9. This account of Stern's dealings with the *LHJ* is related in her son Thomas Noel Stern's memoirs, *Secret Family* (South Dartmouth: T. Noel Stern, 1988), a book that we shall see is not entirely trustworthy as a historical source. It also corresponds to Elizabeth Stern's own fictionalized account of the acceptance of her first story, which she had to edit down to five thousand words (Leah Morton, [Elizabeth Gertrude Stern], *I Am a Woman—and a Jew* [1926; New York: Arno Press, 1969] 120–21).

10. Roosevelt wrote articles for many magazines and served as associate editor for Lyman Abbott's *Outlook* in the years following his presidency. Unlike his role on that journal, his work for the *LHJ* was often secret and has remained virtually unexplored by scholars.

11. Bok, *Americanization* 279.

12. "In this work, Colonel Roosevelt showed his customary promptness and thoroughness," Bok wrote of Roosevelt's efforts. "A manuscript, no matter how long it might be, was in his hands scarcely forty-eight hours, more generally twenty-four, before it was read, a report thereon written, and the article back. His reports were always comprehensive and invariably interesting. There was none of the cut-and-dried flavor of the opinion of the average 'reader'; he always put himself into the report, and, of course, that meant a warm personal touch. If he could not encourage the publication of a manuscript, his reasons were always fully given, and invariably without personal bias" (*Americanization* 279).

13. *LHJ* circulation reached two million in 1919, only two years after Roosevelt's Men's page had come to an end. For circulation rates, see *Short History of the* Ladies' Home Journal; Bok, *Americanization* 374; and *LHJ* May 1919: 1.

14. Amy Kaplan, "Manifest Domesticity," *American Literature* 70 (September 1998): 589ff.

15. For examples of Stern's later writing, see *This Ecstasy* (New York: J. H. Sears, 1927); *The Gambler's Wife* (New York: Macmillan, 1931); *I Am a Woman—and a Jew* (1926; New York: Arno Press, 1969, written under the pseudonym Leah Morton; and *Not All Laughter: A Mirror to Our Times* (Philadelphia: John C. Winston, 1937), written under the pseudonym Eleanor Morton.

16. See Barbara Shollar "Writing Ethnicity/Writing Modernity: Autobiographies by Jewish-American Women," diss., City U of New York, 1992, 129–32; Sally Ann Drucker, "'It Doesn't Say So in Mother's Prayerbook': Autobiographies in English by Immigrant Jewish Women," *American Jewish History* 79.1 (Autumn 1989): 55–71. 69.

17. Bok, *Americanization* 273.

18. *LHJ* February 1907.

19. Roosevelt, "The Woman and the Home" 164–65.

20. Riis, *Peril* 24.

21. Riis, *How the Other Half Lives* 138.

22. Paul Boyer calls this "positive environmentalism" in his *Urban Masses and Moral Order in America* (Cambridge: Harvard UP 1978) 233–83.

23. Roosevelt, "The Woman and the Home" 165.

24. [Robert L. O'Brien], "Mr. Roosevelt's Views on the Strenuous Life," *LHJ* May 1906: 17; Robert Wiebe, *The Search for Order, 1877–1920* (New York: Hill and Wang, 1967).

25. The Progressive movement shifted its orientation in the early twentieth century from encouraging direct popular participation in reform to looking to trained experts to manage such efforts through scientific advice based on much more rigid standards. See Robert Wiebe's analysis of progressivism in *Search for Order*. Gwendolyn Wright applies this claim more specifically to housing reform (*Moralism and the Model Home: Domestic Architecture and Cultural Conflict in Chicago, 1873–1913* [Chicago: U of Chicago P, 1980] 256–73); and Barbara Ehrenreich and Deirdre English examine its effects on housekeeping and mothering advice and techniques (*For Her Own Good: 150 Years of Experts' Advice to Women* [Garden City: Anchor, 1979] 141–209).

26. See *Short History of the* Ladies' Home Journal 19; and Bok, *Americanization* 374. Accounts differ on the exact circulation in Bok's later years at the *LHJ*, but the first page of the May 1919 issue proudly announces the sale of two million copies of the magazine.

27. Subscribers were primarily from households earning between $1,200 and $2,500 per year, with supplementary readers coming from families with earnings from $3,000 to $5,000 per year (Jennifer Scanlon, *Inarticulate Longings: The* Ladies' Home Journal *and the Promises of Consumer Culture* [New York: Routledge, 1995] 14).

28. The *LHJ* has been credited with contributing heavily to the gendering of consumption. It played a major role in shifting the responsibility for household purchasing from men to women. It virtually created mass advertising targeting women, and it helped to define the role of women in the new industrial economy as consumers, rather than producers, while training them to approach their new task "rationally," with attention to quality, brand name, and economy. For an excellent discussion of the *LHJ*'s role in the gendering of commerce and the commercialization of gender, see Helen Damon-Moore, *Magazines for the Millions: Gender and Commerce in the* Ladies' Home Journal *and the* Saturday Evening Post *1880–1910* (Albany: State U of New York P, 1994) 2–3, 54–55, 98–100, 116–17.

29. "Attitudes toward *The Ladies' Home Journal* and *The Saturday Evening Post* as Advertising Mediums," report of the Division of Commercial Research of the Advertising Department of the Curtis Publishing Company (1916) 14, in the Curtis Publishing Company Papers, Special Collections, Van Pelt Library, University of Pennsylvania.

30. See Salme Harju Steinberg's *Reformer in the Marketplace: Edward W. Bok and the* Ladies' Home Journal (Baton Rouge: Louisiana State UP, 1979) xiv–xix.

31. Bok, *Americanization* 240.

32. For the groundbreaking analysis of what he termed the "conspicuous consumption" of America's upper classes, see Thorstein Veblen's *The Theory of the Leisure Class* (1899; New York: Penguin, 1979).

33. For discussions of the ideal of the simple life in the context of the larger reaction to urban industrial and consumer culture, see Jackson Lears, *No Place of Grace: Antimodernism and the Transformation of American Culture, 1880–1920* (New York: Pantheon, 1981); and David E. Shi, *The Simple Life: Plain Living and High Thinking in American Culture* (New York: Oxford UP, 1985) 154–222. Shi talks specifically about

Bok's promotion of the "simple life" within the *Ladies' Home Journal* (181–89, 204–7).

34. Bok, *Americanization* 241–43. For analyses of the shift away from the Victorian parlor, see Wright 136–37; Sally McMurry, "City Parlor, Country Sitting Room: Rural Vernacular Design and the American Parlor, 1840–1900," *Winterthur Portfolio* 20 (Winter 1985): 261–80; and Margaret Marsh, "From Separation to Togetherness: The Social Construction of Domestic Space in American Suburbs, 1840–1915," *Journal of American History* 76 (September 1989): 515–22. See also John Kasson's *Rudeness and Civility: Manners in Nineteenth-Century America* (New York: Hill and Wang, 1990) 170–81.

35. See Carey Edmunds, "The New Home for the Bride," *LHJ* October 1916: 45. For analysis of the revival of the Colonial in this period, see Wright 251–53; and William B. Rhoads, "The Colonial Revival and American Nationalism," *Journal of the Society of Architectural Historians* 35 (December 1976): 239–54.

36. Bok printed pictures of his commissioned houses and "bungalows" in the *LHJ* and sold blueprints by request. This series, which began in 1895 and continued for almost twenty-five years, was a huge success.

37. The only record of this declaration exists in Bok's autobiography, *Americanization* 249–50.

38. Shi 187–88. See also Scott Erbes, "Manufacturing and Marketing the American Bungalow: The Aladdin Company, 1906–1920," *The American Home: Material Culture, Domestic Space, and Family Life*, ed. Eleanor McD. Thompson (Hanover: UP of New England, 1998) 45, 57–59.

39. Bok, *Americanization* 244.

40. Bok, *Americanization* 244. For examples of this column, see the *Ladies' Home Journal* September 1907: 43; and 15 February 1911: 14.

41. See, for instance, "Good and Bad Taste in Window Curtains," *LHJ* March 1906: 23, which is just a few pages away from "Mr. Roosevelt's Views on Factory Laws for Women and Children." The *LHJ* also published the columns "Good Taste and Bad Taste in Hair Dressing," dictating how the proper middle-class woman's body should appear, and "Good Manners and Good Form," telling her how to behave in social situations (e.g., February 1908: 48). Also included in this long-running column were several pieces titled "Good Taste and Bad Taste in College Girls' Rooms" (e.g., October 1911). These articles acknowledged the increasing prevalence of higher education for girls but sought to ensure that these girls retained their domestic values. The greatest concern addressed here is the need for order. Rooms filled with signs of girls' affiliations and activities—such as tennis rackets, snapshots, and banners—were denounced in favor of uncluttered rooms with coordinated wallpaper and furniture, teacups, and flowers.

42. The professionalization of advice was one of the hallmarks of Bok's *Journal*. In its early years, the magazine encouraged reader participation in this area. Its first editor, Louisa Knapp Curtis, encouraged readers to write to the magazine with suggestions for other women, but when he became editor, Bok curtailed this practice, establishing service departments run by experts whom readers could write to for advice. In *Magazines for the Millions*, Helen Damon-Moore argues that the *LHJ* under Louisa Knapp Curtis was a more democratic and feminist text than under Bok, encouraging readers to share ideas and tips (29–58). Christopher P. Wilson places

Bok's approach in the context of the more general shift from the gentleman's journal to the mass-market magazine in "The Rhetoric of Consumption: Mass Market Magazines and the Demise of the Gentle Reader, 1880–1920," *The Culture of Consumption: Critical Essays in American History 1880–1980*, ed. Richard Wrightman Fox and T. J. Jackson Lears (New York: Pantheon, 1983) 39–64.

The shift away from shared advice corresponds to the previously noted general reorientation of the Progressive movement in the early twentieth century from direct popular participation to trained experts. See Robert Wiebe's analysis of Progressivism in *Search for Order*. Gwendolyn Wright applies this claim more specifically to housing reform (256–73), and Ehrenreich and English examine its effects on housekeeping and mothering advice and techniques (141–209).

43. Dr. Coolidge instructed mothers through both personalized letters and her monthly column. Her "Young Mothers' Registry" invited new mothers to fill out information sheets on their babies every month for the first two years of life and receive personalized, "scientific" directions on how to care for them at each stage. Virtually all of Dr. Coolidge's magazine columns similarly insisted on regularity as the key to child rearing. See, for instance, "The Young Mothers' Guide," *LHJ* July 1912; and "The Young Mother's Registry," *LHJ* October 1916: 62.

44. Mrs. Christine Frederick, "The New Housekeeping: How It Helps the Woman Who Does Her Own Work," *LHJ* September 1912: 71. In her later pamphlet, *Come into My Kitchen* (Sheboygan: Vollrath, 1922), Frederick suggests that women paint the walls of their kitchens in light tones of blue, green, tan, or gray to offset the bright whiteness of the rest of the kitchen and the utensils (6–28).

45. Christine Frederick, "The New Housekeeping," *LHJ* October 1912: 100.

46. See, for instance, the *LHJ* of March 1905, where a $750 prize was offered for a photograph of an offensive outdoor advertisement and a photograph of the same spot after the ad had been permanently removed (1). (To prevent cheating, contestants also had to submit signed guarantees from the owner of the property and from the local pastor attesting to the fact that the ad was real and would not be put back after the photo was taken.)

47. In 1903, the *LHJ* began a series called "Beautiful America," written by J. Horace McFarland, president of the American Civic Association. One of its features offered photographic exposés of "ugly places" in cities around the country, meant to embarrass their citizens into taking action to improve the aesthetics of their surroundings. See, for instance, McFarland's "Eyesores That Spoil Memphis," *LHJ* June 1906: 29.

48. Bok, *Americanization* 251.

49. *LHJ* October 1908: 5.

50. Between 1893 and 1897, Curtis and Bok phased out ads for patent medicines in the *LHJ* largely out of concern that more respectable companies with higher revenues would not want to advertise alongside these nostrums and out of a desire to build reader trust in the *LHJ* as a source of sound advice. In 1906, Bok took up a more explicit campaign against patent medicines, warning against the dangers of these unregulated, largely alcoholic elixirs. He even had Roosevelt devote his April 1906 presidential column to the subject.

51. Bok wrote in a March 1906 editorial, "Now there are certain mysteries of life which every man and woman must

understand. We veil them in our ordinary talk as sacred things. They are sacred as part of God's universal plan of life. Only by vicious men and women have they been made to appear vile. It is an absolute necessity that the child should know of these things. His health, his sanity, sometimes life itself will depend upon his right understanding of them" ("The Editorial Page," *LHJ* March 1906: 18). Though the *LHJ* was never explicit about what to tell children, its position on sex education was considered quite radical. Two years after the initial discussion, Bok answered questions on when and how to tell one's children about sex, indicating that his readership had internalized his message and was seeking guidance for implementation (January 1908, 1).

52. For a discussion of the middle-class orientation of Bok's reforms, see Steinberg 40–97, 144–47.

53. See, for instance, *Der idisher froyen zshurnal*, the *Jewish Woman's Home Journal*.

54. For a discussion of the ways in which Bok's *Journal* promoted nationalism, see Kaitlyn Kayer's "Americanizing the American Woman: Symbols of Nationalism in the *Ladies' Home Journal*, 1890–1900," Pell Scholars Honor Thesis, Salve Regina University, 2005, http://escholar.salve.edu/pell_thesis/4.

55. Salme Harju Steinberg writes: "He wanted to become part of America. He outdid his readers in his faith in the myths and hopes of his adopted country" (35). Werner Sollors reads Bok's insistence on writing about himself in the third person in *The Americanization of Edward Bok* as part of the "ethnic transformation" paradigm, in which, like Mary Antin, the immigrant autobiographer insists that his or her ethnic self has been killed off and replaced by a new and improved American self (*Beyond Ethnicity* 32).

56. Edward Bok, *Twice Thirty: Some Short and Simple Annals of the Road* (1922; New York: Scribner's, 1925) 251–52.

57. Bok, *Americanization* 267.

58. Bok, *Americanization* 447.

59. Bok, *Americanization* 445.

60. Bok, *Twice Thirty* 255–56.

61. Riis, *Making* 206–7.

62. See Kaplan on the "domestication of the foreign" ("Manifest Domesticity" 581–91).

63. Isabelle Horton, *The Burden of the City* (New York: F. H. Revell, 1904), Harvard University, Schlesinger On-line Library on the History of Women in America, 183.

64. Horton 57–59.

65. Horton 73ff.

66. Horton 182.

67. Robert A. Woods, ed., *Americans in Process: A Settlement Study* (Boston: Houghton Mifflin, 1902) 303.

68. Lillian D. Wald, *The House on Henry Street* (New York: Henry Holt, 1915) 108.

69. Woods 303. Ironically, while they preached progressive domesticity to immigrant and working-class women, the educated upper-middle-class women who generally became settlement house workers found an escape from the expectations of conventional homemaking through their work. See Jane Addams's discussion on the function of the settlement house for its female workers in *Twenty Years at Hull-House* 90–100.

70. Horton 181. Shannon Jackson analyzes some of the theatrical ways in which Hull House encouraged mimesis in her article "Civic Play-Housekeeping: Gender, Theatre, and American Reform," *Theater Journal* 48 (October 1996): 337–61.

71. Addams 182.

72. Addams 171–83.

73. Andrew R. Heinze, *Adapting to Abundance: Jewish Immigrants, Mass Consumption, and the Search for American Identity* (New York: Columbia UP, 1990) 2–18.

74. Roosevelt, "True Americanism" 22.

75. [Robert L. O'Brien], "The President's View on a Uniform Divorce Law," *LHJ* September 1906: 17.

76. Theodore Roosevelt, "The Home and the Child," *Realizable Ideals, Works* 13:641.

77. Roosevelt, "The Home and the Child" 636, 630.

78. TR to Cass Gilbert, 19 December 1908, in Tony P. Wrenn, "The Eye of Guardianship: Theodore Roosevelt and the American Institute of Architects," *White House History Journal* 11 (1999): 51–61.

79. Roosevelt, *Autobiography* 332.

80. [Roosevelt], "Men," *LHJ* April 1917: 28.

81. [Roosevelt], "Men," *LHJ* October 1916: 32.

82. Bok, *Americanization* 273–74.

83. Bok says that Roosevelt resisted taking on this project, claiming, "I have only half an hour when I am awake, when I am really idle, and that is when I am being shaved" (*Americanization* 274). Bok then proposed that O'Brien interview the president for his column at precisely these moments. The reason given is expediency, yet it is nonetheless fascinating the Roosevelt (through Bok) claims to engage in one of the most gender-defining activities—shaving—while writing for the potentially effeminizing *Ladies' Home Journal*.

84. Bok, *Americanization* 276. The addition of a Men's page to the *LHJ* seems to have been motivated by a continued desire to expand the magazine's audience by appealing to men as well as women. As Helen Damon-Moore describes in her comparative study of the two magazines owned by the Curtis Publishing Company—the *Ladies' Home Journal* and the *Saturday Evening Post*—as the *Post*, originally intended to be a men's magazine, realized it had to appeal to women, too, in order to win readers and advertisers, the *LHJ* sought to expand its readership by targeting men. The *LHJ*'s attempts ultimately failed because of the magazine's gendered name and reputation and the stigmatization of men who read it (141–51).

85. Bok, *Americanization* 276–77.

86. Bok and Roosevelt were dogged about keeping Roosevelt's authorship of this column a secret. Before sending the ex-president's manuscripts to the printer, Bok would recopy them in his own hand. Payments for the articles were sent to Bok, and then he wrote personal checks to Roosevelt. In this way, they were able to keep the author of the column a complete mystery. Most readers believed that the column's author was most likely Charles Eliot, president of Harvard, clergyman Lyman Abbott, or Bok himself (Bok, *Americanization* 278). Bok claims the reason for hiding Roosevelt's identity as author of the Men's page was purely a playful experiment in audience response, but other reasons certainly may have applied, not the least of which was that anonymity provided a loophole through which exclusivity clauses in Roosevelt's contracts with other magazines could be overcome. When revealing the origins of the column in his 1920 autobiography, Bok claimed that only five people (including the two men and their wives) ever knew it before (*Americanization* 277).

The cover letters that accompanied Roosevelt's drafts can be found in the Theodore Roosevelt Collection at Houghton Library, Harvard University, proving undeniably that Roosevelt was indeed the author of the Men's page. These letters also reveal the stress Roosevelt experienced writing these articles, for, as he says in his final letter: "I have not been satisfied with my work; this is the first time I ever tried to write precisely to order, and I am not one of those gifted men who can do so to advantage; generally I find that the 3000 words is not the right-length and that I wish to use 2000 or 4000!—and in consequence feel as if I had either padded or mutilated the article. And I am not always able to feel that every month I have something worth saying on a given subject!" (TR to Bok, 22 January 1917). Clearly Roosevelt was accustomed to dictating the terms and schedule of his own writing.

87. Though generally overlooked in studies of Roosevelt, the president actually wrote and spoke frequently about men's domestic responsibilities. One notable exception is Arnaldo Testi's "The Gender of Reform Politics: Theodore Roosevelt and the Culture of Masculinity," *Journal of American History* 81 (March 1995): 1509–33. This often neglected strain in Roosevelt's ideology necessitates a reconsideration of his notions of gender and the role of the domestic in his larger national visions.

88. [O'Brien], "Mr. Roosevelt's Views on the Strenuous Life" 17.

89. Roosevelt, "The Strenuous Life" 319.

90. Roosevelt, "The Strenuous Life" 320-21.

91. [Robert L. O'Brien], "Mr. Roosevelt's Views on Race Suicide," *LHJ* February 1906: 21.

92. [O'Brien], "Mr. Roosevelt's Views on Race Suicide" 21. Unlike Bok, Roosevelt supported women's suffrage. He saw it as a means by which women could protect themselves from abuse, and he believed that women would be capable voters and would not threaten their families by leaving the home for the polls (Roosevelt, *Autobiography* 167–68).

93. [O'Brien], "Mr. Roosevelt's Views on Race Suicide" 21. The language of O'Brien's piece echoes Roosevelt's earlier speech "The Woman and the Home" 164–65.

94. [O'Brien], "Mr. Roosevelt's Views on Race Suicide" 21.

95. [O'Brien], "Mr. Roosevelt's Views on Race Suicide" 21.

96. [O'Brien], "The President's Views on a Uniform Divorce Law" 17.

97. Bederman 205.

98. The problem of men shirking their home duties is explored in Anna Igra's "Likely to Become a Public Charge: Deserted Women and the Family Law of the Poor in New York City, 1910–1936," *Journal of Women's History* 11.4 (2000): 59–81; and Igra's "Marriage and Manhood in the U.S. Jewish Community," unpublished conference paper, Third Scholars' Conference on American Jewish History, Cincinnati, Ohio, 10 June 1998. See also Martha May's "The 'Problem of Duty': Family Desertion in the Progressive Era," *Social Service Review* 62.2 (March 1988): 40–60; and May's *Home Life: Progressive Social Reformers' Prescriptions for Social Stability, 1890–1920*, diss., State U of New York at Binghamton, 1984.

99. [Roosevelt], "Men," *LHJ* November 1916: 26.

100. In her article "Suburban Men and Masculine Domesticity, 1870–1915," *American Quarterly* 40 (January 1988): 165–86, Margaret Marsh reevaluates the notion of the early twentieth-century "cult of masculinity," arguing that, in fact, with the increased job security of the corporation, the rise of the suburbs, and the ideal of companionate marriage, men were more involved in home life than ever before. Although she examines how imperialist senator Albert Beveridge encouraged male involvement in parenting, Marsh still holds

out Theodore Roosevelt as "the symbol of rugged masculinity in his time" (165). In light of his writings about male "homemaking" and parenting in the *LHJ*, as well as his self-representation as a father in his autobiography (355), Roosevelt's notion of manhood must be reexamined.

101. [Roosevelt], "Men," *LHJ* December 1916: 30.

102. Girls must be allowed the "freedom to choose for [themselves] with in certain quite natural and inevitable limits." They must to learn on their own what men want really want, which is, Roosevelt declares, quite surprisingly, considering his dominant notions of masculinity, that "every man wishes in his heart to be well taken care of" ("Men," *LHJ* February 1917: 28).

103. See [Roosevelt], "Men" *LHJ* March 1917: 24; and April 1917: 28.

104. Testi 1521–22.

105. Kaplan, "Manifest Domesticity" 581–606.

106. [Roosevelt], "Men" *LHJ* October 1917: 153.

107. For more on Roosevelt and the rhetoric of civilization, see Bederman 170–215.

108. Bok to TR, Roosevelt Papers, 8 May 1916.

109. "My Mother and I" 21. Roosevelt's foreword also prefaces the 1917 book *My Mother and I* with slight changes. Instead of saying that it tells the story of "an immigrant girl," it says "of a young girl" (perhaps indicating that Roosevelt discovered something he did not know earlier about the background of the author and the nature of her first-person narrative), and instead of calling immigrants "starved and noble souls," it calls them "starved and eager souls," a less laudatory description of the newcomers who were increasingly held suspect as the United States entered World War I (9).

110. As Magdalena Zaborowska comments, the lack of old-world comparisons, transatlantic passage scenes, nostalgia for a mother country or mother tongue, and expressions of gratitude to America in this work serves as a dramatic rewriting of the more typical immigrant narrative in which the immigrant frequently positions him- or herself as an outsider requesting permission or expressing thanks for acceptance into American life. Instead, the narrator, who says she arrived in the United States at age two and knew no other life, boldly demands a place for herself in America, claims it as her only country, and demonstrates her belonging (*How We Found America: Reading Gender through East European Immigrant Narratives* [Chapel Hill: U of North Carolina P, 1995] 80–81, 85–91). In the book version of her text, Stern writes: "I had always felt that America was my birthright. . . . My mother country had always been—America. It was only my home that had not been American" (147). Interestingly, these lines and the scene where they appear, in which the narrator compares herself to Jewish immigrants from Russia who have a strong sense of Russian identity, are not included in the *Ladies' Home Journal* story. Her declaration of belonging in the United States is more muted in the *LHJ*.

111. "My Mother" 86; *My Mother* 168.

112. There had never been a consensus on how to classify these texts, but they were generally considered autobiographical if not outright autobiography. The *Nation* assumed that *My Mother and I* is an autobiography and demanded more details from the author about how she was able to assimilate so easily ("America's Possibilities" 224). The reviewer for the *New York Times* was not sure what to make of the work, saying, "Her progress . . . is told

vividly and with so great an affect of reality that one is often impelled to wonder whether this is not, in essentials at least, a genuine autobiography rather than a work of fiction" ("Latest Works of Fiction," *New York Times* 8 July 1917: 255). The *New York Times* reviewer of *I Am a Woman—and a Jew* was equally confused about the generic status of this work, writing: "If it is what it purports and appears to be, the actual experiences of a real woman, it has interest and value far beyond its portrayal of one woman's contacts with life and the world" ("A Jewish Woman," *New York Times* 3 March 1927: BR 12). He or she believes that the book would have more merit and sociological utility if it were historical rather than fictional. The *Herald Tribune*, however, felt that Stern's later work was awful, no matter what its genre: "It has neither the searching quality of good exposition nor the intensity of fine imaginative writing, nor yet the vitality which glows like blood in the cheek on the pages of enduring autobiography" (Babette Deutsch, "An Unimpressive Autobiography," review of *I Am a Woman—and a Jew, New York Herald Tribune Books* 19 December 1926: 17).

Later critics have engaged in the same debates about how to classify Stern's work. In her article "'It Doesn't Say So in Mother's Prayerbook'" 65, Sally Ann Drucker defines both books as autobiographical accounts of the life of Elizabeth Gertrude Levin Stern. Mary Dearborn discusses Stern's work in terms of the autobiographical novel in her book *Pocahontas's Daughters: Gender and Ethnicity in American Culture* (New York: Oxford UP, 1986). And in her introduction to the 1986 reprinted edition of *I Am a Woman—and a Jew*, Ellen Umansky claimed that *My Mother and I* is an autobiography, whereas Stern's later work is an autobiographical novel (viii). Ellen Serlen Uffen, basing herself on Umansky, makes the same claim about Stern's later work (Uffen, *Strands of the Cable: The Place of the Past in Jewish American Women's Writing* [New York: Peter Lang, 1992] 27).

The debate has continued even after Ellen Umansky's 1993 revelation of Thomas Noel Stern's claims about his mother's life. Continued confusion about the texts has resulted partly out of a lack of awareness of T. Noel Stern's book and of Umansky's article on the subject, but largely because of the unreliability of his narrative and the impossibility of proving its veracity. In her 1997 entry on Stern for *Jewish Women in America: An Historical Encyclopedia* (ed. Paula E. Hyman and Deborah Dash Moore, vol. 2 [New York: Routledge, 1997] 1334), Kirsten Wasson refers to *My Mother and I* and *I Am a Woman and a Jew* as autobiographical novels and states that Stern was born in Skedel, Poland, in 1889 to the Levin family. In 1999, Wendy Zierler identified *My Mother and I* as an autobiography and *I Am* as fictional autobiography (Zierler, "In(ter)dependent Selves: Mary Antin, Elizabeth Stern, and Jewish Women's Autobiography," *The Immigrant Experience in North American Literature: Carving Out a Niche*, ed. Katharine B. Payant and Toby Rose [Westport: Greenwood Press, 1999] 2). Basing themselves on Umansky's claims, Laura Browder identifies Stern's work as "impersonator ethnic autobiography"; Barbara Shollar deals with both texts as autobiographical in genre, if not in fact; and Susanne Amy Shavelson insists that since we cannot be sure about the truth value of Stern's work, we must concentrate on the texts rather than how they reflect the life of the author. See Browder, *Slippery Characters: Ethnic Impersonators and American Identities* (Chapel Hill: U of

North Carolina P, 2000) 165–70; Shollar, 195–201; and Shavelson 118–19.

Interestingly, the only person before 1993 to claim without question that *My Mother and I* is entirely a work of fiction was Edward Bok's wife, Mary Louise Curtis Bok, who wrote in her introduction to the 1937 collection of Stern's pseudonymous newspaper columns, *Not All Laughter: A Mirror to Our Times*: "They are contributions from a career as writer, begun twenty years ago, in 1917, when my husband, Edward Bok, first published an imaginary biography, tender, and yet keenly interpretive of a great problem in America, under the title *My Mother and I*, later to become a book with an introduction by President Theodore Roosevelt" (Mary Louise Bok, introduction, *Not All Laughter: A Mirror to Our Times*, Eleanor Morton [Elizabeth Gertrude Stern] [Philadelphia: John C. Winston, 1937]). One must wonder what Mary and Edward Bok knew about Stern's life to call her first work an "imaginary autobiography."

113. See Ellen M. Umansky, "Representations of Jewish Women in the Works and Life of Elizabeth Stern," *Modern Judaism* 13 (1993): 165–76. According to Thomas Noel Stern, his mother was taken in at the age of seven by Sarah Leah and Aaron Levin, Russian Jewish immigrants who raised her as their daughter and gave her their name. Sarah became a loving mother to the abandoned child, but Aaron repeatedly raped Elizabeth until she became pregnant with his child at the age of fourteen. The son's account of his mother's life cannot be taken entirely at face value. He is not a reliable narrator of her story. He tells us outright that as a child, "I realized that the telling of fables was the way of the world. . . . It was 'ok' for me to tell tales about myself," and it is impossible for the reader to determine when he is telling tales and when he is not (*Secret* 5). Furthermore, he is not a trustworthy recorder of family history. All of what he recounts in this book occurred before he was fourteen years old, and he never corroborated any of it with his mother or her family before recording it more than sixty years later. Documents external to his book fail to provide definitive proof as to who his mother really was. Also, much of his work reads like recovered memory, written in the name of therapy. Even more problematic is T. Noel Stern's second agenda for his book: he desperately desires to prove that he is not Jewish.

Still, it is possible that, as her son suggests, Elizabeth Stern invented herself as a Jewish immigrant through her writings as a way to create for herself a more acceptable American identity. She preferred to be an assimilable foreigner than a permanently "stained" bastard (7, 33). The genre of the immigrant autobiography, with its trope of the assimilating immigrant as the adopted or foster child of America, replacing foreign fathers with founding fathers, could have afforded her with the ideal literary means through which to talk about her experience. As an actual foster child taking on the voice of the immigrant, Stern could have doubled the metaphor over onto itself so that the immigrant represents the foster child representing the immigrant.

114. Thomas Noel Stern claims that his mother burned all records of her past, and indeed, the Leon and Elizabeth Stern archives housed at Haverford College contain little pertaining to Elizabeth's life before the 1920s. (See Leon and Elizabeth Stern Papers, Quaker Collection, Magill Library, Haverford College, Haverford, Pennsylvania. The Stern papers were donated to Haverford in 1975 by their son

Richard because in their later years, his parents had joined the Quaker community of Philadelphia.) No birth or emigration certificates can be located, and records at the St. Paul orphanage, where T. Noel Stern claims his mother resided for a short time, fail to list her as a resident (Rev. David B. Lady, *History of St. Paul's Orphans' Home* [Philadelphia: Sunday School Board, 1917], and personal communication with St. Paul Homes, now located in Greenville, Pennsylvania). While Ellen Umansky has found a marriage certificate indicating that Elizabeth and Leon were married by an Orthodox rabbi in Pittsburgh ("Representations" 166), this evidence can be interpreted in multiple ways. Thomas Noel Stern claims that wishing to keep her illegitimate birth a secret, Elizabeth used the secret of Aaron's rape to blackmail her foster father into making a Jewish wedding for her and thereby proclaiming her Jewish to the world (3–4). However, the marriage certificate could, of course, also indicate that Elizabeth was Aaron and Sarah Leah's natural daughter and that Leon was in fact of Jewish birth as well.

The only documents I have located outside of T. Noel Stern's book that might corroborate at least part of his story are U.S. census records. In both the 1900 and 1910 censuses, place of birth for Elizabeth is recorded as Russia, while in the 1920 census, after she had married and left the Levin house, it is recorded as Pittsburgh. While this does not prove where Elizabeth actually was born, it does reveal that different stories about who she was were being told at different times.

Interestingly, one of the items preserved in Stern's papers is a letter from a James A. Montgomery Jr., librarian of the Library of the Supreme Court of Pennsylvania, praising Stern for a piece in her regular newspaper column, which he calls a "castigation of the biographical debunkers." "The debunking habit has grown to be a disgraceful national excrescence which needs just such treatment as yours," he declares (28 February 1931). With this column, Stern left behind an attack on those who would call into question her own version of her biography.

115. Kirsten Anna Wasson, "Daughters of Promise, Mothers of Revision: Three Jewish American Immigrant Writers and Cultural Inscriptions of Identity," diss., U of Wisconsin, 1992, 226–27. While Wasson carefully distinguishes between the voices of the narrator and the protagonist, she problematically views both as identical to the author and refers to all as "Elizabeth" or "Stern."

116. *My Mother* 124.

117. "My Mother" 86; *My Mother* 168.

118. Anzia Yezierska, *Bread Givers* (1925; New York: Persea Books, 1975) 66.

119. "My Mother" 22; *My Mother* 112–13.

120. *My Mother* 118. Interestingly, in the *Ladies' Home Journal* story, her Americanness is ungendered here, for she says, "I was accepted as, and become, an American in its friendly white walls" (80). However, she will go on to detail how she became part of the "strange, new womanhood of America" (22).

121. *My Mother* 117.

122. *My Mother* 143; "My Mother" ("In New York I studied in an American college, one of America's most wonderful, majestic institutions. I lived—lived!—in an American home") 82.

123. Shollar, 155–57. Wendy Zierler shares this view of the centrality of middle-class femininity to the child's definition of self (11).

124. "My Mother" 22; *My Mother* 110, which adds to the description of this mother: "She romped through the two-steps with us, and judged the forfeits."

125. "My Mother" 22; *My Mother* 107; Sigmund Freud, "The Family Romance," *The Standard Edition of the Complete Psychological Works of Sigmund Freud*, trans. James Strachey, vol. 9 (London: Hogarth, 1959) 237–41.

126. See Ruth Schwartz Cowan's study of housework in the United States, *More Work for Mother: The Ironies of Household Technology from the Open Hearth to the Microwave* (New York: Basic Books, 1983) 171–72.

127. "My Mother" 80; *My Mother* 136, with minor revisions ("And at college were opened to my eyes windows upon splendid and beautiful visions").

128. "My Mother" 22; *My Mother* 84.

129. "My Mother" 80; *My Mother* 114–15, with minor changes ("Whom could she marry if she became so learned?").

130. In *Alma Mater: Design and Experience in the Women's Colleges from Their Nineteenth-Century Beginnings to the 1930s* (1985; Amherst: U of Massachusetts P, 1993), Helen Lefkowitz Horowitz demonstrates how the very architectural designs of the early women's colleges sought to reconcile the idea of women's higher education with the desire of parents and educators to preserve the femininity and domestic ideals of those who enrolled (28–41, 69–81).

131. See, for instance, Thomas I. Masson, "Can Parents and Children Get Together?" *LHJ* October 1916: 43, 98.

132. "One of the most pitiable of all Life's ironies is that . . . the young do not appreciate their mothers at their full until they are gone from them," he writes (Editorial, *LHJ* November 1916: 8).

133. Editorial, *LHJ* (November 1916) 42.

134. Paula Hyman, "Culture and Gender: Women in the Immigrant Jewish Community," *The Legacy of Jewish Migration: 1881 and Its Impact*, ed. David Berger (New York: Brooklyn College, 1983) 163.

135. "My Mother" 22; *My Mother* 74.

136. "My Mother" 80; *My Mother* 116.

137. "My Mother" 86. The text is slightly altered in *My Mother*, where she writes: "We have this woman that I am, this woman mother has helped me to become. And I shall always remember that, though my life is now part of my land's, yet, if I am truly part of America, it was mother, she who does not understand America, who made me so" (168).

138. According to Linda Rosenzweig, what distinguished "new women" most from the generation of their mothers were "new jobs, new fashions, new social behaviors, and particularly new educational experiences" (*The Anchor of My Life: Middle-Class American Mothers and Daughters, 1880–1920* [New York: New York UP, 1993] 136).

139. "My Mother" 84; *My Mother* 153.

140. "My Mother" 84; *My Mother* 161.

141. "My Mother" 82.

142. "My Mother" 21; *My Mother* 12–13.

143. "My Mother" 86; *My Mother* 164.

144. "My Mother" 21; *My Mother* 15.

145. "My Mother" 22; *My Mother* 78.

146. "My Mother" 22; *My Mother* 79.

147. "My Mother" 22; *My Mother* 78.

148. Jacob Riis frequently photographed young children holding or carrying younger siblings in this awkward position. These photographs implicitly criticize parents who leave their babies in the incapable hands of their older children and "deny childhood" to all their offspring. See, for instance, Riis's photos "Girl and Baby on Doorstep" and "Minding the Baby—Scene in Gotham Court" in Riis's *How the Other Half Lives* 120, 125.

149. The other illustrations on the first page of Stern's *Ladies' Home Journal* story are entitled "At Eight I Was Writing the Letters Sent from Soho to Russia by My Illiterate Neighbors" and "Finally Father, Choosing His Words with Difficulty, Said to the Doctor: 'Sir, Do You Know You Are the First American Gentleman Who Has Spoken to Me in America?'" In the first of these pictures, five people crowd into Mammele's kitchen. Mammele does housework while conversing with a neighbor in the background as the child sits writing at the table with a disheveled man with beard, hat, and hook nose leaning over the table, telling her what to write as another seated woman looks on. This image is interesting, for while it illustrates the three sentences describing the girl's letter writing in the *Ladies' Home Journal*, it runs counter to the full description of letter writing in Stern's unabridged text, where she writes that she wrote for men in their own homes. Only women came to her mother's house to have their letters written, and Mammele always helped her with the task. While the book explains that writing is a collaborative act of ethnic women, the *LHJ* text and illustration give great power to the literate, Americanizing child over her old-world elders. The illustration of the "American Gentleman," the girl's high school principal, conversing at the table with her parents provides an interesting transition between the illustrations of the ghetto home and the single picture of the daughter's own American home. The artist portrays the parents' kitchen very differently in this illustration than in the earlier ones. Here, the usually cluttered table is clear of everything but wine glasses and a plate of cake. A feeling of greater space in the kitchen is conveyed by the distance at which the principal sits from the parents, and orderliness is portrayed by the large, neat bookcase and coats and hats on hooks in the background. Though this is the first meeting between the immigrant parents and the American gentleman, they and their house are clearly improved by the contact.

There are no illustrations where the piece continues into the back pages of the magazine. However, on each of the four pages where Stern's story continues, a single column of text is surrounded by illustrated advertisements, depicting corsets providing "perfect figure and perfect ease," Pyrex ovenware that allows for thorough cooking and attractive service, disinfectants enabling housewives to "fight disease as they do in hospitals," vacuum sweepers, tooth cleansers, and beauty schools. Stern's story and the ads surrounding it mutually reinforce a single image of the good, healthy, and beautiful American woman, family, and home attainable through education and a proper assortment of consumer products.

150. "My Mother" 86; *My Mother* 168.
151. *My Mother* 74.
152. *My Mother* 106.
153. *My Mother* 79.
154. *My Mother* 109.
155. *My Mother* 17. Kirsten Wasson reads this unusual clock as both a symbol of American liberty and a sign of the family's resistance to secular, American standards of measuring time (212). The erratic kitchen clock can also be seen as resisting the rules of home economics, which demanded, in Christine Frederick's words, that the household "work like a clock."
156. *My Mother* 99.
157. *My Mother* 99.
158. Drucker interprets this room in Woolfian terms, as expressing the female

author's need for "literal and figurative space for the ... room of her own" (65–67). Shollar sees the isolated room as a signal of the development of the protagonist's peculiarly American self-consciousness, which requires and demands privacy (148).

159. The book also provides a history of the protagonist's yearning for a particular kind of middle-class American home, recounting her first exposure to such a home in the little gray house in the ghetto where she grew up (57–63). This episode is surprisingly omitted from the *LHJ* despite the fact that it details the requirements of a proper *Journal* home. Its absence cannot be explained in ideological terms.

160. "My Mother" 86.

161. Lizabeth A. Cohen, "Embellishing a Life of Labor: An Interpretation of the Material Culture of American Working-Class Homes, 1885–1915," *Journal of American Culture* 3 (Winter 1980): 762–75.

162. Cohen, "Embellishing" 763.

163. Cohen, "Embellishing" 764. See also McMurry 268–74 for an analysis of rural resistance to the Victorian parlor and the persistent use of the kitchen as social center in rural homes of the period.

164. Heinze (*Adapting* 133–134) uses Stern's narrative as historical evidence in his analysis of the ways in which immigrants Americanized their domestic space. However, the subtext of her story as well as what she and Cohen reveal to be a serious discrepancy between the construction of space and its uses warn against using Stern's narrative uncritically in this way.

165. "My Mother" 82; *My Mother* 143.

166. *My Mother* 166.

167. The same conflict between the utility and beauty versus the exoticism of one's grandmother's functional art is described most poignantly in Alice Walker's story "Everyday Use" (1973), where the grandmother's quilt symbolizes the creative legacy of ethnic female ancestors (*Everyday Use*, ed. Barbara T. Christian [New Brunswick: Rutgers UP, 1994] 23–35).

168. "My Mother" 86; *My Mother* 166; here the comparison of the sterile kitchen to a drugstore is omitted.

169. "My Mother" 86; *My Mother* 164.

170. "My Mother" 86; *My Mother* 164–65.

171. "My Mother" 86; *My Mother* 168.

172. *My Mother* 168–69.

173. "My Mother" 21; *My Mother* 9.

174. Zaborowska asserts that the child's choice to leave parents behind in order to conquer new frontiers partakes in a very American tradition. In making this choice, Stern's protagonist writes herself as an American heroine (103–6).

175. "America's Possibilities" 228.

176. "My Mother" 80; *My Mother* 133.

177. As Kirsten Wasson says, "Stern's focus on her mother upsets the 'natural' movement of autobiography, wherein growth and development lead to adult identity defined by separation.... Consequently, the reader's investment in reading for linear progression within her life story is problematized; despite her success and happiness we are asked to evaluate the cost of the autobiographer's Americanization" ("Daughters" 225). Wasson's idea of the mother's perspective disrupting our usual course of reading narratives of development can apply whether or not Stern's text is autobiography. Instead of seeing Stern's double consciousness as interrupting the usual progression of the autobiographical form, Wendy Zierler views it as emblematic of the nature of female autobiography, which, she claims, typically combines its story of the development of the individual self with that of the development of the female self in relation to others (10).

178. *My Mother* 11.

179. *My Mother* 14.

180. "My Mother" 21. The text in *My Mother and I* reads slightly differently, with a bit less emphasis on the journey of parents to America ("I am writing to those sons and daughters of immigrant fathers who are now in America and to those who will come after this devastating war to America, and to those who will receive them" [12]).

181. "My Mother" 21. In the book version, Stern clarifies that she is referring to the daring immigrant parents (not native-born Americans) as the openers of the gates of America for their children. "I am writing this for myself and for those who, like me, are America's foster-children, to remind us of them, through whose pioneer courage the bright gates of this beautiful land of freedom were opened to us, and upon whose tumuli of grey and weary years of struggle, we their children rose to our opportunities," she says here (11–12).

182. In a reading of women's autobiography (which is how she classifies Stern's text) based on Nancy Chodorow's theories of female relationships, Wasson writes that by recording her life and that of her mother, Stern in fact becomes mother to her mother, re-creating her life through the text ("Daughters" 228).

183. Wasson, "Daughters" 218–19.

184. "My Mother" 21; *My Mother* 31.

185. *My Mother* 38–39.

186. *My Mother* 43.

187. *My Mother* 31–32.

188. *My Mother* 33.

189. *My Mother* 33.

190. *My Mother* 34.

191. *My Mother* 36.

192. *My Mother* 36. Stern's 1917 articulation of an ethnic women's artistic tradition anticipates the attempt of contemporary minority feminist authors to recognize the artistry of latent in their mothers' daily language, activities, gardens, and kitchens (see, for instance, Paule Marshall, "From the Poets in the Kitchen," *Merle: A Novella and Other Stories* [London: Virago, 1983] 3–12; and Alice Walker, "In Search of Our Mothers' Gardens," *In Search of Our Mothers' Gardens: Womanist Prose* [New York: Harcourt Brace, 1983] 231–43).

193. The girl's role as communal letter writer is mentioned in the *LHJ* as follows: "However, it was difficult to hold my incurable wickedness [tomboyishness] against me, for as mother astutely told my detractors I wrote the best Yiddish letter composed by a female of any age in Soho. Indeed at the ripe age of eight, I was writing most of the love letters, filial letters, marital letters and letters of condolence sent from Soho to Russia by my illiterate neighbors. I was paid two cents a letter, the paper being furnished by me" (21).

194. See, for instance, Stern's 1926 book *I Am a Woman—and a Jew*. In this work, the Jewish protagonist believes that marriage to a Christian man will solidify her identity as an American. But she discovers the failure of marriage both to satisfy her personal ambitions and to blur the markers of her former identity, which she now understands in terms of the increasingly popular discourse of race:

> Now I knew . . . what every Jew is and does, is something which must, indeed, belong to his people; that no other people living have our peculiar quality, which is not individual, but racial, and which gives to each of us who accomplished with genius, the ability to express through himself only the

accumulated genius of the race, so that every Jewish writer, statesman, actor, is not only himself, but the mirror of his people, the voice of his people.

I did not feel part of the Jewish State. I did not need it. But the Jewish nation does not need the boundaries of a land, it does not require the frontier of a physical country. Each of us carries the boundaries, the acknowledgment of its sovereignty, in our hearts, in our blood. (358–59)

By locating Jewishness in her blood, the narrator seeks to transform her own apparently inescapable Jewishness into a positive identity that she then forcibly affixes to her children, claiming it as a physical and immutable reality. She completely removes the element of choice from her definition of Jewish identity, proclaiming: "The citizen chose his country, with reason, with love. But the Jew in me could, by no choice, no reasoning, elect to be anything but a Jew: that was part of the life which poured through my veins; it had come to be in my mother's womb, before I had thought, before I had being" (359–60). By separating the citizen from the Jew, nation from race, she overturns the idea of assimilation, arguing that even when one chooses to become an American, one nevertheless always remains a Jew, in a very different way than posited by *My Mother and I*.

CHAPTER 4

1. Roosevelt, "True Americanism" 26.
2. [Finley Peter Dunne], "A Book Review," 19 November 1899, *Mr. Dooley's Philosophy* (New York: R. H. Russell, 1900) 15.
3. [Dunne], "A Book Review" 13, 17, 18.

4. TR to Dunne, 28 November 1899, Roosevelt Papers. Unless otherwise indicated, all quotations from the Roosevelt-Dunne correspondence are taken from this collection.
5. Dunne to TR, 10 January 1900.
6. The claim to be speaking for the people against special interest is James J. Connolly's definition of Progressivism, which he understands as a style of political discourse and behavior that was adopted by multiple interest groups for their own ends. See Connolly's *Triumph of Ethnic Progressivism*.
7. Gerstle 25–43; Slotkin 104.
8. Theodore Roosevelt, "The Reunion of the Rough Riders," 7 April 1905, *Rough Riders*, Appendix, *Works* 11:177.
9. For a broader discussion of the role of military service in establishing equal rights, particularly for minorities, see Ronald R. Krebs, *Fighting for Rights: Military Service and the Politics of Citizenship* (Ithaca: Cornell UP, 2006).
10. [Dunne], "A Book Review" 15. Dunne would comment in his memoirs that at the time that he wrote his "Book Review," the "picture I had of him in my mind was that of a dude rancher, noisy, something of a bully, class proud, who pretended to a sentiment of democracy that he by no means felt.... I was ready to ridicule him to the limit" (Philip Dunne, ed., *Mr. Dooley Remembers: The Informal Memoirs of Finley Peter Dunne* [Boston: Little, Brown, 1963] 185).
11. Connolly 8–9.
12. In examining Boston municipal politics, James Connolly finds that progressivism was not solely the attempt of the middle class to critique and depose corrupt ethnic politicians; it simultaneously included the attempts of ethnic groups to use the rhetoric of progressivism to critique the larger system and to insist on their

place within. What Connolly calls "ethnic Progressivism" often worked by exposing Anglo-American reformers as a special interest group and claiming the superior legitimacy of ethnic politicians to speak for the people and to uphold progressive American values. Connolly's work on ethnic progressivism in Boston has provided me with the framework for this analysis of Mr. Dooley's ethnic critique of "True Americanism"; I am grateful to the anonymous reader for NYU who pointed me in this direction. See Connolly 39–76.

13. Grace Eckley, *Finley Peter Dunne* (Boston: Twayne, 1981) 36. Other critics who question the "Irishness" of Mr. Dooley include Barbara C. Schaaf, *Mr. Dooley's Chicago* (Garden City: Anchor/Doubleday, 1977); Finley Peter Dunne's son Philip Dunne in *Mr. Dooley Remembers*; and, to a more limited degree, Charles Fanning in *Mr. Dooley and the Chicago Irish: An Anthology* (New York: Arno Press, 1976).

14. In memory of his mother, Dunne took her maiden name, Finley, as his middle name in 1886. In 1888, he reversed the order, signing his name FP Dunne.

15. Dunne's wife, Margaret Abbott, was the daughter of Mary Ives Abbott, a widowed Bostonian who moved to Chicago, where she worked with Dunne on the *Chicago Evening Post* as the art and book review editor. Mary Abbot served as hostess to many of Chicago's social and literary elite, including Dunne. According to Elmer Ellis, Dunne credited her with advancing his social status (*Mr. Dooley's America: A Life of Finley Peter Dunne* [New York: Knopf, 1941] 55).

16. Finley Peter Dunne, introduction, *Mr. Dooley at His Best*, ed. Elmer Ellis (1936; New York: Scribner's, 1938) xxiii.

17. Upon the death of financier Jay Gould, the *Chicago Evening Post* printed Dunne's first column written in the voice of a Chicago Irish barkeep, then called Col. McNeery. Through the voice of Col. McNeery, Dunne expressed views about Gould that he had originally heard from a real saloonkeeper named James McGarry, who owned a pub Dunne frequented. The device worked, and Dunne expanded his use of Col. McNeery, employing this character as a mask behind which to critique Chicago politics. The real James McGarry complained, however, that readers were attributing all the fictional McNeery's comments to him. In October 1893, Dunne changed his character's name to Martin Dooley and altered the location of the bar.

18. Finley Peter Dunne, "The Annual Freedom Picnic," 18 August 1894, rpt. in Fanning, *Mr. Dooley and the Chicago Irish* 414.

19. Schaaf 2. Schaaf argues that Dunne wrote neither as "a professional Irishman, nor did he write as a hyphenated American"

20. Philip Dunne, *Mr. Dooley Remembers* 50–51.

21. Philip Dunne, *Mr. Dooley Remembers* 270.

22. Philip Dunne, *Mr. Dooley Remembers* 269.

23. Letter from Philip Dunne to Grace Eckley, 12 March 1978, rpt. in Eckley 36. Apparently embarrassed by the very voice that won his family entrée into the upper echelons of American society, Philip Dunne repudiates the Irish American context, function, and meanings of his father's legacy by erasing Mr. Dooley's dialect.

24. Connolly 4–14. Histories of progressivism that have cast it as a middle-class attack on the ethnic machine include, among others, Richard Hofstadter's *Age of Reform* (1955); Robert Wiebe's *Search for Order* (1967); Paul Boyer's *Urban Masses and Moral Order in America* (1978); Gabriel Kolko's *The Triumph*

of Conservativism: A Reconsideration of American History, 1900–1916 (New York: Free Press, 1963); and Robert Crunden's *Ministers of Reform: The Progressives' Achievement in American Civilization, 1889–1920* (New York: Basic Books, 1982).

25. Dunne, introduction, *Mr. Dooley at His Best* xxiii–xxiv.

26. Fanning, *Mr. Dooley and the Chicago Irish*.

27. F[inley] P[eter] D[unne], *Mr. Dooley in Peace and in War* (1898; New York: Greenwood Press, 1968) viii.

28. [Dunne], *Peace and War* ix. As Dunne explained further in an 1899 interview, he sought to "make Dooley talk as an Irishman would talk who has lived thirty or forty years in America, and whose natural pronunciation had been more or less affected by the slang of the streets" (Irving Way, "Mr. Martin Dooley of Chicago," *Bookman* [May 1899]: 217).

29. Dunne, "Poverty and Pride in the Callaghan Family," 24 November 1894, rpt. in Fanning, *Mr. Dooley and the Chicago Irish* 239–41.

30. Dunne, "Naming the Hogan Baby," 17 November 1894, rpt. in Fanning, *Mr. Dooley and the Chicago Irish* 198–201.

31. Dunne, "Molly Donahue and the Divided Skirt," 22 September 1894, rpt. in Fanning, *Mr. Dooley and the Chicago Irish* 201–4.

32. Dunne, "The Popularity of Firemen," 23 November 1895, rpt. in Fanning, *Mr. Dooley and the Chicago Irish* 161–65.

33. Dunne, "The Pullman Strike: Lemons and Liberty," 7 July 1894, rpt. in Fanning, *Mr. Dooley and the Chicago Irish* 266–69; Dunne, "The Pullman Strike: The Tragedy of the Agitator," 14 July 1894, rpt. in Fanning, *Mr. Dooley and the Chicago Irish* 269–71; Dunne, "The Pullman Strike: What Does He Care," 25 August 1894, rpt. in Fanning, *Mr. Dooley and the Chicago Irish* 271–75.

34. Dunne, "Hanging Alderman: How Boodle Is Dispensed," 17 December 1898, rpt. in Fanning, *Mr. Dooley and the Chicago Irish* 330–35; Dunne, "Political Appointments by the Spoils System," 6 January 1894, rpt. in Fanning, *Mr. Dooley and the Chicago Irish* 326–30.

35. Dunne, "An Irish-German Alliance in Bridgeport," 11 January 1896, rpt. in Fanning, *Mr. Dooley and the Chicago Irish* 388–91.

36. For a discussion of the shifting balance between Bridgeport and the larger world in the columns over time, see Charles Fanning, *Finley Peter Dunne and Mr. Dooley* (Lexington: UP of Kentucky, 1978) 175–85.

37. In a 1919 review of Dunne's final book of collected columns, Frances Hackett argued that Dunne was no longer "sufficiently disreputable" to be writing satire; he was no longer an outsider to the world of the rich and powerful whom he satirized ("Mr. Dooley," *New Republic* 24 September 1919: 235–36). Recent critics have argued much the same. See, for instance, Fanning, *Finley Peter Dunne and Mr. Dooley* 175–77, 242–45; Charles Fanning, *The Irish Voice in America: 250 Years of Irish-American Fiction*, 2nd ed. (Lexington: UP of Kentucky, 2000) 236; Joseph Boskin and Joseph Dorinson, "Ethnic Humor: Subversion and Survival," *American Quarterly* 37 (Spring 1985): 85.

38. Boskin and Dorinson 85.

39. Fanning, *Finley Peter Dunne and Mr. Dooley* 210.

40. Arthur Power Dudden is one of the few critics to recognize that Dooley's Irishness affords him the perspective to uncover America's "democratic pretensions" and "nativist contradictions" ("The Record of Political Humor," *American Quarterly* 37 [Spring 1985]: 56).

41. In his study of the linguistic politics of vernacular literature, Gavin Roger Jones has demonstrated the conflict inherent in dialect literature of the late nineteenth and early twentieth centuries. Vernacular language could simultaneously create and destroy national identity. The profusion of dialect writing in this period celebrated the multiplicity of the American voice and citizenry, suggesting that America's essence lay in its variety. Yet at the same time, this very diversity endangered the unity of the nation. It undermined any linguistic, social, and political hegemony. While vernacular writing could evoke "rural quaintness," it could also evoke the mass immigration and urbanization that threatened the nation's identity. It made the English language alien to its native speakers, forcing them to translate within their own language. For further discussion, see Gavin Roger Jones's *Strange Talk: The Politics of Dialect Literature in Gilded Age America* (Berkley: U of California P, 1999) 37–55.

42. For a history and analysis of the "crackerbox philosopher" in American literature, see Jennette Tandy, *Crackerbox Philosophers in American Humor and Satire* (1924; Port Washington: Kennikat Press, 1964).

43. As Walter Blair points out, Dunne was not the first to give his funny man a foreign accent (*Horse Sense in America: From Benjamin Franklin to Ogden Nash* [1942; New York: Russell and Russell, 1962] 241–43). Dunne was, however, incredibly successful at it and used his character's voice to provide an ethnic critique of America as he found it.

44. For a discussion of the ways in which Dooley turns Bridgeport into small-town America, see James DeMuth, *Small Town Chicago: The Comic Perspective of Finley Peter Dunne, George Ade, and Ring Lardner* (Port Washington: Kennikat Press, 1980) 3, 28–30, 44–45.

45. John Lowe, "Newsprint Masks: The Comic Columns of Finley Peter Dunne, Alexander Posey, and Langston Hughes," *Beyond the Binary: Reconstructing Cultural Identity in a Multicultural Context*, ed. Timothy B. Powell (New Brunswick: Rutgers UP, 1999) 214.

46. Sollors, *Beyond Ethnicity* 251. Sollors adds that by assuming the form of an in-group conversation, the ethnic author can be freed from observing linguistic, generic, and ideological conventions.

47. Theodore Roosevelt, "Race Decadence," *Outlook*, 8 April 1911, *Works*, memorial edition, 14:155.

48. [Finley Peter Dunne], "Immigration," *Boston Globe*, 15 December 1901, rpt. in *Observations by Mr. Dooley* (1902; New York: Greenwood Press, 1969) 50–51.

49. [Dunne], "Immigration" 50.

50. [Finley Peter Dunne], "Americans Abroad," *Boston Globe* 28 January 1900, rpt. in *Philosophy* 22.

51. [Dunne], "Americans Abroad" 26.

52. [Dunne], "Americans Abroad" 24.

53. See Øverland (1–22, 120–44) on the rhetorical modes of claiming a place for the immigrant in America.

54. Roosevelt, "Colonial Survival" 368.

55. Roosevelt, "True Americanism" 18.

56. Roosevelt, "Colonial Survival" 368.

57. Roosevelt, "Race Decadence" 155.

58. For analyses of the politics of the frame in vernacular literature, see Alan Trachtenberg, *The Incorporation of America: Culture and Society in the Gilded Age* (New York: Hill and Wang, 1982) 189–90. For immigrant and African American writers, the standard English-speaking narrator could also be a means through which to assert

their own mainstream American identities within their dialect texts—something Dunne, as a second-generation Irish American, did not feel pressure to prove. For a discussion of this phenomenon, see Aviva Taubenfeld, "'Only an "L"': Linguistic Borders and the Immigrant Author in Abraham Cahan's *Yekl* and *Yankel der Yankee*," *Multilingual America: Transnationalism, Ethnicity, and the Languages of American Literature*, ed. Werner Sollors (New York: New York UP, 1998) 154–56. In *Cultures of Letters: Scenes of Reading and Writing in Nineteenth-Century America* (Chicago: U of Chicago P, 1993), Richard Brodhead discusses other ways in which the foreign is managed and controlled in dialect literature of this period (120–41).

59. [Dunne], "On a Speech by President McKinley," *Peace and War* 81.

60. [Dunne], "On a Speech" 83.

61. In reality, McKinley said: "My countrymen, the currents of destiny flow through the hearts of the people; who will check them? Who will divert them? Who will stop them? And the movements of men, planned and designed by the Master of Men, will never be interrupted by the American people" (quoted in Fanning, *Finley Peter Dunne and Mr. Dooley* 203).

62. [Dunne], "On a Speech" 85–86.

63. [Dunne], "On a Speech" 86.

64. Matthew Frye Jacobson demonstrates this paradigm of immigrant responses to the Spanish-American War and its aftermath in *Special Sorrows*.

65. Fanning, *Finley Peter Dunne and Mr. Dooley* 185–206.

66. *Chicago Journal* 18 March 1899, cited in Fanning, *Finley Peter Dunne and Mr. Dooley* 200.

67. Though Mack can be a general, informal way of addressing a man, Dooley uses it to indicate Irishness. In his piece "The Irishman Abroad," for instance, he comments: "There's Mac's an' O's in ivry capital iv Europe atin' off silver plates whin their relations is staggerin' under th' creels iv turf in th' Connaught bogs.... Why don't they do as much for their own counthry?" (*Mr. Dooley in the Hearts of His Countrymen* [Boston: Small, Maynard, 1899] 204).

68. [Dunne], "On His Cousin George," *Peace and War* 20.

69. [Dunne], "On Fitz-Hugh Lee," *Peace and War* 10.

70. Interestingly, Dooley's pronunciation of Roosevelt's surname Judaicized the president rather than making him Irish. Referring to Roosevelt consistently as "Rosenfelt," which, Dunne said, he "thought was about the way a Mr. Dooley would pronounce the name," seems to have left some readers confused about the president's ethnicity. In his memoir, Dunne recounts that the *London Spectator* took him to task for "'alluding to the President's Jewish ancestry.'" When he showed this article to Roosevelt, the president laughed and responded, "'No. So far as I know I haven't a trace of Jewish blood in me. I wish I had a little. But I'm straight Dutch and Irish,'" and he sang his "favorite song": "'The Irish, the Irish, they don't amount to much, but they're a damned sight better than the Goddammned Dutch'" (Philip Dunne, *Mr. Dooley Remembers* 39).

71. Though often dominating urban municipal politics, Irish Americans were excluded from national power. As Dunne writes to Roosevelt: "Irishmen are the most unsuccessful politicians in the country. Although they are all there is to politics in the North between elections, there is not, with one exception, a single representative Irish man in any important cabinet, diplomatic, judicial, or administrative office....

[A]ppointed office is one of the recognized ways of demonstrating political friendship. In this respect every administration has managed to dissemble its love even if it has not actually kicked us downstairs" (Dunne to TR, 1 December 1904).

72. Ralph Ellison, "An Extravagance of Laughter," *The Collected Essays of Ralph Ellison*, ed. John Callahan (New York: Modern Library, 1995) 656–57.

73. Ellison 658.

74. Ellison 613–14.

75. [Finley Peter Dunne], "Youth and Age," *Mr. Dooley's Opinions* (New York: R. H. Russell, 1901) 182, 186.

76. [Finley Peter Dunne], "The Booker Washington Incident," *Opinions* 208–9. Dunne went further, arguing that in fact, Roosevelt did a disservice to Washington and his race by inviting him to dine. To really help the "naygur," Dooley says, "I'd take way his right to vote an' his right to ate at th' same table an' his right to ride on th' cars an' even his sacred right to wurruk. I'd take thim all away an' give him th' on'y right he needs nowadays in th' South. . . . th' right to live. . . . If he cud start with that he might make something iv himsilf" (212). In effect, Dooley argues that though Roosevelt made a social statement through his dinner with Washington, he was not doing enough to defend the basic rights of African Americans.

77. See Roosevelt's letters to Dunne dated 16 January 1900, 22 November 1900, 24 June 1900, and 26 August 1901. After Roosevelt took up residence in the White House, however, Dunne came several times to visit, dine, and discuss.

78. Dunne to TR, 7 January 1907.

79. From the earliest examinations of Roosevelt's reception of Dooley and Dunne, critics have argued that Roosevelt courted the satirist "because he feared that scourge of princes, Mr. Dooley" (Ellis 204). Elmer Ellis suggests that such claims have come from "some of Roosevelt's enemies" and suggests Roosevelt's "good temper" at much of Dooley's swipes, but he concluded that "Theodore Roosevelt's assiduous cultivation of Dunne was probably not alone due to his appreciation of wisdom and humor" (Ellis, *Mr. Dooley's America: A Life of Finley Peter Dunne* [New York: Knopf, 1941] 293). Charles Fanning states similarly that Roosevelt conducted a "long campaign to disarm Mr. Dooley by proffering friendship to his creator" (*Finley Peter Dunne and Mr. Dooley* 212).

80. TR to Dunne, 9 January 1907.

81. [Finley Peter Dunne], "Swearing," *Observations* 223, 225–26.

82. [Finley Peter Dunne], "The Food We Eat," *Dissertations by Mr. Dooley* (New York: Harper, 1906) 249.

83. [Dunne], "White House Discipline," *Observations* 60–61.

84. [Dunne], "The News of a Week," *Observations* 186–87.

85. For a discussion of the Roosevelt White House as a salon, see Richard Collin's *Theodore Roosevelt, Culture, Diplomacy and Expansion: A New View of American Imperialism* (Baton Rouge: Louisiana State UP, 1985) 25–26, 33–47.

86. Bederman 170–87; Testi, 1509–33; Sarah Watts, *Rough Rider in the White House: Theodore Roosevelt and the Politics of Desire* (Chicago: U of Chicago P, 2003) 14–16.

87. Roosevelt, *Autobiography* 150–51.

88. Roosevelt, *Autobiography* 59.

89. Testi 1517. For discussions of the virility associated with the working class, see, for instance, Keith Gandal's *Virtues of the Vicious*.

90. Roosevelt, *Autobiography* 59.

91. [Robert L. O'Brien], "The Man President Roosevelt Works For," *LHJ* June 1906: 19.

92. "Practical Politics" is the title of the third chapter of Roosevelt's autobiography. Roosevelt uses dialect similarly in the chapter entitled "In Cowboy Land," which first appeared in the *Century* in 1893. Roosevelt admitted to finding the art of representing spoken speech far more difficult than it appeared. "I began to be a little doubtful about my own dialect accuracy," he wrote to his friend the Columbia English professor Brander Matthews. "The things I have been trained to observe I can observe all right, but it is astonishing how difficult it is to record even what one is familiar with if one is not accustomed to recording it" (TR to Brander Matthews, 5 May 1894, in Oliver, *Letters* 78). Like many realist and local-color writers, Roosevelt was further disappointed to be told by the *Century* that his use of dialect might offend its genteel readers and to "have all the snap taken out of his speech" by the editors (TR to Brander Matthews, 8 June 1893, Oliver, *Letters* 58).

93. Roosevelt, *Autobiography* 61.

94. Roosevelt, *Autobiography* 92–93. In another instance of Roosevelt's use of dialect, he quotes at length the motion of the legislator whom he tellingly calls "Brogan," who rose and pronounced, "I rise to a point of ordher under the rules!" Being informed that there are no rules to object to, he responds, "Thin I move that they be amended until there ar-r-re!" (93). In this case, dialect becomes a way to mock and discount the Irish American politician, who presents a threat to the system, and to make clear the need for politicians like Roosevelt.

95. [Dunne], "Swearing," *Observations* 223.

96. [Dunne], "Swearing," *Observations* 224.

97. [Dunne], "White House Discipline," *Observations* 61.

98. TR to Dunne, 9 January 1907.

99. Theodore Roosevelt, "The Manly Virtues and Practical Politics," 1894, *American Ideals*, *Works* 13:33.

100. TR to Dunne, 23 November 1904.

101. [Dunne], "The Anglo-Saxon Triumph," *Dissertations* 213–18.

102. Brander Matthews to TR, 27 November 1904, cited in Oliver, *Letters* 150.

103. Roosevelt, *The Naval War of 1812* 23.

104. Roosevelt, *Winning of the West* 1:1. See also Roosevelt, "Joseph Hodges Choate," *Works*, memorial edition, 11:264.

105. Roosevelt, "Children of the Crucible" 30.

106. Dyer 68. Updating his science, Roosevelt substituted the notion of relatedness through pure blood with an idea of linguistic relatedness. In addition to replacing the term "Anglo-Saxon" with the "English-speaking race," he argued in 1910 that the terms "Aryan" and "Teuton" were linguistic designations rather than physical ones ("Biological Analogies" 83).

107. For histories of the rhetoric, theories, and uses in foreign affairs of American claims to Anglo-Saxon identity, see Reginald Horseman, *Race and Manifest Destiny: The Origins of American Racial Anglo-Saxonism* (Cambridge: Harvard UP, 1981); and Stuart Anderson, *Race and Rapprochement: Anglo-Saxonism and Anglo-American Relations, 1895–1904* (Rutherford: Fairleigh Dickinson UP, 1981).

108. [Dunne], "On the Anglo-Saxon," *Peace and War* 54–55.

109. Jacobson, *Special Sorrows* 189.

110. Jacobson, *Whiteness* 39–52. For examples of claims of America as an Anglo-Saxon nation, see, for instance, Franklin H. Giddings, "The American People," *International Quarterly* 7 (June 1903): 281–99; and John Burgess, "Germany, Great Britain and the United States," *Political Science Quarterly*

19 (March 1904): 1–19. Burgess argues here for closer relationships among the "three great Teutonic nations" based on their racial relatedness (1). Brander Matthews discusses this article with Roosevelt in a letter dated 10 October 1904 (Oliver, *Letters* 144).

111. [Finley Peter Dunne], "International Amenities," *Observations* 33.

112. [Dunne], "International Amenities," *Observations* 33.

113. Assimilating into an Anglo-American identity appears to have been problematic for Dunne as well as for Dooley.

114. [Dunne], "Amateur Ambassadors," *Opinions* 37.

115. [Finley Peter Dunne], "Lord Charles Beresford," *Hearts* 18.

116. [Dunne], "Amateur Ambassadors," *Opinions* 41.

117. [Dunne], "International Amenities," *Observations* 34.

118. [Dunne], "International Amenities" 36.

119. [Dunne], "Lord Charles Beresford" 19–20.

120. [Dunne], "Lord Charles Beresford" 21.

121. [Dunne], "Lord Charles Beresford" 21

122. [Dunne], "The Anglo-Saxon Triumph" 214.

123. [Dunne], "The Anglo-Saxon Triumph" 214–15.

124. [Dunne], "The Anglo-Saxon Triumph" 215–16.

125. [Dunne], "The Anglo-Saxon Triumph" 216–17.

126. [Dunne], "The Anglo-Saxon Triumph" 218.

127. TR to Dunne, 23 November 1904.

128. TR to Dunne, 23 November 1904.

129. Roosevelt, "True Americanism" 25.

130. I am grateful to Robert A. Ferguson for pointing out this slippage.

131. Dunne to TR, 1 December 1904.

132. Roosevelt, "True Americanism" 23.

133. Dunne to TR, 23 November 1904.

134. *New York Sun*, 20 November 1904. It is noteworthy that Zangwill, who had been in the United States at this time, kept an article reporting this speech in his files (Zangwill Papers A120/165). Perhaps it was on the basis of Roosevelt's atypically broad claims here to American hybridity that Zangwill believed his racial melting-pot vision corresponded to Roosevelt's own.

EPILOGUE

1. Roosevelt, "True Americanism" 22.

2. Theodore Roosevelt, preface, "My Mother and I" 21.

BIBLIOGRAPHY

ARCHIVAL COLLECTIONS

Curtis Publishing Company Papers, Special Collections, Van Pelt Library, University of Pennsylvania, Philadelphia, Pennsylvania

John Hay Papers, Cornell University, Ithaca, New York

Jacob A. Riis Collection, Library of Congress, Washington, DC

Jacob A. Riis Collection, Museum of the City of New York, New York, New York

Jacob A. Riis Collection, New York Public Library (NYPL), New York, New York

Theodore Roosevelt Collection, Houghton Library, Harvard University, Cambridge, Massachusetts

Theodore Roosevelt Papers, Library of Congress, Washington, DC

Leon and Elizabeth Stern Papers, Quaker Collection, Magill Library, Haverford College, Haverford, Pennsylvania

Israel Zangwill Papers, Central Zionist Archives (CZA), Jerusalem, Israel

PUBLISHED WORKS

Abu-Laban, Yasmeen, and Victoria Lamont. "Crossing Borders: Interdisciplinarity, Immigration and the Melting Pot in the American Cultural Imaginary." *Canadian Review of American Studies* 27.2 (1997): 23–43.

Addams, Jane. *Twenty Years at Hull-House*. 1910. New York: Signet, 1982.

Alland, Alexander, Sr. *Jacob A. Riis, Photographer and Citizen*. Millerton: Aperture, 1974.

"America's Possibilities for the Immigrant." Rev. of *My Mother and I, Nation* 30 August 1917: 225.

Ammons, Elizabeth, and Valerie Rohy. Introduction. *American Local Color Writing, 1880–1920*. Ed. Elizabeth Ammons and Valerie Rohy. New York: Penguin, 1998.

Anderson, Benedict. *Imagined Communities: Reflections of the Origin and Spread of Nationalism*. Rev. ed. London: Verso, 1991.

Anderson, Stuart. *Race and Rapprochement: Anglo-Saxonism and Anglo-American Relations, 1895–1904*. Rutherford: Fairleigh Dickinson UP, 1981.

Antin, Mary. *The Promised Land*. 1912. New York: Penguin, 1997.

"Attitudes toward *The Ladies' Home Journal* and *The Saturday Evening Post* as Advertising Mediums." Report of the Division of Commercial Research of the Advertising Department of the Curtis Publishing Company, 1916.

Balibar, Etienne, and Immanuel Wallerstein. *Race, Nation, Class: Ambiguous Identities*. Trans. Chris Turner. London: Verso, 1991.

Bederman, Gail. *Manliness and Civilization: A Cultural History of Gender and Race in the United States, 1880–1917*. Chicago: U of Chicago P, 1995.

Bellah, Robert. "Civil Religion in America." *Daedalus* 96 (Winter 1967): 1–21.

Bercovitch, Sacvan. *The American Jeremiad*. Madison: U of Wisconsin P, 1978.

Bhabba, Homi K., ed. *Nation and Narration*. New York: Routledge, 1990.

Biale, David. "The Melting Pot and Beyond: Jews and the Politics of American Identity." *Insider/Outsider: American Jews and Multiculturalism*. Ed. David Biale, Michael Galchinsky, and Susannah Heschel. Berkeley: U California P, 1998. 17–33.

Blair, Walter. *Horse Sense in America: From Benjamin Franklin to Ogden Nash*. 1942. New York: Russell and Russell, 1962.

Bodnar, John. *The Transplanted: A History of Immigrants in Urban America*. Bloomington: Indiana UP, 1985.

Boelhower, William. "The Brave New World of Immigrant Autobiography." *MELUS* 9 (Summer 1982): 5–23.

Boggs, Coleen Glenney. *Transnationalism and American Literature*. New York: Routledge, 2007.

Bok, Edward. *The Americanization of Edward Bok: The Autobiography of a Dutch Boy Fifty Years After*. 1920. New York: Scribner's, 1924.

———. *Successward: A Young Man's Book for Young Men*. 2nd ed. New York: Fleming H. Revell, 1895.

———. *Twice Thirty: Some Short and Simple Annals of the Road*. 1922. New York: Scribner's, 1925.

Bok, Mary Louise. Introduction. *Not All Laughter: A Mirror to Our Times*. Eleanor Morton, [Elizabeth Gertrude Stern]. Philadelphia: John C. Winston, 1937.

Boskin, Joseph, and Joseph Dorinson. "Ethnic Humor: Subversion and Survival." *American Quarterly* 37 (Spring 1985): 81–97.

Bourne, Randolph S. "Trans-national America." 1916. *Theories of Ethnicity: A Classical Reader*. Ed. Werner Sollors. New York: New York UP, 1996. 93–108.

Bowler, Peter. *The Eclipse of Darwinism: Anti-Darwinian Evolution Theories in the Decades around 1900*. Baltimore: Johns Hopkins UP, 1983.

Boyer, Paul. *Urban Masses and Moral Order in America*. Cambridge: Harvard UP, 1978.

Brace, Charles Loring. *The Dangerous Classes of New York and Twenty Years' Work among Them*. New York: Wynkoop and Hallenbeck, 1872.

Bramen, Carrie Tirado. *The Uses of Variety: Modern Americanism and the Quest for National Distinctiveness*. Cambridge: Harvard UP, 2000.

Brands, H. W. *T.R.: The Last Romantic*. New York: Basic Books, 1997.

Braziel, Jana Evans, and Anita Mannur, eds. *Theorizing Diaspora*. New York: Blackwell, 2003.

Broca, Paul. *On the Phenomena of Hybridity in the Genus Homo*. London: Longman, Green, 1864.

Brodhead, Richard H. *Cultures of Letters: Scenes of Reading and Writing in Nineteenth-Century America*. Chicago: U of Chicago P, 1993.

Brodkin, Karen. *How the Jews Became White Folks and What That Says about Race in America*. New Brunswick, NJ: Rutgers UP, 1998.

Browder, Laura. *Slippery Characters: Ethnic Impersonators and American Identities*. Chapel Hill: U of North Carolina P, 2000.

Burgess, John W. "Germany, Great Britain and the United States." *Political Science Quarterly* 19 (March 1904): 1–19.

Camfield, Gregg. *Necessary Madness: The Humor of Domesticity in Nineteenth-Century American Literature*. New York: Oxford UP, 1997.

Chapin, E. H. *Humanity in the City*. New York: DeWitt and Davenport, 1854.

Cohen, Lizabeth A. "Embellishing a Life of Labor: An Interpretation of the Material Culture of American Working-Class Homes, 1885–1915." *Journal of American Culture* 3 (Winter 1980): 762–75.

Cohen, Mitchell. "In Defense of Shaatnez: A Politics for Jews in a Multicultural America." *Insider/Outsider: American Jews and Multiculturalism*. Ed. David Biale, Michael Galchinsky, and Susannah Heschel. Berkeley: U of California P, 1998. 34–54.

Cohen, Naomi W. *A Dual Heritage: The Public Career of Oscar S. Straus*. Philadelphia: Jewish Publication Society, 1969.

Cohen, Robin. *Global Diasporas: An Introduction*. Seattle: U of Washington P, 1997.

Collin, Richard H. *Theodore Roosevelt, Culture, Diplomacy and Expansion: A New View of American Imperialism*. Baton Rouge: Louisiana State UP, 1985.

Commons, John R. "Racial Composition of the American People: Amalgamation and Assimilation." *Chautauquan* 39 (May 1904): 217–227.

Connolly, James J. *The Triumph of Ethnic Progressivism: Urban Political Culture in Boston, 1900–1925*. Cambridge: Harvard UP, 1998.

Cooper, John Milton. *The Warrior and the Priest: Woodrow Wilson and Theodore Roosevelt*. Cambridge: Harvard UP, 1983.

Cowan, Ruth Schwartz. *More Work for Mother: The Ironies of Household Technology from the Open Hearth to the Microwave*. New York: Basic Books, 1983.

Crèvecoeur, J. Hector St. John de. *Letters from an American Farmer*. 1782. New York: Dutton, 1957.

Crunden, Robert. *Ministers of Reform: The Progressives' Achievement in American Civilization, 1889–1920*. New York: Basic Books, 1982.

Dainotto, Roberto Maria. "'All the Regions Do Smilingly Revolt': The Literature of Place and Region." *Critical Inquiry* 22 (Spring 1996): 486–505.

Dalton, Kathleen. *Theodore Roosevelt: A Strenuous Life*. New York: Vintage, 2003.

Damon-Moore, Helen. *Magazines for the Millions: Gender and Commerce in the* Ladies' Home Journal *and the* Saturday Evening Post *1880–1910*. Albany: State U of New York P, 1994.

Daniels, Roger. *Guarding the Golden Door*. New York: Farrar, Straus and Giroux, 2005.

Dearborn, Mary. *Pocahontas's Daughters: Gender and Ethnicity in American Culture*. New York: Oxford UP, 1986.

DeMuth, James. *Small Town Chicago: The Comic Perspective of Finley Peter Dunne, George Ade, and Ring Lardner*. Port Washington: Kennikat Press, 1980.

Deutsch, Babette. "An Unimpressive Autobiography." Review of *I Am a Woman—and a Jew*. *New York Herald Tribune Books* 19 December 1926: 17.

Drucker, Sally Ann. "'It Doesn't Say So in Mother's Prayerbook': Autobiographies in English by Immigrant Jewish Women." *American Jewish History* 79.1 (Autumn 1989): 55–71.

Dudden, Arthur Power "The Record of Political Humor." *American Quarterly* 37 (Spring 1985): 50–70.

[Dunne, Finley Peter]. *Dissertations by Mr. Dooley*. New York: Harper, 1906.

———. *Mr. Dooley at His Best*. Ed. Elmer Ellis. 1936. New York: Scribner's, 1938.

———. *Mr. Dooley in Peace and in War*. 1898. New York: Greenwood Press, 1968.

———. *Mr. Dooley in the Hearts of His Countrymen*. Boston: Small, Maynard, 1899.

———. *Mr. Dooley's Opinions*. New York: R. H. Russell, 1901.

———. *Mr. Dooley's Philosophy*. New York: R. H. Russell, 1900.

———. *Observations by Mr. Dooley* 1902. New York: Greenwood Press, 1969.

Dunne, Philip, ed. *Mr. Dooley Remembers: The Informal Memoirs of Finley Peter Dunne*. Boston: Little, Brown, 1963.

Dunton, Edith Kellogg. Rev. of *The Making of an American*, *Dial* 1 January 1902: 8.

Dyer, Thomas. *Theodore Roosevelt and the Idea of Race*. Baton Rouge: Louisiana State UP, 1980.

Eckley, Grace. *Finley Peter Dunne*. Boston: Twayne, 1981.

Edmunds, Carey. "The New Home for the Bride." *Ladies' Home Journal* October 1916: 45.

Ehrenreich, Barbara, and Deirdre English. *For Her Own Good: 150 Years of Experts' Advice to Women*. Garden City, NY: Anchor, 1979.

Elliott, Michael A. *The Culture Concept: Writing and Difference in the Age of Realism*. Minneapolis: U of Minnesota P, 2002.

Ellis, Elmer. *Mr. Dooley's America: A Life of Finley Peter Dunne*. New York: Knopf, 1941.

Ellison, Ralph. "An Extravagance of Laughter." *The Collected Essays of Ralph Ellison*. Ed. John Callahan. New York: Modern Library, 1995. 613–58.

Erbes, Scott. "Manufacturing and Marketing the American Bungalow: The Aladdin Company, 1906–1920." *The American Home: Material Culture, Domestic Space, and Family Life*. Ed. Eleanor McD. Thompson. Hanover: UP of New England, 1998. 45–69.

Fairchild, Henry Pratt. *Melting Pot Mistake*. Boston: Little, Brown, 1926.

Fanning, Charles. *Finley Peter Dunne and Mr. Dooley: The Chicago Years*. Lexington: UP of Kentucky, 1978.

———. *The Irish Voice in America: 250 Years of Irish-American Fiction*. 2nd ed. Lexington: UP of Kentucky, 2000.

———, ed. *Mr. Dooley and the Chicago Irish: An Anthology*. New York: Arno Press, 1976.

Fetterley, Judith. "'Not in the Least American': Nineteenth-Century Literary Regionalism." *College English* 56 (December 1994): 877–95.

Fetterley, Judith, and Marjorie Pryse. *Writing Out of Place: Regionalism, Women, and American Literary Culture*. Urbana: U of Illinois P, 2003.

Foner, Nancy. *From Ellis Island to JFK: New York's Two Great Waves of Immigration*. New Haven: Yale UP, 2000.

Frederick, Christine. *Come into My Kitchen*. Sheboygan: Vollrath, 1922.

Freud, Sigmund. "The Family Romance." *The Standard Edition of the Complete Psychological Works of Sigmund Freud*. Trans. James Strachey. Vol. 9. London: Hogarth, 1959. 236–41.

Fried, Louis. *Makers of the City*. Amherst: U of Massachusetts P, 1990.

Gandal, Keith. *The Virtues of the Vicious: Jacob Riis, Stephen Crane, and the Spectacle of the Slum*. New York: Oxford UP, 1997.

Garland, Hamlin. *Crumbling Idols*. 1894. Gainesville,: Scholars Facsimiles, 1952.

Gatewood, Willard B., Jr. *"Smoked Yankees" and the Struggle for Empire: Letters from Negro Soldiers 1898–1902*. Fayetteville: U of Arkansas P, 1987.

———. *Theodore Roosevelt and the Art of Controversy: Episodes of the White House Years*. Baton Rouge: Louisiana State UP, 1970.

Gerstle, Gary. *American Crucible: Race and Nation in the Twentieth Century*. Princeton: Princeton UP, 2001.

Giddings, Franklin H. "The American People." *International Quarterly* 7 (June 1903): 281–99.

Gilman, Sander. *Multiculturalism and the Jews*. New York: Routledge, 2006.

Glazer, Nathan, and Daniel Patrick Moynihan. *Beyond the Melting Pot: The Negroes, Puerto Ricans, Jews, Italians and Irish of New York City*. Cambridge: MIT and Harvard UP, 1963.

Gleason, Philip. "Confusion Compounded: The Melting Pot in the 1960s and 1970s." *Ethnicity* 6 (1979): 10–20.

———. "Melting-Pot: Symbol of Fusion or Confusion." *American Quarterly* 16 (1964): 20–46.

Goldstein, Eric L. *The Price of Whiteness: Jews, Race, and American Identity*. Princeton: Princeton UP, 2006.

Gordon, Milton. *Assimilation in American Life: The Role of Race, Religion, and National Origins*. New York: Oxford UP, 1964.

Grant, Madison. *The Passing of the Great Race*. 1916. New York: Scribner's, 1921.

Grewal, Inderpal. *Transnational America: Feminisms, Diasporas, Neoliberalism*. Durham: Duke UP, 2005.

Grondahl, Paul. "*I Rose Like a Rocket*": *The Political Education of Theodore Roosevelt*. New York: Free Press, 2004.

Guglielmo, Thomas. *White on Arrival: Italians, Race, Color, and Power in Chicago, 1890–1945*. New York: Oxford UP, 1998.

Gurock, Jeffery. "Jacob A. Riis: Christian Friend or Missionary Foe: Two Jewish Views." *American Jewish History* 71 (September 1981): 29–47.

Hackett, Frances. "Mr. Dooley." *New Republic* 24 September 1919: 235–36.

Handlin, Oscar. *The Uprooted: The Epic Story of the Great Migrations That Made the American People*. 1951. Boston: Little, Brown, 1996.

Heinze, Andrew R. *Adapting to Abundance: Jewish Immigrants, Mass Consumption, and the Search for American Identity*. New York: Columbia UP, 1990.

———. *Jews and the American Soul: Human Nature in the 20th Century*. Princeton: Princeton UP, 2004.

Herzl, Theodore. *The Complete Diaries of Theodore Herzl*. Ed. Raphael Pati. Trans. Harry Zohn. New York: Herzl Press and Thomas Yoseloff, 1960.

Higham, John. *Strangers in the Land: Patterns of American Nativism, 1860–1925*. 1955. New Brunswick: Rutgers UP, 1994.

Hofstadter, Richard. *The Age of Reform*. New York: Vintage, 1955.

Horowitz, Helen Lefkowitz. *Alma Mater: Design and Experience in the Women's Colleges from Their Nineteenth-Century Beginnings to the 1930s*. 1985. Amherst: U of Massachusetts P, 1993.

Horseman, Reginald. *Race and Manifest Destiny: The Origins of American Racial Anglo-Saxonism*. Cambridge: Harvard UP, 1981.

Horton, Isabelle. *The Burden of the City*. New York: F. H. Revell, 1904. Harvard University, Schlesinger On-line Library on the History of Women in America.

Howard, June. "Unraveling Regions, Unsettling Periods: Sarah Orne Jewett and American Literary History." *American Literature* 68 (June 1996): 365–84.

Howells, William Dean. *Literature and Life*. New York: Harper, 1902.

Hyman, Paula. "Culture and Gender: Women in the Immigrant Jewish Community." *The Legacy of Jewish Migration: 1881 and Its Impact*. Ed. David Berger. New York: Columbia UP, 1983.

Ignatieff, Michael. *Blood and Belonging: Journeys into New Nationalism*. 1993. New York: Noonday Press, 1995.

Ignatiev, Noel. *How the Irish Became White*. New York: Routledge, 1995.

Igra, Anna. "Likely to Become a Public Charge: Deserted Women and the Family Law of the Poor in New York City, 1910–1936." *Journal of Women's History* 11.4 (2000): 59–81.

———. "Marriage and Manhood in the U.S. Jewish Community." Unpublished conference paper. Third Scholars' Conference on American Jewish History. Cincinnati, OH, 10 June 1998.

Jackson, Shannon. "Civic Play-Housekeeping: Gender, Theatre, and American Reform." *Theater Journal* 48 (October 1996): 337–61.

Jacobs, Joseph. "The Tragedy of Kishineff: Israel Zangwill's 'Melting Pot.'" *American Hebrew* 10 September 1909: 407–8.

Jacobson, Matthew Frye. *Special Sorrows: The Diasporic Imagination of Irish, Polish and Jewish Immigrants in the United States*. Cambridge: Harvard UP, 1995.

———. *Whiteness of a Different Color: European Immigrants and the Alchemy of Race*. Cambridge: Harvard UP, 1998.

Jacoby, Tamar, ed. *Reinventing the Melting Pot: The New Immigrants and What It Means to Be American*. New York: Basic Books, 2004.

James, Henry. *The American Scene*. 1907. New York: Penguin, 1994.

Jeffers, H. Paul. *Commissioner Roosevelt: The Story of Theodore Roosevelt and the New York City Police, 1895–1897*. New York: Wiley, 1994.

"A Jewish Woman." Review of *I Am a Woman—and a Jew*. *New York Times* 13 March 1927: BR 12.

Johnson, James Weldon. *The Autobiography of an Ex-Colored Man*. 1912. Rpt. in *Three Negro Classics*. New York: Avon, 1965.

Jones, Gavin Roger. *Strange Talk: The Politics of Dialect Literature in Gilded Age America*. Berkeley: U of California P, 1999.

Jones, W. Glyn. *Denmark: A Modern History*. London: Croom Helm, 1986.

Kallen, Horace. "Democracy versus the Melting Pot." Pts. 1 and 2. *Nation* 18 February 1915: 190–94; 25 February 1915: 217–20.

Kaplan, Amy. "Black and Blue on San Juan Hill." *Cultures of US Imperialism*. Ed. Amy Kaplan and Donald E. Pease. Durham: Duke UP, 1993. 219–36.

———. "Manifest Domesticity." *American Literature* 70 (September 1998): 581–606.

———. "Nation, Region, Empire." *Columbia Literary History of the American Novel*. Ed. Emory Elliott. New York: Columbia UP, 1991. 240–66.

Kasson, John. *Rudeness and Civility: Manners in Nineteenth-Century America*. New York: Hill and Wang, 1990.

Kayer, Kaitlyn. "Americanizing the American Woman: Symbols of Nationalism in the *Ladies' Home Journal*, 1890–1900." Pell Scholars Honor Thesis, Salve Regina University, 2005. http://escholar.salve.edu/pell_thesis/4.

Keane, A. H. *Man Past and Present*. 1899. Cambridge: Cambridge UP, 1920.

King, Desmond. *Making Americans: Immigration, Race, and the Origins of the Diverse Democracy*. Cambridge: Harvard UP, 2000.

Klauber, Adolph. "A Spread Eagle Play by Israel Zangwill." *New York Times* 2 September 1909: 10.

Kobrin, Rebecca Amy. *Between Exile and Empire: Jewish Bialystock and Its Diaspora*. Bloomington: Indiana UP, forthcoming.

Kolko, Gabriel. *The Triumph of Conservatism: A Reconsideration of American History, 1900–1916*. New York: Free Press, 1963.

Kramer, Michael P. "New English Typology and the Jewish Question." *Studies in Puritan American Spirituality* 3 (December 1992): 97–124.

Kraus, Joe. "How *The Melting Pot* Stirred America: The Reception of Zangwill's Play and Theater's Role in the American Assimilation Experience." *MELUS* 24 (Autumn 1999): 3–19.

Krebs, Ronald R. *Fighting for Rights: Military Service and the Politics of Citizenship*. Ithaca: Cornell UP, 2006.

Kuhn, Thomas S. *The Structure of Scientific Revolutions*. 1962; Chicago: U of Chicago P, 1996.

The Ladies' Home Journal. Philadelphia: Curtis Publishing Company, 1906–20.

Lady, David B. *A History of the St. Paul's Orphans' Home*. Philadelphia: Sunday School Board, 1917.

Lane, James B. *Jacob A. Riis and the American City*. Port Washington: Kennikat Press, 1974.

Larson, Edward John. *Sex, Race, and Science: Eugenics in the Deep South*. Baltimore: Johns Hopkins UP, 1995.

"Latest Works of Fiction." Review of *My Mother and I*. *New York Times* 8 July 1917: 255.

Lauring, Palle. *A History of the Kingdom of Denmark*. Trans. David Hohnen. Copenhagen: Host and Son, 1968.

Lears, Jackson. *No Place of Grace: Antimodernism and the Transformation of American Culture, 1880–1920*. New York: Pantheon, 1981.

Leslie, Amy. "Grave Play at Grand." Review of the *Melting Pot*. *Chicago Daily News* 21 October 1908.

Leviatin, David. "Framing the Poor: The Irresistibility of How the Other Half Lives." Introduction to *How the Other Half Lives*. New York: Bedford, 1996.

Lowe, John. "Newsprint Masks: The Comic Columns of Finley Peter Dunne, Alexander Posey, and Langston Hughes." *Beyond the Binary: Reconstructing Cultural Identity in a Multicultural Context*. Ed. Timothy B. Powell. New Brunswick: Rutgers UP, 1999. 205–35.

Lubove, Roy. *The Progressives and the Slums: Tenement House Reform in New York City, 1890–1917*. Westport: Greenwood Press, 1974.

Mann, Arthur. "The Melting Pot." *Uprooted Americans: Essays to Honor Oscar Handlin*. Ed. Richard L. Bushman, Neil Harris, David Rothman, et al. Boston: Little, Brown, 1979.

Marsh, Margaret Marsh. "From Separation to Togetherness: The Social Construction of Domestic Space in American Suburbs, 1840–1915." *Journal of American History* 76 (September 1989): 515–22.

———. "Suburban Men and Masculine Domesticity, 1870–1915." *American Quarterly* 40 (January 1988): 165–86.

Marshall, Paule. "From the Poets in the Kitchen." *Merle: A Novella and Other Stories*. London: Virago, 1983. 3–12.

Matthews, Brander. *An Introduction to the Study of American Literature*. 1890. Rev. ed. New York: American Book Company, 1918.

May, Martha. "Home Life: Progressive Social Reformers' Prescriptions for Social Stability, 1890–1920." Diss., State U of New York at Binghamton, 1984.

———. "The 'Problem of Duty': Family Desertion in the Progressive Era." *Social Service Review* 62.2 (March 1988): 40–60.

McCullough, David. *Mornings on Horseback: The Story of an Extraordinary Family, a Vanished Way of Life, and the Unique Child Who Became Theodore Roosevelt*. 1981. New York: Simon and Schuster, 2001.

McFarland, J. Horace. "Eyesores That Spoil Memphis." *Ladies' Home Journal* June 1906: 29.

McGerr, Michael E. *A Fierce Discontent: The Rise and Fall of the Progressive Movement in America, 1870–1920*. New York: Simon and Schuster, 2003.

McMurry, Sally. "City Parlor, Country Sitting Room: Rural Vernacular Design and the American Parlor, 1840–1900." *Winterthur Portfolio* 20 (Winter 1985): 261–80.

Meyer, Edith Patterson. *"Not Charity, but Justice": The Story of Jacob A. Riis*. New York: Vanguard, 1974.

Michaels, Walter Benn. *Our America: Nativism, Modernism, and Pluralism*. Durham: Duke UP, 1995.

Miller, Kerby. *Emigrants and Exiles: Ireland and the Irish Exodus to North America*. New York: Oxford UP, 1985.

Miller, Nathan. *Theodore Roosevelt: A Life*. New York: Morrow, 1992.

Morris, Edmund. *The Rise of Theodore Roosevelt*. New York: Coward, McCann, and Geoghegan, 1979.

Morton, Eleanor [Elizabeth Gertrude Stern]. *Not All Laughter: A Mirror to Our Times*. Philadelphia: John C. Winston, 1937.

Morton, Leah [Elizabeth Gertrude Stern]. *I Am a Woman—and a Jew*. 1926. New York: Arno Press, 1969.

Nahshon, Edna. *From the Ghetto to the Melting Pot: Israel Zangwill's Jewish Plays*. Detroit: Wayne State UP, 2006.

"New Zangwill Play Cheap and Tawdry." *New York Times* 7 September 1909: 9.

Nickel, John. "Eugenics and the Fiction of Pauline Hopkins." *Evolution and Eugenics in American Literature and Culture, 1880–1940: Essays on Ideological Conflict and Complicity*. Ed. Lois A. Cuddy and Claire M. Roche. Lewisburg: Bucknell UP, 2003.

Nielsen, George R. *The Danish Americans*. Boston: Twayne, 1984.

Nott, Josiah Clark, and George R. Gliddon. *Indigenous Races of the Earth*. Philadelphia: Lippincott, 1897.

———. *Types of Mankind*. Philadelphia: Lippincott, 1854.

O'Brien, Robert L. "The President: A Department in Which Will Be Presented the Attitude of the President on Those National Questions Which Affect the Vital Interests of the Home by a Writer Intimately Acquainted and in Close Touch with Him." *Ladies' Home Journal* February 1906–February 1907.

Oliver, Laurence J. *Brander Matthews, Theodore Roosevelt and the Politics of American Literature 1880–1920*. Knoxville: U of Tennessee P, 1992.

———. *The Letters of Theodore Roosevelt and Brander Matthews*. Knoxville, U of Tennessee P, 1995.

O'Toole, Patricia. *When Trumpets Call: Theodore Roosevelt after the White House*. New York: Simon and Schuster, 2005.

Øverland, Orm. *Immigrant Minds, American Identities: Making the United States Home, 1870–1930*. Champaign: U of Illinois P, 2000.

Prichard, James Cowles. *The Natural History of Man; Comprising Inquiries into the Modifying Influence of Physical and Moral Agencies on the Different Tribes of the Human Family*. 1843. 2 vols. London: H. Bailliere, 1855.

Rauchway, Eric. *Murdering McKinley: The Making of Theodore Roosevelt's America*. New York: Hill and Wang, 2003.

Renan, Ernest. "What Is a Nation?" Lecture delivered at the Sorbonne, 11 March 1882. Trans. Martin Thom. *Nation and Narration*. Ed. Homi K. Bhabha, New York: Routledge, 1990. 8–22.

Reports of the Immigration Commission. Washington: GPO, 1911.

Rhoads, William B. "The Colonial Revival and American Nationalism." *Journal of the Society of Architectural Historians* 35 (December 1976): 239–54.

Riis, Jacob A. *The Battle with the Slum*. 1902. New York: Dover, 1998.

———. "Children of the Danish Heath." *Century* July 1912: 449–54.

———. *The Children of the Poor*. New York: Scribner's, 1892.

———. *Children of the Tenements*. 1903. Upper Saddle River, NJ: Gregg Press, 1970.

———. *Christmas Stories*. New York: Macmillan, 1923.
———. *Hero Tales of the Far North*. 1910. New York: Macmillan, 1919.
———. *How the Other Half Lives*. 1890. New York: Dover, 1971.
———. *The Making of an American*. 1901. New York: Macmillan, 1928.
———. *Nibsy's Christmas*. 1893. Freeport: Books for Libraries Press, 1969.
———. *The Old Town*. New York: Macmillan, 1909.
———. *Out of Mulberry Street: Stories of Tenement Life in New York City*. New York: Century, 1898.
———. *The Peril and Preservation of the Home*. Philadelphia: George W. Jacobs, 1903.
———. *The Ten Years' War: An Account of the Battle with the Slum in New York*. Boston: Houghton Mifflin, 1900.
———. *Theodore Roosevelt the Citizen*. New York: Outlook, 1904.
Ripley, William Z. *The Races of Europe: A Sociological Study*. 1896. London: K. Paul Trench, 1913.
[Roosevelt, Theodore.] "Men: In Answer to the Oft-Asked Question: Why Do You Not Have Just One Page for Men in the Home Journal." *Ladies Home Journal* October 1916–October 1917.
———. *Literary Essays*. Philadelphia: Pavilion Press, 2004.
———. *The Winning of the West*. Presidential edition. 1889–96. 4 vols. Lincoln: Bison Books, 1995.
———. *The Works of Theodore Roosevelt*. Memorial edition. Ed. Hermann Hagedorn. 24 vols. New York: Scribner's, 1923–26.
———. *The Works of Theodore Roosevelt*. National edition. Ed. Hermann Hagedorn. 20 vols. New York: Scribner's, 1923–26.
Rosenzweig, Linda. *The Anchor of My Life: Middle-Class American Mothers and Daughters, 1880–1920*. New York: New York UP, 1993.
Scanlon, Jennifer. *Inarticulate Longings: The Ladies' Home Journal and the Promises of Consumer Culture*. New York: Routledge, 1995.
Schaaf, Barbara C. *Mr. Dooley's Chicago*. Garden City: Anchor/Doubleday, 1977.
Schiller, Nina Glick, Linda Basch, and Cristina Szanton Blanc. "From Immigrant to Transmigrant: Theorizing Transnational Migration." *Anthropological Quarterly* 68.1 (1995): 48–63.
———. *Nations Unbound: Transnational Projects, Postcolonial Predicaments, and Deterritorialized Nation States*. New York: Gordon and Breach, 1994.
———. *Towards a Transnational Perspective on Migration: Race, Class, Ethnicity and Nationalism Reconsidered*. New York: New York Academy of Sciences, 1992.
Schultz, Alfred P. *Race or Mongrel: A Brief History of the Rise and Fall of the Ancient Races of Earth: A Theory That the Fall of Nations Is Due to Intermarriage with Alien Stocks: A Demonstration That a Nation's Strength Is Due to Racial Purity: A Prophecy That America Will Sink to Early Decay Unless Immigration Is Rigorously Restricted*. Boston: L. C. Page, 1908.
Scott, Emmett J., and Lyman B. Stowe. *Booker T. Washington, Builder of a Civilization*. Garden City: Doubleday, Page, 1916.
Shapiro, James. *Shakespeare and the Jews*. New York: Columbia UP, 1996.
Shavelson, Susanne Amy. "From Amerike to America: Language and Identity in the Yiddish and English Autobiographies of Jewish Immigrant Women." Diss., U of Michigan, 1996.
Shi, David E. *The Simple Life: Plain Living and High Thinking in American Culture*. New York: Oxford UP, 1985.

Shollar, Barbara. "Writing Ethnicity/Writing Modernity: Autobiographies by Jewish-American Women." Diss., City U of New York, 1992.

A Short History of the Ladies' Home Journal. Philadelphia: Curtis Publications, 1953, Curtis Publishing Company Papers, Special Collections, University of Pennsylvania.

Shumsky, Neil Larry. "Zangwill's *The Melting Pot*: Ethnic Tensions on Stage." *American Quarterly* 27 (March 1975): 29–41.

Skardal, Dorothy Burton. *The Divided Heart: Scandinavian Immigrant Experience through Literary Sources*. Lincoln: U of Nebraska P, 1974.

Slotkin, Richard. *Gunfighter Nation: The Myth of the Frontier in Twentieth-Century America*. Norman: U of Oklahoma P, 1998.

Smith, Rogers. *Civic Ideals: Conflicting Visions of Citizenship in U.S. History*. New Haven: Yale UP, 1997.

Sollors, Werner. *Beyond Ethnicity: Consent and Descent in American Culture*. New York: Oxford UP, 1986.

———. *Neither Black Nor White Yet Both: Thematic Explorations of Interracial Literature*. New York: Oxford UP, 1997.

———. "The Rebirth of All Americans in the Great Melting Pot: Notes toward the Vindication of a Rejected Popular Symbol; or: An Ethnic Variety of Religious Experience." *Prospects: The Annual of American Cultural Studies* 5 (1980): 79–110.

———. *Theories of Ethnicity: A Classical Reader*. Ed. Werner Sollors. New York: New York UP, 1996.

Steffens, Lincoln. *The Autobiography of Lincoln Steffens*. 1931. New York: Harcourt, Brace, and World, 1958.

Stein, Harry H. "Theodore Roosevelt and the Press: Lincoln Steffens." *Mid-America* April 1972: 94–107.

Steinberg, Salme Harju. *Reformer in the Marketplace: Edward W. Bok and the Ladies' Home Journal*. Baton Rouge: Louisiana State UP, 1979.

Steiner, Edward. *From Alien to Citizen*. 1914. New York: Arno Press, 1975.

Stepan, Nancy. *The Idea of Race in Science: Great Britain 1800–1960*. London: Macmillan, 1982.

Stern, Elizabeth Gertrude. *The Gambler's Wife*. New York: Macmillan, 1931.

———. *My Mother and I*. New York: Macmillan, 1917.

———. "My Mother and I: The Story of How I Became an American Woman." *Ladies' Home Journal* October 1916: 21ff.

———. *This Ecstasy*. New York: J. H. Sears, 1927.

Stern, T[homas] Noel. *Secret Family*. South Dartmouth: T. Noel Stern, 1988.

Stocking, George W., Jr. *Race, Culture, and Evolution: Essays in the History of Anthropology*, 1968. Chicago: U of Chicago P, 1982.

———. *Victorian Anthropology*. New York: Free Press, 1987.

Stokes, Claudia Aron. "The American Messiah: Assimilation and Cultural Exchange in Israel Zangwill's *The Melting Pot*." MA essay, Columbia U, 1994.

Strong, Josiah. *Our Country: Its Possible Future and Its Present Crisis*. 1885. Cambridge, MA: Belknap, 1963.

Sundquist, Eric. "Realism and Regionalism." *Columbia Literary History of the United States*. Ed. Emory Elliott. New York: Columbia UP, 1988. 501–24.

Szuberla, Guy. "Zangwill's *The Melting Pot* Plays Chicago." *MELUS* 20 (Autumn 1995): 3–20.

Takaki, Ronald. *A Different Mirror: A History of Multicultural America*. Boston: Little, Brown, 1994.

Tandy, Jennette. *Crackerbox Philosophers in American Humor and Satire*. 1924. Port Washington: Kennikat Press, 1964.

Tansill, Charles Callan. *The Purchase of the Danish West Indies*. New York: Greenwood Press, 1968.

Taubenfeld, Aviva. "'Only an "L"': Linguistic Borders and the Immigrant Author in Abraham Cahan's *Yekl* and *Yankel der Yankee*." *Multilingual America: Transnationalism, Ethnicity, and the Languages of American Literature*. Ed. Werner Sollors. New York: New York UP, 1998. 144–65.

Testi, Arnaldo. "The Gender of Reform Politics: Theodore Roosevelt and the Culture of Masculinity." *Journal of American History* 81 (March 1995): 1509–33.

Topinard, Paul. *Anthropology*. 1880. London: Chapman and Hall, 1890.

Trachtenberg, Alan. *The Incorporation of America: Culture and Society in the Gilded Age*. New York: Hill and Wang, 1982.

Tulis, Jeffrey. *The Rhetorical Presidency*. Princeton: Princeton UP, 1987.

Turner, Frederick Jackson. "The Significance of the Frontier in American History." 1893. *The Frontier in American History*. New York: Henry Holt, 1920. 1–38.

Udelson, Joseph H. *Dreamer of the Ghetto: The Life and Works of Israel Zangwill*. Tuscaloosa: U of Alabama P, 1990.

Uffen, Ellen Serlen. *Strands of the Cable: The Place of the Past in Jewish American Women's Writing*. New York: Peter Lang, 1992.

Umansky, Ellen. Introduction. *I Am a Woman—and a Jew*. Leah Morton. New York: Markus Wiener, 1986.

———. "Representations of Jewish Women in the Works and Life of Elizabeth Stern." *Modern Judaism* 13 (1993): 165–76.

Veblen, Thorstein. *The Theory of the Leisure Class*. 1899. New York: Penguin, 1979.

Vought, Hans P. *The Bully Pulpit and the Melting Pot: American Presidents and the Immigrant, 1897–1933*. Macon: Mercer UP, 2004.

Wald, Lillian D. *The House on Henry Street*. New York: Henry Holt, 1915.

Wald, Priscilla. *Constituting Americans: Cultural Anxiety and Narrative Form*. Durham: Duke UP, 1996.

———. "Of Crucibles and Grandfathers: The East European Immigrants." *The Cambridge Companion to Jewish American Literature*. Ed. Michael P. Kramer and Hana Wirth-Nesher. New York: Cambridge UP, 2003.

Walker, Alice. "Everyday Use." *Everyday Use*. Ed. Barbara T. Christian. New Brunswick: Rutgers UP, 1994. 23–35.

———. "In Search of Our Mothers' Gardens." *In Search of Our Mothers' Gardens: Womanist Prose*. New York: Harcourt Brace, 1983. 231–43.

Ware, Emma Louise. *Jacob A. Riis: Police Reporter, Reformer, Useful Citizen*. New York: Appleton-Century, 1939.

Wasson, Kirsten. "Daughters of Promise, Mothers of Revision: Three Jewish American Immigrant Writers and Cultural Inscriptions of Identity." Diss., U of Wisconsin, 1992.

———. "Elizabeth Gertrude Stern." *Jewish Women in America: An Historical Encyclopedia*. Ed. Paula E. Hyman and Deborah Dash Moore. New York: Routledge, 1997.

Watts, Sarah. *Rough Rider in the White House: Theodore Roosevelt and the Politics of Desire*. Chicago: U of Chicago P, 2003.

Way, Irving. "Mr. Martin Dooley of Chicago." *Bookman* May 1899: 217.

Westergaard, Waldemar. *Denmark and Slesvig, 1848–1864*. London: Oxford UP, 1946.

Who's Who in America 1936–1937, 1948–1950. Chicago: A. N. Marquis, 1937, 1950.

Wiebe, Robert. *The Search for Order, 1877–1920*. New York: Hill and Wang, 1967.

Wilson, Christopher P. "The Rhetoric of Consumption: Mass Market Magazines and the Demise of the Gentle Reader, 1880–1920." *The Culture of Consumption: Critical Essays in American History 1880–1980*. Ed. Richard Wrightman Fox and T. J. Jackson Lears. New York: Pantheon, 1983. 39–64.

Wohlgelernter, Maurice. *Israel Zangwill: A Study*. New York: Columbia UP, 1964.

Woods, Robert A., ed. *Americans in Process: A Settlement Study*. Boston: Houghton Mifflin, 1902.

Wrenn, Tony P. "The Eye of Guardianship: Theodore Roosevelt and the American Institute of Architects." *White House History Journal* 11 (1999): 51–61.

Wright, Gwendolyn. *Moralism and the Model Home: Domestic Architecture and Cultural Conflict in Chicago, 1873–1913*. Chicago: U of Chicago P, 1980.

Yezierska, Anzia. *Bread Givers*. 1925. New York: Persea Books, 1975.

Young, Robert J. C. *Colonial Desire: Hybridity in Theory, Culture and Race*. New York: Routledge, 1995.

Zaborowska, Magdalena. *How We Found America: Reading Gender through East European Immigrant Narratives*. Chapel Hill: U of North Carolina P, 1995.

Zangwill, Edith Ayrton. Foreword. *Speeches, Articles and Letters of Israel Zangwill*. London: Soncino Press, 1937.

Zangwill, Israel. Afterword. *The Melting Pot: Drama in Four Acts*. 1914. New York: Macmillan, 1917.

———. *Chosen Peoples: The Hebraic Ideal versus the Teutonic*. New York: Macmillan, 1919.

———. *Dreamers of the Ghetto*. 1898. Philadelphia: Jewish Publication Society, 1938.

———. *The East African Question: Zionism and England's Offer*. Rpt. from *The Maccabaean*. New York: Maccabaean Publishing Company, 1904.

———. *The Melting Pot*. 1909. New York: Arno Press, 1975.

———. *The Principle of Nationalities*. Conway Memorial Lecture, Delivered at South Place Institute, 8 March 1917. New York: Macmillan, 1917.

———. *The Problem of the Jewish Race*. New York: Judean Publishing Company, 191[2].

———. *Speeches, Articles and Letters of Israel Zangwill*. London: Soncino Press, 1937.

———. *The Voice of Jerusalem*. New York: Macmillan, 1921.

———. *The War for the World*. London: William Heinemann, 1916.

———. *Watchman, What of the Night*. New York: American Jewish Congress, 1923.

Zierler, Wendy. "In(ter)dependent Selves: Mary Antin, Elizabeth Stern, and Jewish Women's Autobiography." *The Immigrant Experience in North American Literature: Carving Out a Niche*. Ed. Katharine B. Payant and Toby Rose. Westport, CT: Greenwood Press, 1999. 1–16.

INDEX

Abbott, Lyman, 191n10, 196n86
Addams, Jane, 7, 48, 90
African Americans: Mr. Dooley on, 211n76; Roosevelt and, Theodore, 37; vernacular literature, 138, 209n58; Zangwill and, Israel, 172n82. *See also* Washington, Booker T.
African immigrants, 5
Alderson, Clifton, *31*
amalgamation: hybridity (*see* hybridity); intermarriage (*see* intermarriage); race, 16, 18, 20–21, 24, 26–27, 29–30; Zangwill and, Israel, 20–21, 22, 28, 34
American Anglo-Saxonism, 145–153; Dunne on, Finley Peter, 145–155; Mr. Dooley on, 146–152; Roosevelt and, Theodore, 146, 152–153, 212n106; Schultz and, Alfred P., 6
American literature: immigrant autobiographies (*see* immigrant autobiographies); immigrant writers, 9, 11–12, 160, 209n58; native-born writers, 9, 10; Roosevelt's national literature program, 3–4, 8–10
American race: Mr. Dooley on, 150–151; Roosevelt and, Theodore, 16, 17, 33–34, 36–38, 61–62, 94, 146, 155–156, 164n24, 187n107; sexuality, 21; Zangwill, Israel, 17, 21, 27–29; Zangwill's *The Melting Pot*, 16, 18, 20–21, 26, 29
Americanism: hyphenated Americanism, 7, 42, 43, 52; Riis and, Jacob, 66; Roosevelt on, Theodore, 2, 3, 5, 9–10, 15, 41, 124, 153–154; Roosevelt's "True Americanism" (*see* "True Americanism")
Americanization: Addams and, Jane, 90; Bok and, Edward, 87, 90 (see also *Americanization of Edward Bok*); class and, 90, 101; home and, 111; melting pot (*see* melting pot model of Americanization);

of Mr. Dooley, 133; Roosevelt and, Theodore, 90; Roosevelt's "True Americanism" (*see* "True Americanism"); sitting rooms, 111; Stern and, Elizabeth, 87, 90, 97–98; Stern's "My Mother and I," 100
Americanization of Edward Bok (Bok), 87, 195n55
Americanness: class, 80, 101; need for definition of, 2; Roosevelt and, Theodore, 175n101
"The Anglo-Saxon Triumph" (Dunne), 145–146, 155
Anglo-Saxonism. *See* American Anglo-Saxonism
Antin, Mary, *The Promised Land,* 69, 116, 166n43, 195n55
Asian immigrants: Chinese immigrants, 5, 37, 60, 186n95; Japanese immigrants, 5, 37
assimilation: amalgamation, 16, 22, 28; assimilable races, 5–6, 15, 34, 36, 37–38, 160; assimilative performances, 28; Roosevelt on, 5–6; Zangwill and, Israel, 22, 28. *See also* Americanization
Astor, William Waldorf, 133–134, 154
autobiography. *See* immigrant autobiographies; women autobiographies
The Autobiography of an Ex-Colored Man (Johnson), 175n108
Autobiography (Roosevelt): on armchair reformers, 142; dialect speech in, 143, 212n92, 212n94; New York City Police Department, 46; on Riis (Jacob), 48
Ayrton, Edith, 173n95

Baltimore Jewish Comment (newspaper), 172n88
Battle with the Slum (Riis), 76, 187n101, 189n153

Becher, Arthur E., 107
Bederman, Gail, 20, 142, 168n27
Beveridge, Albert, 197n100
Beyond Ethnicity (Sollors), 25, 166n44
Billings, Josh, 132
"Biological Analogies in History" (Roosevelt), 35–36
Bismarck, Otto von, 50, 181n50
Boas, Franz, 165n30
Boelhower, William, 188n130
Bok, Edward, 83–87; Americanization, 87, 90; *Americanization of Edward Bok*, 87, 195n55; architectural plans for model homes, 84–85, 111; criticism of Americans, 87; on daughters' respect for their mothers, 103; dual loyalty, 86–87; home, definition of, 92; on ideal family environment, 83–87; immigrant conversion narrative, 69; *Ladies' Home Journal*, 78, 83–87, 88, 105, 111, 193n36, 193n42, 194n50, 194n51; Roosevelt and, Theodore, 78, 81, 86–87, 92, 97, 196n83, 196n86; Roosevelt on, Theodore, 84–85; on sex education, 194n51; Stern's *My Mother and I*, 78, 80–81, 101; Stern's "My Mother and I," 78, 100, 115, 116, 119; women's suffrage, 86, 197n92
Bok, Mary Louise Curtis, 198n112
"A Book Review" (Dunne), 121, 139, 143, 206n10
Booker T. Washington, Builder of a Civilization (Scott and Stowe), 175n108
Boskin, Joseph, 131
Bourne, Randolph, 6–7, 59
Bread Givers (Yezierska), 100
Bridgeport neighborhood, Chicago, 130
Browder, Laura, 198n112

Catholic Knights of Columbus, 42
Chicago Evening Post (newspaper), 207n17
"Children of the Crucible" (Roosevelt), 13
Chinese immigrants, 5, 37, 60, 186n95
Choate, Joseph Hodges, 149

Christian, King of Denmark, 50, 180n47
citizenship, 74–76, 82, 91
civic nationalism, 170n65
Civil War, 1, 9
Clark, P. Percival, *31*
class: altering class mentality, 88; alternatives to progressive middle-class domesticity, 108–109; Americanization, 90, 101; Americanness, 80, 101; domesticity, 80; middle-class domestic life in *Ladies' Home Journal*, 83–87; progressive middle-class American domesticity to Stern, 98, 99; working-class immigrant men, 143
Cohen, Lizabeth A., 111
Connolly, James J., on progressivism, 124, 163n5, 179n29, 206n6, 206n12
Coolidge, Emelyn L., 85, 86, 109, 194n43
Cortelyou, George, 152
cosmopolitanism, immigration and, 6–7
Crèvecoeur, J. Hector St. John de, 16, 169n30
"cultural pluralism," 6
"culture," 165n30
Curtis and, Louisa Knapp, 193n42

Dagmar, dowager empress of Russia, 52, 182n59
Dalton, Kathleen, 179n32
Damon-Moore, Helen, 196n84
Danish immigrants, 43, 44, 50, 51, 72, 182n54, 182n55. *See also* Riis, Jacob
Darwin, Charles, 20, 60
Davenport, Charles, 26
Dearborn, Mary, 198n112
Democratic Party, 142
dialect literature: Dunne and, Finley Peter, 209n58; by Roosevelt, Theodore, 143, 212n92, 212n94; unity of the nation, 209n41. *See also* vernacular literature
diasporas: Danish diaspora, 43, 44, 59, 60, 61, 72; diasporic national literature, 57–58; Jewish diaspora, 30
diversity, 11

INDEX

domesticity: alternatives to progressive middle-class domesticity, 108–109; class and, 80; domestication of the foreigner, 90, 96–97; domestication of the strenuous life, 90–97; middle-class domestic life, 83–87, 98, 99; reorganization of domestic space, 111; Stern and, Elizabeth, 11
Dorinson, Joseph, 131
Drucker, Sally Ann, 198n112
dual loyalty, 52–59, 66–71; Bok and, Edward, 86–87; Riis and, Jacob, 11, 43, 44, 52–59, 63, 66–71, 176n8; Roosevelt on, Theodore, 53; Roosevelt's "True Americanism," 41
Dudden, Arthur Power, 208n40
Dunne, Finley Peter: "A Book Review," 121, 139, 143, 206n10; alliance between United States and Britain, 154–155; American Anglo-Saxonism, 145–155; "The Anglo-Saxon Triumph," 145–146, 155; anti-imperialism, 137, 148–150; brogues in Bridgeport neighborhood of Chicago, 130; character by, Callaghan family, 130; character by, Colonel McNeery, 126, 207n17; character by, Hogan and wife, 130; character by, Immanuel Kant Gumbo, 141; character by, Malachi Hennessy, 122, 132, 134, 135, 136, 140, 142, 152; character by, Mr. Dooley (see Mr. Dooley); character by, Molly Donahue, 130; childhood, 125; dialect, 209n58; on English government, 154–155; on expatriates, 134; Hackett on, Frances, 208n37; influence on public, 153; Irish Americanness, 124; on Irish Americans, 130, 155, 156, 210n71; Irish hatred of England, 154; Irish nationalism, 127, 137, 155; McGarry and, James, 207n17; *Mr. Dooley Remembers*, 127–128; move from Chicago to New York, 131; "On a Speech by President McKinley," 135–136; "On the Irish," 127; portrait of, *126*; on Roosevelt, Theodore, 139, 156, 206n10; Roosevelt and, Theodore, 10, 11, 134, 145, 148, 150–151, 152, 154–155, 156–157, 210n70, 210n71, 211n79; Roosevelt on, Theodore, 153; satire, 122, 208n37; sons, 125; "Swearing," 140, 144; vernacular literature, 131–132; wife, 125
Dunne, Philip, 127–128, 155, 207n23
Dunton, Edith Kellogg, 182n67
Dyer, Thomas, 34, 146

Eastern European Jews, 16, 187n101
Effen, Ellen Serlen, 198n112
Eliot, Charles, 196n86
Ellis, Elmer, 211n79
Ellison, Ralph, 138
environment: environment's effect on immigrants, 7, 34–37, 60–61; ideal family environment, 83–87
Esther (Biblical), 30
ethnic accommodation and cooperation, 22–23
ethnic authors, 209n46
ethnic literature, 25
ethnic/national loyalties, tropes describing, 53
ethnic politics, 72, 152, 153
"ethnic progressivism," 206n12
"ethnic transformation" paradigm, 166n44, 195n55
ethnic wives, 54, 182n66
ethnicization, linguistic, 137–138
ethnicization of the "crackerbox philosopher," 132
eugenics movement, 7
European immigrants, 186n95. *See also specific nationalities, such as "Danish immigrants"*
Evans, Thomas, 183n72
Evening Sun (newspaper), 43
evolution, 36, 168n27

Fanning, Charles, 130, 131, 211n79
feminism, 80, 82
First Universal Races Congress (1911), 27–28, 171n72

Fiske, Virginia (Jacob Riis's granddaughter), 190n157
Fiske, William (Jacob Riis's son-in-law), 182n67
Frederick, Christine, 85, 86, 109
Frederick, Crown Prince of Denmark, 52, 73
Freeman, Mary Wilkins, 3

Garland, Hamlin, *Crumbling Idols,* 166n37
gender: domesticity (*see* domesticity); feminism, 80, 82; masculinity (*see* masculinity); race, 21, 79; Zangwill's *The Melting Pot,* 21
gendering of consumption, 192n28
German Americans, 150–151
Gerstle, Gary, 123, 167n27, 170n65
Gjortz, Elisabeth. *See* Riis, Elisabeth
Glazer, Nathan, *Beyond the Melting Pot* (with Moynihan), 168n16
Gould, Jay, 207n17
Gouverneur Morris (Roosevelt), 3, 62
Grant, Madison, 6, 7

Hackett, Frances, 208n37
Harris, Joel Chandler, 3, 8
Hay, John, 148–149, 167n13
Heinze, Andrew R., 111
Henry Street Settlement (New York City), 89. *See also* Wald, Lillian
Herald Tribune (newspaper), 198n112
heredity: Lamarckism (*see* Lamarckism); Mendelianism, 29–30
Hero Tales from American History (Roosevelt and Lodge), 3, 177n10
Hero Tales of the Far North (Riis), 43, 57–58, 177n10
Herzl, Theodore, 172n82
the home: architecture and, 84, 85; Bok and, Edward, 92; domestic life (*see* domesticity); idealization of American home, 77, 98, 106; immigrant homes, 49, 55–56, 82, 88–90, 97, 106, 108–112; influence on future generations, 82–83; public spaces mirroring middle-class homes, 86; Riis on ideal home, Jacob, 82, 88, 185n83; Roosevelt on, Theodore, 77, 82, 83, 91, 92; settlement houses, 88–90; White House, 91; yearning for middle-class American home, 204n159. *See also Ladies' Home Journal; My Mother and I;* "My Mother and I"
Horowitz, Helen Lefkowitz, 202n130
Horton, Isabelle, 88–89, 109
"How I Became a Progressive" (Roosevelt), 179n32
How the Other Half Lives (Riis): beginning, 44–45; fame of, 42; poverty and opportunity, 60; Roosevelt and, Theodore, 43, 45, 48; sentimentalism, 54; success of, 75
Howells, William Dean, 166n37
Hull House (Chicago), 88, 90
Hull-House Labor Museum, 90
hybridity, 16, 18, 26–27, 29–31, 171n71. *See also* amalgamation; intermarriage
Hyman, Paula, 104

I Am a Woman—and a Jew (Stern), 100, 205n194
immigrant autobiographies: "ethnic transformation" paradigm, 166n44, 195n55; immigrant as foster child of America, 200n113; influence of Riis's *Making of an American,* 69; similarities, 188n130
immigrants: African immigrants, 5; biological essence of, 6, 16–17; Chinese immigrants, 5, 37, 60, 186n95; Crèvecoeur on, 169n30; Danish immigrants, 43, 44, 50, 51, 72, 182n54, 182n55 (*See also* Riis, Jacob); Eastern European Jews, 16, 187n101; environment's effect on, 7, 34–37, 60–61; ethnic wives, 54, 182n66; European immigrants, 186n95 (*see also specific nationalities, such as "Danish immigrants"*); German immigrants, 96–97; Irish immigrants, 96–97, 134, 153; Italian immigrants, 60, 97; Japanese

immigrants, 5, 37; Jewish immigrants, 26, 167n13, 170n59, 173n95; loyalty to United States, 25–26; Norwegian immigrants, 187n112; number (1880-1924), 1–2; Polish immigrants, 97; Polish Jews, 60; Roosevelt and, Theodore, 4–6, 7, 8, 9, 11–12, 17, 24, 25, 34–37, 73–74, 96–97, 143; Spanish-American War, reaction to, 56–57, 185n86

immigration: anxiety among native-born, 1, 2; cosmopolitanism, 6–7; polygenism, 171n73; restrictions on, 37, 38, 171n73; Roosevelt on, Theodore, 4, 5, 37, 90–91; Zangwill and, Israel, 38

intermarriage: degeneration, 171n73; race, 16, 18, 20–21, 24, 26–27, 29–30; Schultz and, Alfred, 27; sterility, 27, 171n69; "vigor," 171n71; Zangwill and, Israel, 169n34; Zangwill's *The Melting Pot*, 18, 21, 30. *See also* amalgamation; hybridity

Irish Americans: Dunne on, Finley Peter, 130, 155, 156, 210n71; Dunne's Irish Americanness, 124; exclusion from positions of power, 151–152, 153–154, 155, 156

Irish immigrants, 96–97, 134, 153

Italian immigrants, 60, 97

Jacobson, Matthew Frye: American Anglo-Saxonism, 147; immigrants' reaction to Spanish-American War, 185n86; *Special Sorrows*, 56–57, 181n49

James, Henry, 1, 2, 32

Japanese immigrants, 5, 37

Jewett, Sarah Orne, 3

Jewishness: as recessive traits, 29–30; Roosevelt and, Theodore, 210n70; Stern on, Elizabeth, 205n194; Zangwill and, Israel, 28, 29–30, 173n95

Jews: diaspora, 30; Eastern European Jews, 16, 187n101; Jewish immigrants, 26, 167n13, 170n59, 173n95; Jewish sense of justice, 33; patriotism of, 28; physiognomy, 30–33; Polish Jews, 60; Riis and, Jacob, 60, 187n101; Roosevelt and, Theodore, 52; Russian persecution, 52; Stern and, Elizabeth (see *My Mother and I*); Zangwill and, Israel, 16, 28, 29, 33; Zionism, 167n13, 173n95

Johnson, James Weldon, 175n108

Jones, Gavin Roger, 131, 209n41

The Jungle (Sinclair), 140–141

Kallen, Horace, 6–7, 17, 66

Kaplan, Amy, 96

Kellogg, P., 183n72

Kobrin, Rebecca, 42, 170n59

Ladies' Home Journal, 83–88, 92–108; Americanizing mission, 86, 87; architectural plans for model homes, 84–85, 111; "Beautiful America" (column), 194n47; Bok and, Edward, 78, 83–87, 88, 105, 111, 193n36, 193n42, 194n50, 194n51; child rearing tips, 85; circulation, 190n7, 191n13, 192n26; commissioned houses in, 193n36; Curtis and, Louisa Knapp, 193n42, 194n50; exposés of ugly cities, 194n47; gendering of consumption, 192n28; "Good Manners and Good Form" (column), 193n41; "Good Taste and Bad Taste in Hair Dressing" (column), 193n41; higher education for girls, 193n41; housekeeping tips, 85–86; "In Other People's Homes" (column), 85; influence, 83–84; "Inside Other Women's Homes" (column), 85; kitchens in, 118; long-running series, 85; McFarland and, J. Horace, 194n47; "Men: In Answer to the Oft-Asked Question: Why Do You Not Have Just One Page for Men in the Home Journal?" (column), 92–97, 196n84, 196n86; middle-class domestic life, 83–87; O'Brien and, Robert L., 92, 94; outdoor advertisements, campaigns against, 86, 194n46;

Ladies' Home Journal (*continued*), patent medicine advertisements, campaign against, 86, 194n50; professionalization of advice, 85, 193n42; progressive American womanhood, 80; public spaces mirroring middle-class homes, support for, 86; reader participation, 193n42; Roosevelt and, Theodore, 78–79, 88, 92–97, 105, 191n12, 196n83, 196n86; sex education, support for, 86, 194n51; Stern's *My Mother and I,* 78, 101–102, 109; Stern's "My Mother and I" (*see* "My Mother and I"); subscribers, 192n27; "The President" (column), 92, 93; "Young Mothers' Registry" (column), 194n43

Lamarck, Jean-Baptist, 7

Lamarckism: progressivism, 82–83; Riis and, Jacob, 45, 56; Roosevelt and, Theodore, 7, 34–35

Lane, Grace, *19, 31*

Leah, Sarah, 200n113, 200n114

Lee, Fitzhugh, 137

Leslie, Amy, 172n86

Letters from an American Farmer (Crèvecoeur), 169n30

Levin, Aaron, 200n113, 200n114

Levitan, David, 54

linguistic ethnicization, 137–138

literary regionalism, 8, 166n37

Lodge, Henry Cabot, *Hero Tales from American History* (with Roosevelt), 177n10

Making of an American (Riis), 64–70; conversion narrative, 64–71, 74–75; on Denmark, 60–61; dual loyalty, 41, 42, 50, 53–54; Elisabeth Riis in, 54, 55, 67, 183n72, 183n78; final scene, 64–70, 74–75; illustration from, *47, 65;* manuscript page from, *68;* as a romance, 183n72; Roosevelt in, Theodore, 41; sentimentality, 52, 54

manliness, 177n10, 177n12

Marsh, Margaret, 197n100

masculinity: domestication of the strenuous life, 90–97; Men's page in *Ladies' Home Journal,* 92–97, 196n84, 196n86; Roosevelt and, Theodore, 4, 9, 11, 96, 123, 142, 177n10, 177n12, 197n100, 198n102

Matthews, Brander, 145–146, 166n37, 175n108

McFarland and, J. Horace, 194n47

McGarry, James, 207n17

McKinley, William, 135–136, 137, 139, 210n61

melting pot model of Americanization: civic nationalism, 170n65; forgetting pre-American enemies, 24; physical features of children of, 30; racial nationalism, 170n65; replacement by transnationalism, 42; Riis's vision of, Jacob, 59; Roosevelt's vision of, Theodore, 17, 33–35, 38, 39; Zangwill's vision of, Israel, 10–11, 17–21, 27, 39

The Melting Pot (Zangwill), 13–27, 30–33; afterword, 29; on America as a crucible, 17–18, 23; America as promised land, 20; character in, David Quixano, 18–21, 22, 23–24, 25, 26, 30, 33, 132, 170n59; character in, Frau Quixano, 21–23, 31, 33; character in, Herr Pappelmeister, *31;* character in, Kathleen, 21–23, 24, 30, *31,* 33; character in, Quincy Davenport, 18, 25, 26, *31,* 53–54, 134; character in, Uncle Mendel Quixano, 18, 21, 29, 30, 33; character in, Vera Revendal, 18–21, 23–24, 25, 26, 30, *31,* 33; character in, Vera's father (the Butcher of Kishineff), 18, 23; characters' noses, 172n86; compassion, 21; denouement, 18–20; empathy, 22–24; ethnic accommodation and cooperation, 22–23; European Jewry, 167n13; forgetting the past, 23–24; friendship *vs.* desire, 24; gender, 21; immigrants' loyalty to United States, 25–26; influence, 10; intermarriage, 18, 21, 30; Jewish customs, 172n86, 172n88; Jewish physiognomy, 30–33; Leslie on, Amy, 172n86; millennialism, 20; power of, 39; premiere, 13–15, 16, 166n1, 168n15; Purim festival scene, 30–33; race, 16, 18, 20–21, 26, 29; racial fusion/intermixing, 20–21, 22, 28; on real Americans, 13, 18; reviews of, 172n86, 172n88; Roosevelt and, Theodore, *14*, 15–16, 25, 35, 38–39, 167n6; Roosevelt on, Theodore, 14, 39; Roosevelt's "true Americanism," 15; scenes from, *19, 31;* sexuality, 21; Sollors on, Werner, 26; Straus on, Oscar, 167n14

Mendel, Gregor, 29

Mendelianism, 29–30

middle-class domestic life, 83–87

Mr. Dooley, 125–157, 153, 157; on African Americans, 211n76; alliance between United States and Britain, 145–146, 148–149; on American Anglo-Saxonism, 146–152; on American race, 150–151; American values, 132; Americanization of, 133; "The Anglo-Saxon Triumph" column, 145–146, 155; anti-imperialism, 137, 148–150; antithesis of stereotypical Irishman, 132; on Astor, William Waldorf, 133–134; "A Book Review" column, 121, 139, 143, 206n10; on Choate, Joseph Hodges, 149; critics of, 125–128; Democratic Party, 142; on Dewey, George, 137; Dunne on, Finley Peter, 208n28; Dunne on, Philip, 132, 207n23; ethnicization of the "crackerbox philosopher," 132; exclusion of Irish Americans from positions of power, 151–152; failure of native-born to uphold founding principles, 133; as a force of communal censure, 128–131; on German voters, 150–151; on Hay, John, 148–149; Irish American military leaders, 137–138; Irish nationalism, 127, 137; on Irish voters, 150–151; Irishness, 208n40, 210n67; Irishness of, 125–131; on Lee, Fitzhugh, 137; linguistic ethnicization strategy, 137–138; on McKinley, William, 135–136, 137; municipal reform in Chicago, 128–130; national and international affairs, 131, 138; "On a Speech by President McKinley" column, 135–136; original name, 126, 207n17; portrayals of, *129;* on Roosevelt, Theodore, 124, 137, 139, 144–145, 149–152, 150–151, 206n12, 211n76; Roosevelt and, Theodore, 121–122, 123–125, 140–142, 142–144, 157; Roosevelt on, Theodore, 140; Roosevelt's "True Americanism," 11, 145, 156, 206n12; on Spanish-American War, 136–137; structure of the columns, 135–136; superiority of Irish immigrants as Americans, 134; "Swearing" column, 140, 144

Mr. Dooley Remembers (Dunne), 127–128

Mortensen, Enok, *Saaledes blev jeg hjemlos* (Thus I Became Homeless), 66

Moynihan, Daniel Patrick, *Beyond the Melting Pot* (with Glazer), 168n16

multiculturalism, 7

Murray, Joe, 143

My Mother and I (Stern) (book version), 108–119; alternative to progressive middle-class domesticity, 106, 108–110; audience, 205n181; on belonging in United States, 198n110; Bok and, Edward, 78, 80–81, 101; class, 101; distinction between narrator and protagonist, 100; education as a private affair, 110; ethnic female tradition, 118–119; genre of, 198n112; kitchen as center of life, 111, 117, 119; kitchen clock, 110; *Ladies' Home Journal*, 78, 101–102, 109; letter writing in, 117–118, 202n149; marital home, 112; marital home, sitting room in, 110–112; mealtimes, 109; opening, 116; progressive American ("New") womanhood, 80–81, 102–103; protagonist, 101–103, 110, 115; protagonist's alienation from her mother, 113–115; protagonist's Americanness, 201n120; protagonist's father, 103–104;

My Mother and I (*continued*), protagonist's mother (Mammele), 112–113, 113, 117–118; protagonist's rejection of her mother's home, 112; protagonist's son, 113; reviews of, 198n112; Roosevelt and, Theodore, 78, *79*, 101, 114, 119, 190n8; Shollar on, Barbara, 101; Thanksgiving celebration, 109–110; Wasson on, Kirsten, 100, 117, 119n112; weekly cleaning for the Sabbath, 109; writing as a tie between mother and daughter, 116–119; yearning for middle-class American home, 204n159

"My Mother and I" (Stern) (*Ladies' Home Journal* story), 98–108; ads surrounding, 202n149; American feminine identity, support for, 100; Americanization, support for, 100; Becher and, Arthur E., 107; on belonging in United States, 198n110; Bok and, Edward, 78, 100, 115, 116, 119; genre of, 198n112; idealization of American home, 77, 98, 106; illustrations for, 106–107, *107*, *108*, 202n149; *Ladies' Home Journal*, 98–99, 101–102, 110–111; letter writing in, 202n149, 205n193; letting neighbors use family's bathtub, 106; progressive American ("New") womanhood, 80–81, 100–103, 104–105; progressive middle-class American domesticity, 98, 99; protagonist, 101–105, 115; protagonist's alienation from her mother, 103–104, 113–115; protagonist's father, 103–104; protagonist's higher education, 100–101, 103, 104; protagonist's husband, 105; protagonist's mother (Mammele), 103–104, 106–108, 112–113, 115, 202n149, 204n177, 205n182; Roosevelt and, Theodore, 78, 98–100, 115, 116; subtitle, 115; suburban marital home, 105–106, 107–108; traditional American ideas of womanhood, 104–105; Wasson on, Kirsten, 204n177, 205n182

Nasby, Petroleum V., 131
nation, 163n7, 164n24
The Nation (magazine), 198n112
nationalism: civic nationalism, 170n65; Danish nationalism, 59–52, 71; dual loyalty (*see* dual loyalty); European nationalists, 3; Irish nationalism, 127, 137, 155; racial nationalism, 170n65, 187n107 (*see also* American Race); Riis and, Jacob, 55–57, 59, 186n87; transnationalism, 11, 42
"new women," 202n138
New York (Roosevelt), 3
New York Sun (newspaper), 46
Nielsen, George R., 182n55
Norwegian immigrants, 187n12
Nott, Josiah Clark, 171n69

O'Brien, Robert L., 92, 94, 196n83
O'Connor, E. Noland, *31*
Old Town (Riis), 52, 70–71, 180n47
"On a Speech by President McKinley" (Dunne), 135–136
"On the Irish" (Dunne), 127
Outlook (magazine), 67, 191n10
Øverland, Orm, 63, 187n112

Parkhurst, Charles, 178n24
patriotism: of Jews, 28; Riis and, Jacob, 176n8, 186n87, 188n119; Roosevelt and, Theodore, 177n10. *See also* dual loyalty; nationalism
Peril and Preservation of the Home (Riis), 82
Polish immigrants, 97
Polish Jews, 60
polygenism, 171n73
Powers, John, 128
progressivism: alliance between United States and Britain, 154; altering class mentality, 88; American womanhood, 80; boss politics, 128; Connolly on, James, 163n5, 179n29, 206n6, 206n12; "ethnic progressivism," 206n12; ideal

family environment, 83–87; Lamarckism, 82–83; orientation of, 192n25, 193n42; publicity, 179n29; Stern and, Elizabeth, 11

The Promised Land (Antin), 69, 116, 166n43, 195n55

race: amalgamation, 16, 18, 20–21, 24, 26–27, 29–30; American Anglo-Saxonism (*see* American Anglo-Saxonism); American race (*see* American race); assimilable races, 5–6, 15, 34, 36, 37–38, 160; assimilative performances, 28; as biological phenomenon, 21; intermarriage, 16, 18, 20–21, 24, 26–27, 29–30; polygenism, 171n73; racial development, 21; Riis and, Jacob, 60–64; Roosevelt and, Theodore, 6, 11, 15, 16, 17, 33–34, 37, 168n27, 175n101; Zangwill and, Israel, 17, 21, 27–29; Zangwill's *The Melting Pot*, 16, 18, 20–21, 26, 29. *See also* amalgamation; hybridity

"Race Decadence" (Roosevelt), 9

"race suicide," 35, 94

racial nationalism, 170n65, 187n107. *See also* American race

Rauchway, Eric, 186n98, 190n154

Renan, Ernest, "What Is a Nation?", 24, 163n7

Republican Association, 142, 143

Ribe, Denmark, 55–56, 180n47, 188n132

Riis, Clara (Jacob's daughter): Danish immigrants, 182n54; daughter, 190n157; letter from Elisabeth Riis, 55; marriage, 182n67; Slesvig, 185n85, 185n86

Riis, Edward (Jacob's son), 182n67

Riis, Elisabeth (nee Elisabeth Gjortz; Jacob's first wife): class status, 179n42; on Denmark, 55–56; engagement to Danish army lieutenant, 179n42, 184n77; as ethnic wife, 182n67; Frederick and, Crown Prince of Denmark, 52; in *Making of an American*, 54, 55, 67, 183n72, 184n78; marriage to Jacob, 49; as representative of success in two worlds, 182n66; return trips to Denmark, 49, 71; Ribe, Denmark, 55–56; Roosevelt and, Theodore, 52

Riis, Emma (Jacob's sister), 180n47, 186n87

Riis, Florence (Jacob's daughter-in-law), 182n67

Riis, Jacob, 41–76; Addams and, Jane, 48; Americanism, 66; anti-German sentiments, 60, 71; articles for Danish newspapers, 186n87; *Battle with the Slum*, 76, 187n101, 189n153; birthplace, 185n85; blood inheritance, unalterable, 60; on boardinghouses, 182n67; childhood, 61; children, 49; Chinese immigrants, 60, 186n95; as citizen, 74–76; on citizenship, 82; class status, 179n42; correspondence, destruction of, 182n60; Cross of Dannebrog, 50; Cuba, self-determination for, 185n86; on Danes, 64; on Danish flag, 50; Danish nationalism, 49–52, 71; Danishness, 53, 54, 55, 60, 63–64, 67, 186n87; diasporic national literature, 57–58; dual loyalty, 11, 43, 44, 52–59, 63, 66–71, 176n8; early years in United States, 49; on Eastern European Jews, 187n101; environment's effect on immigrants, 35, 60–61; essentialism, 60–61; ethnic wives to, 182n66; Eurocentrism, 186n95; European immigrants to, 186n95; *Evening Sun* (newspaper), 43; family life, 182n67; Gjortz family and, 179n42; heaven to, 188n132; *Hero Tales of the Far North*, 43, 57–58, 177n10; on his children, 180n45; home, feeling of, 56; *How the Other Half Lives* (see *How the Other Half Lives*); hyphenated Americanism, 43, 52; ideal family environment, 83; on ideal home, 82, 88, 185n83; immigrant conversion narratives, 64–71, 74–75; Italian immigrants, 60; Jeffersonianism, 185n83; Jews, 60; Kallen and, Horace, 66; King Christian and, 50, 180n47;

Riis, Jacob, (*continued*), Lamarckism (inheritance of acquired characteristics), 45, 56; land, real estate ownership, 185n83; love for homeland, 185n85; *Making of an American* (see *Making of an American*); malaria, 66; manliness, 177n12; marriage to Elisabeth, 49; melting pot, vision of, 59; missionizing tendency, 185n86; mother, 55; municipal politics, 74; nationalism, 56–57, 59, 186n87; *New York Sun* (newspaper), 46; *Old Town*, 52, 70–71, 180n47; Pan-Scandinavianism, 186n89; patriotism, 176n8, 186n87, 188n119; *Peril and Preservation of the Home*, 82; Philippines, self-determination for, 185n86; photographs of young children, 202n148; on poverty, 60; public perception of, 182n54; race, 60–64; return trips to Denmark, 49, 60, 63, 71; Ribe, Denmark, 180n47, 188n132; on Roosevelt, Theodore, 43, 179n37, 181n48; Roosevelt and, Theodore, 10, 11, 43–49, 47, 50–52, 67–69, 71–73, 75–76, 177n12, 179n36, 179n38, 180n47, 181n48, 188n127, 189n137, 190n154, 190n157, 190n158; Roosevelt compared to, Theodore, 59; Roosevelt on, Theodore, 41, 48, 71, 72, 73, 178n16, 179n32; sentimentalism, 54, 183n70; Slesvig, 42–43, 57; slums, 56; Spanish-American War, 186n87; *The Ten Year's War*, 76, 190n158; *Theodore Roosevelt the Citizen*, 48, 72, 177n12; transnationalism, 11; urban poor, 45; Zangwill compared to, Israel, 59, 64

Riis, John (Jacob's son), 182n67

Riis, Mary (Jacob's second wife), 182n67, 185n83

Riis, Niels Edward (Jacob's father), 184n77

Riis, William (Vivi) (Jacob's son), 182n67

Robinson, Edward Arlington, 3

Rockefeller, John D., Sr., 138

Roosevelt, Edith, 91

Roosevelt, Theodore

Roosevelt, Theodore — ancestry, his, 210n70

Roosevelt, Theodore — gender, 81–82

Roosevelt, Theodore — influence of Riis's *How the Other Half Lives*, 45, 48

Roosevelt, Theodore — libel suit, 179n36

Roosevelt, Theodore — opinions, his of: advancement of humanity through conquest, 20; African Americans, 37; American citizens, 74; Americanism, 2, 3, 5, 9–10, 15, 153–154; Americanization, 90; Americanness, 175n101; anarchism, 4, 186n98; Bok, Edward, 84–85; citizenship, 91; Danes, 61; dual loyalty, 53; Dunne, Finley Peter, 153; the Dutch, 210n70; England, 153; Englishmen, 61–62; expatriates, 9, 134; family life, 91; Founding Fathers, 62–63; Garland's *Crumbling Idols*, 166n37; Harris, Joel Chandler, 8; himself, 3, 179n32; his contributions to *Ladies' Home Journal*, 196n86; the home, 77, 82, 83, 91, 92; hyphenated Americans, 7, 42; "ideal American citizen," 73–74, 76; ideal family environment, 83; immigrants, 4–6, 8, 17, 25, 37, 73–74; immigrants, Chinese, 37; immigrants, environment's effect on, 34–37; immigrants, German, 96–97; immigrants, Irish, 96–97, 153; immigrants, Italian, 97; immigrants, Japanese, 5, 37; immigrants, Polish, 97; immigration, 4, 5, 37, 90–91; Johnson's *Autobiography of an Ex-Colored Man*, 175n108; Latin nations, 187n111; literary regionalism, 8, 166n37; the "man he works for," 142–143; men, 93, 94, 95–97; Mr. Dooley, 140; motherhood, 95; native-born lovers of Europe, 25, 134–135; native-born writers, 9; problem of color, 175n108; progress of society, 175n101; public schools, 74; race, American, 16, 61–62, 94, 146, 155–156, 164n24, 187n107; "race suicide," 35, 94; races, assimilable,

5–6, 15, 34, 36, 37–38, 160; races, equipotentiality of all, 37; reversion to ancient types, 36; Riis, Jacob, 41, 48, 71, 72, 73, 178n16, 179n32; Rough Riders, 122–123; "strenuous life," 93; sweatshops, 46; "true American," 73–74; Twain, Mark, 8; white middle class, 94–95; women, 93, 94; writing spoken speech, 212n92; Zangwill's *Melting Pot*, 14, 39

Roosevelt, Theodore — opinions of him: Dunne's, Finley Peter, 139, 156, 206n10; Marsh's, Margaret, 197n100; Mr. Dooley's, 124, 137, 139, 140–142, 144–145, 149–152, 150–151, 206n12, 211n76; Riis's, Jacob, 43, 179n37, 181n48

Roosevelt, Theodore — organizational relationships: Catholic Knights of Columbus, 42; Lexow Committee, 45, 178n24; Manhattan Elevated Railroad Company, 46; New York City Police Department, 45, 46–48, 72, 178n24; New York Health Board, 48; Republican Association, 142, 143

Roosevelt, Theodore — personal relationships: Addams, Jane, 48; Bok, Edward, 78, 81, 86–87, 92, 97, 196n83, 196n86; Cortelyou, George, 152; Dunne, Finley Peter, 10, 11, 134, 145, 148, 150–151, 152, 154–155, 156–157, 210n70, 210n71, 211n79; Hay, John, 167n13; Johnson, James Weldon, 175n108; Matthews, Brander, 145–146, 166n37, 175n108; Murray, Joe, 143; O'Brien, Robert L., 196n83; Riis, Elisabeth, 52; Riis, Jacob, 10, 11, 43–49, 47, 50–52, 67–69, 71–73, 75–76, 177n12, 179n36, 179n38, 180n47, 181n48, 188n127, 189n137, 190n154, 190n157, 190n158; Robinson, Edward Arlington, 3; Roth, Cecil Spring, 189n137; Strong, William, 178n24; Twain, Mark, 3; Washington, Booker T., 37, 139, 175n108, 179n37, 211n76; Wister, Owen, 3; Zangwill, Israel, 10–11, 13–16, 25, 38–39, 167n13, 170n58, 213n134

Roosevelt, Theodore — personality: laughing at himself, 145; manliness, 177n10; masculinity, 4, 9, 11, 96, 123, 142, 177n10, 177n12, 197n100, 198n102; rhetorical and physical violence, 141, 142; self-image, 140; sobriety, 179n36

Roosevelt, Theodore — photo of, *8*

Roosevelt, Theodore — publicity/press, 47, 91

Roosevelt, Theodore — social and political issues: alliance between United States and Britain, 145–146, 148–149, 154, 156; American Anglo-Saxonism, 146, 152–153, 212n106; Americanism, 2, 3, 5, 9–10, 15, 153–154; Chinese immigrants, 5; civil responsibility, 5; cross-cultural socialization, 97; Darwinism, 168n27; domestication of foreigners, 90, 96–97; domesticity, 90–92; ethnic politics, 72, 152, 153; eugenics, 175n101; evolution, 36, 168n27; exclusion of Irish Americans from positions of power, 151–152, 153–154, 155, 156; immigrants, environment's effect on, 7, 34–37; immigrants' forgetting about pre-American enemies, 24; individual rights, defense of, 177n10; intimidation as political method, 144–145; Lamarckism (inheritance of acquired characteristics), 7, 34–35; "master race," 177n10; melting pot, vision of, 17, 33–35, 38, 39; national liberation movements overseas, 51; national literature program, 3–4, 8–10; national rights, defense of, 177n10; patriotism, 177n10; progressive American womanhood, 80; race, 11, 17, 33–34, 37, 168n27, 175n101; races, assimilable, 6, 15, 34, 160; Russian persecution of Jews, 52; Square Deal, 2, 10, 75, 156; strenuous life, domestication of, 90–97; treaty with Germany, 156; trusts, 144; women's suffrage, 197n92; working-class immigrant men, 143

Roosevelt, Theodore — writings, his: *Autobiography* (see *Autobiography*); "Biological Analogies in History" (lecture), 35–36; "Children of the Crucible," 13; dialect literature by, 143, 212n92, 212n94; ghostwriting by, 92; *Gouverneur Morris*, 3, 62; *Hero Tales from American History* (with Lodge), 3, 177n10; "How I Became a Progressive," 179n32; for *Ladies' Home Journal*, 78–79, 88, 92–97, 105, 191n12, 196n83, 196n86; *New York*, 3; for Outlook magazine, 67, 191n10; "Race Decadence" (speech), 9; "Social Evolution," 168n27; "True Americanism" (*see* "True Americanism"); *Winning of the West*, 2–3, 61–62; "Woman and the Home," 77

Roosevelt, Theodore — writings, other people's: Dunne's *Mr. Dooley*, 121–122, 123–125, 142–144, 157; Riis's *How the Other Half Lives*, 43; Sinclair's *The Jungle*, 140–141; Stern's *My Mother and I*, 78, 79, 101, 114, 119, 190n8; Stern's "My Mother and I," 78, 98–100, 115, 116; Zangwill's *Melting Pot*, 14, 15–16, 25, 35, 38–39, 167n6

Rosenzweig, Linda, 202n138
Roth, Cecil Spring, 189n137
Rough Riders, 122–123

Saaledes blev jeg hjemlos (Thus I Became Homeless) (Mortensen), 66
Saturday Evening Post (magazine), 196n84
Schaaf, Barbara, 127
Schiff, Jacob, 185n83
Schultz, Alfred P., 6, 7, 17, 27
Scott, Emmett J., *Booker T. Washington, Builder of a Civilization* (with Stowe), 175n108
Secret Family (Stern), 191n9
settlement house workers, 195n69
settlement houses, 88–90; Henry Street Settlement, 89. See also Hull House
sexuality, 21
Shafter, William, 136
Shavelson, Susanne Amy, 198n112
Shollar, Barbara, 101, 198n112
Sinclair, Upton, *The Jungle*, 140–141
Slesvig (Schleswig), Denmark: German occupation, 50, 51, 181n50; Riis and, Clara, 185n85, 185n86; Riis and, Jacob, 42–43, 57
Slotkin, Richard, 123, 167n27
Smith, Rogers, 170n65
"Social Evolution" (Roosevelt), 168n27
social workers, 89, 106, 112
Sollors, Werner: *Alma Mater* metaphor, 169n30; *Beyond Ethnicity*, 25, 166n44; Bok's *Americanization of Edward Bok*, 195n55; ethnic authors, 209n46; ethnic literature, 25; ethnic wives, 182n66; immigrant autobiographies, 166n44, 195n55; Riis's Danishness, 60; tropes describing ethnic/national loyalties, 53; Zangwill's *Melting Pot*, 26
Spanish-American War: immigrants' reaction to, 56–57, 185n86; Mr. Dooley on, 136–137; Riis and, Jacob, 186n87; Rough Riders, 122–123
Special Sorrows (Jacobson), 56–57, 181n49
Spencer, Herbert, 60
Steiner, Edward, 69
Stern, Elizabeth, 97–119; Americanization, 87, 90, 97–98; archives, 200n114; birth, 100, 200n114; childhood, 100, 200n113; feminism, 80; foster parents, 100, 200n113; on her audience, 116–117; *I Am a Woman—and a Jew*, 100, 205n194; immigrant conversion narratives, 69; Jewish identity, 200n113; on Jewishness, 205n194; later writings, 119; marriage, 200n114; *My Mother and*

I (see *My Mother and I*); "My Mother and I" (*see* "My Mother and I"); parents, 200n113; progressive American womanhood, 80–81; progressive domesticity, questioning of, 11; pseudonyms, 119; Roosevelt and, Theodore, 10, 78, 80; son, 100; Umansky on, Ellen, 100, 190n8, 200n114
Stern, Leon, 200n114
Stern, Richard, 200n114
Stern, Thomas Noel, 100, 191n9, 198n112
Stocking, George, Jr., 171n73
Stowe, Lyman B., *Booker T. Washington, Builder of a Civilization* (with Scott), 175n108
Straus, Oscar, 16, 167n14
Strong, William, 178n24
"Swearing" (Dunne), 140, 144

The Ten Year's War (Riis), 76, 190n158
Tennyson, Alfred, 60
Testi, Arnaldo, 142
Theodore Roosevelt the Citizen, 48, 72, 177n12
Three Negro Classics (Johnson), 175n108
Tocqueville, Alexis de, 87
transnationalism, 11, 42. *See also* dual loyalty
"True Americanism" (Roosevelt): on Americanism, 2; assimilable races, 5–6, 15; as call to literary arms, 8; dual loyalty, 41; on immigration, 4; Mr. Dooley's critique of, 11, 145, 156, 206n12; working together for common country, 121
Twain, Mark, 3, 8

Umansky, Ellen, 100, 190n8, 198n112, 200n114

Valdemar II, King of Denmark, 63–64
vernacular literature, 131–132, 138, 209n41, 209n58. *See also* dialect literature

Wald, Lillian, 89, 109
Wald, Priscilla: "conversion narratives," 166n44; "official stories" of national movements, 165n33; Riis's *Making of an American*, 54, 65, 66, 75
Ward, Artemus, 132
Washington, Booker T. and Roosevelt, Theodore, 37, 139, 175n108, 179n37, 211n76
Wasson, Kirsten, on Stern's works, 100, 117, 198n112, 204n177, 205n182
Watts, Sarah, 142
Wendell, Barrett, 2
"What Is a Nation?" (Renan), 24, 163n7
Whiteside, Walker, *19*
Wiebe, Robert, 83
Winning of the West (Roosevelt), 2–3, 61–62
Wister, Owen, 3
"Woman and the Home" (Roosevelt), 77
women and Theodore Roosevelt, 81–82
women autobiographies, 204n177. *See also My Mother and I; Promised Land*
women's colleges, architecture of, 202n130
women's suffrage, 86
World Zionist Congress, 16

Yezierska, Anzia, *Bread Givers*, 100
"You're All Right, Teddy" (Johnson), 175n108

Zaborowska, Magdalena, 198n110
Zangwill, Edith Ayrton, 173n95
Zangwill, Israel, 13–21, 27–33; African Americans, 172n82; amalgamation, 20–21, 22, 28, 34; assimilation, 22, 28; Ayrton and, Edith, 173n95; on blacks and whites, 172n82; children of, 173n95; First Universal Races Congress (1911), 27–28, 171n72; forgetting pre-American enemies, 24; Hebraism, 173n95; Herzl on, Theodore, 172n82; hybrid superiority, 171n71; immigration restriction, 38; intermarriage, 169n34; Jewish immigrants, 167n13,

170n59, 173n95; Jewish sense of justice, 33; Jewishness, 28, 29–30, 173n95; on Jews, 28, 29, 33; Jews, Eastern European, 16; *The Melting Pot* (see *The Melting Pot*); melting pot, vision of, 10–11, 17–21, 27, 39; Mendelianism, 29–30; obligations of immigrants, 17; physical features of children of the melting pot, 30; on prognathous faces, 172n82; race, 17, 21, 27–29; racial equality, 171n72; Riis compared to, Jacob, 59, 64; Roosevelt and, Theodore, 10–11, 13–16, 25, 38–39, 167n13, 170n58, 213n134; twin visions of, 173n95; wife, 169n31, 173n95; World Zionist Congress, 16; Zionism, 167n13, 173n95

Zierler, Wendy, 198n112, 204n177

ABOUT THE AUTHOR

AVIVA TAUBENFELD is Assistant Professor of Literature at Purchase College, State University of New York.